THE PhotoshopWorld DREAMTEAM BOOK

Pete Bauer

Russell Brown

Rod Harlan

Todd Morem

Scott Kelby

Taz Tally

Vincent H. E. Versace.com

PHOTOSHOP WORLD EAST 2003 ATTENDEES

A special note of thanks to: You, the attendees of 2003's PhotoshopWorlds, West Coast and East Coast editions. When we decided to do this book (after PhotoshopWorld West, but before PhotoshopWorld East), we thought it would be cool to ask attendees if they'd like to see their names in this book. Nearly 500 of you took us up on the offer... Cheers.

Adrian Demoret	Bernard Ottley Jr	Wattananusit	David Rogers	Ellen Sutter	Hortensia Cesar
Aimee Roberts-Mazurek	Betsy Walton	Cheri Craft	David Russin	Enrique Zuniga	Howard Silver
Aimee Wheaton	Beverly Wodicka	Chet Kelley	Dawn Sealy	Eran Borochov	Ian Aberle
Albert Holland	Bill Durrence	Chris Acuna	Debbie Frazee	Erik Colonese	Iraida Carrion
Alberto Fernandez	Bill Pollac	Chris Bain	Debbie Zotfor	Errol DeSilva	Iris F Lopez
Alejandra Ramirez	Blake Fisher	Chris D'Angelo	Debora Berberich	Evelyn Fernandez	Israel Carunungan
Alessandra Beckmann	Bob Leinbaugh	Chris Grinnell	DeBora Watts	Fabianna Diaz	J.P. Kabala
Alex Montano	Bonnie Jacobs	Christina Moss	Deborah Meyer	Fernando Ramos	Jack Papandreou
Alexandra Barnard	Bonnie Youngs	Christina Nash	deLancey Funsten Whitmer	Francisco Cardarelli	James Jackson
Alexandra Gebhardt	Brandon Langton	Christopher Duque	Dennis Fox	Francisco E. Carballo	James Petts
Alexandre Keese	Brandon Sofsky	Chuck Kacin	Diana Teeters	Frank Bisono	James Pritchett
Alexia Jokisch	Brandy Snyder	Chuck Szachta	Diane Jackson	Gabriel Mas	jamie hipple
Ali Carlton	Brenda B. Daigre	Ciara Young	Dick Henrichon	Gary Leive	Jane Gordon
Alina Balaguero	Brenda Belliveau	Cindy Doyle	Dina Coyle	Gary-Paul Prince	Jane Janovsky
Allan Weitz	Brenda Sorrells	Cindy Moore	Dinah Edmonson	Gaye Smith	Janee Aronoff
Allen Kalka	Brian Hurlburt	Clarence R. Brown	Dolores A. Russo	Gene McCree	Janeene Holly
Allen Kane	Brian Payne	Claudia Cary	Dominic Thomas	Gene Scott	Jannet Martell
Amy Eileen Koester	Brian Sullivan	Claudia Hose	Don Cooper	Gerald Barron	Jarvis Grant
Ana M. Avila	Brian Walker	Clay Ritchings	Don Fraser	Gerry Robins	Jasson Ryals
Ana Saltos	Bridgette Barger	Colette Stemple	Donna Bouzagni	Gil Roeder	Javier Hernandez
Andrea Ainley	Brittany Rhodes	Cristina Strader	Donna Clute	Giles Hooper	Jeff Toorish
Andresa Frizzera	Bruce Wetherbee	Curtis Chan	Donna Prejean	Gina Masi	Jeff Weisberg
Andressa Sily	Butler Perkins	Curtis Loftis	Dorinda McCarthy	Gina Morelli	Jennifer Cleary
Andrew Rodriguez	Byron Tracy	Cynthia Krebs	Dougl Abernethy	Glenn Levy	Jennifer Munson
Angela Gates	Camila Palomo	Cyrus Bowman	Dustin Goodman	Glyn W. Jackson	Jennifer Panland
Ann Bennett	Camilo Rozo	Dale O'Dell	Ed Linn	Greg Burton	Jennifer Randolph
Ann Halbrooks	Carlos A. Fernandez	Dalila Brooks	Ed Mineuc	Greg Gackle	Jennifer Reynolds
Anna Iadowski	Carlos Baquero	Dan Chase	Eileen Courtright	Greg Otto	Jeremy Vest
Anna Navarro	Carlos Hueso	Dan Doll	Elaine Escotto	Greg Stapleton	Jim Blakely
Anna Pacheco	Carmen P. Caldero	Dan Kingcaid	Elana Lazar	Guido Vosu	Jim Magill
Aous Asfar	Caroline Zaffery	Daniela Afonso	Elena Perez	Gustavo Monte	Jim Urick
Arliene Sports	Carolyn Anne Ryan	Darrel Hoo	Elisa Knataitis	Guy Halligan	Jim White
Art Swenson	Cary Perez	Darrin Waterbury	Elizabeth Matzko	Handler Jay	Jing Jing Zeng
Barbara Russ	Caslyn Daniel	Dave Myers	Elizabeth Miller	Harrol Porter	Jodie Sinclair
Bernard Matz	Catherine Meggison	David Billings	Elizabeth Phillips	Heather Matkowsky	Joel Schreck
	Chad Eidschun	David Holland	Elizabeth Schrader	Heather Protz	Joelle Almodovar
	Charkkrit	David N. Gant		Herbie Martin	John Burdick

John Campoli	Larry Stuart	Mark Benno	Nick Lebeda	Ryan Dausay	Steve Shore
John Davis	Larry Thaw	Mark Blank	Nick Truden	Ryan N Harvey	Steve Tanzeb
John Geyer	Laura Herrmann	Mark Borosch	Nicky Guthrie	Sabrina Ocner	Steven Rankin
John Greske	Laura Spofford	Mark Hanson	Nicole Cox	salehi armaghan	Susan Bailey
John Monterrey	Laurie Senroa	Mark Harris	NW Smith	Sally Smollar	Susan Emanuel
John Taylor	Lavzi Mnnermaa	Mark Johnson	Om Upadhya	Samantha Farias	Susanne Loomis
John Wilson	LeAnn Campbell	MarKos Leave	Orestes Vega Jr	Samuel Hall	Susy Thielen
Jonathan Summers	Lee Krull Gullett	Marlene Parness	Orvulle Wilson	Sandi Knight	Suzan Charnock
Jose Francisco	Lee Van Gnack	Martha Olson	Pablo Gehr	Sandi Knight	Suzanne Lambert
Salgado,PhD	Leika Nakamura	Mary Lyons	Pablo Rodriguez	Sandra Anderson	Syed Reza Ali
Joseph De Gregorio	Leo Mennitt	Matthew Moore	Paola Valverde	Sara Martinez	Tal Ninio
Joseph Szymczyk	Leonard J. Rall	Matthew Morris	Patti Steib	Sarah John	Tania Untulis
Joy Hwang	Lerida Perez	Mauricio Viana	Paul Camhi	Sarah Perez	Tara Bones
Juan Reyes	LeRoy Borofsky	Meg Murphy	Paul Feder	Scott Cowlin	Taylor Smith
Judith S.Kessler	Leslie Allen	Melinda Bashen	Paula Buncy	Scott Norman	Ted Penland
Judy Jordan	Leslie Line	Melissa Drake	Paweena Pimkwan	Sean Matheson	Teonne Daye
Judy Morse	Lillian Mogavero	Mercedes Hanabergh	Pekka Caesar	Sebastian Aczka	Teresa Bowsman
Juilio G Torres	Linda Carter	Michael Aronoff	Philip Marraccini	Sebastian Maczka	Terry Rieckhoff
Julie Fox	Linda King	Michael Burge	R. O. Porter	Sergio Diment	Thomas Quinn
Julio Balaguero	Linda Welch	Michael Collins	Rachael Hixon	Shan DeSilva	Tim Gill
Julio Gonzalez	Lisa Bonnes	Michael Davis	Rachel Tiley	Shane Emenheiser	Tim Johnson
Karel Welles	Lisa Papandreou	Michael Dvoravic	Raul De La Cruz	Shannon E. Coffey	Todd Onsa
Karen Chevarria	Logan Perkins	Michael Mitz	Raul Montaqno	Shannon Patel	Trish Johnson
Karen Young	Lolanda Brewster	Michael Porterfield	Ray Amos	Shari Staiger	Valladares Malisa
Iwamoto	Loren Greenblatt	Michelle Franceschi	Rebecca Nimmer	Sharon Bruce	Vanessa Beltran
kat Moran	Lori Laming	Mickey Winter	Rebecca Punet	Shawna Braunstein	Veronica Lima
Kat Ziagos	Lucrecia Pinero	Mike Jones	Rena Bernstein	Sheila Delemos	Vesko Urukov
Kathey Fatica	Lucy Perez	Mike McKenney	Rene Granado	Sherry Romain	Vicki Fernandez
Kathryn Lightcap	Luis Giron	Mike Radel	Rick English	Sherry White	Victor Paul
Kathryn Parker	Mallie Williams	Mike Stone	Rick Guilfoil	Sheryl Molloy	victoria didonato
Kathy Durkee	Mamie Lingo	Mimi Alonso	Rick Hermosillo	Shirley Allen	Victoria Mohblatt
Katia Dumont	Marage Navratil	Mitch Kloorfain	Rick Nelsom	Skip Pennington	Virginia Bruce
Ken Ogrodowski	Marcia Braunstein	Mitzi Smith	Rick Stare	Sonia Vazquez	Vivianne Bonsall
Kim Horvath	Maria Bencomo	Monica A. Rodriguez	Robby Davis	Stacy Gorman	Walter Vinci
Kim Hulsizer	Marianne Rodriguez	Nancy Gold	Robert Belfon	Stan Chmielewski	Wendy Castleberry
Kirsten Andreason	Marie Sarich	Naomi Salz	Robert Campell	Stan Wagner	William Wolf
Konrad Poth	Marilyn Antram	Natalia E. Weigandt	Robert V Capalbo	Stani Henriques	Windy Barrett
Kris Chavez	Marilyn Cook	Natalia Trovato	Roberta M Smith	Stephanie Cole	Yanira Cardarelli
Kyla Swart	Marion Saunders	Natasha Whitted	Roberto Chiuz	Stephen Depetro	Yoli Salen
Kyle Bennett	Maritza S. Radbill	Neil Patel	Roberto Rodiguez	Steve Ratkowski	Yong W. Lee
Kyle Miller	Mark Allen	Neka Wilson	Rosemarie Szedula	Steve Schraer	

The PhotoshopWorld Dream Team Book, Volume 1
PhotoshopWorld Dream Team

Published by New Riders Publishing/Peachpit Press
1249 Eighth Street
Berkeley, CA 94710
510/524-2178
800/283-9444
510/524-2221 (fax)

Find us on the World Wide Web at: www.peachpit.com
To report errors, please send a note to errata@peachpit.com

Peachpit Press is a division of Pearson Education

Editor: Steve Weiss
Project Editor: Becky Morgan
Production Editor: Connie Jeung-Mills
Copyeditor: Elissa Rabellino
Technical Editor: Seán Duggan
Compositors: Ted LoCascio, David Van Ness
Indexer: Judy Walthers von Alten
Cover design: Felix Nelson
Interior design: Felix Nelson, Ted LoCascio

ISBN 0-7357-1421-5

9 8 7 6 5 4 3 2 1

Printed and bound in the United States of America

TABLE OF CONTENTS

TABLE OF CONTENTS

TABLE OF CONTENTS

TABLE OF CONTENTS

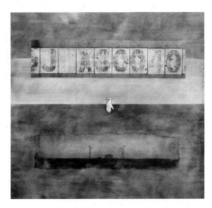

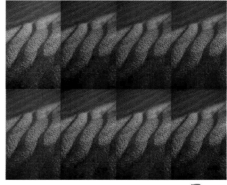

TABLE OF CONTENTS

Downloadable project files are available for you to work along with your Dream Team instructor. Please go to www.peachpit.com/dreamteam.html and click on this chapter.

DREAM TEAM ACKNOWLEDGEMENTS

 One of the things that I believe makes PhotoshopWorld such a special event is that each year it brings together five entirely different groups of people: instructors, students, Adobe, industry vendors, and NAPP's own event staff. Each group plays a separate role in making PhotoshopWorld happen, as well as making this book happen, but even though we're separate groups we all come together through a common bond—Adobe Photoshop.

I'd like to start by thanking the PhotoshopWorld instructors who've lent their expertise, shared their wisdom, and given us a glimpse inside their sessions by contributing to this book. As Conference Technical Chair for PhotoshopWorld, my goal has always been to seek out instructors who absolutely love to teach. To find those who gladly share their best techniques and hold nothing back. To find instructors who care deeply about their students, who work hard to craft their message, and deliver it in a way that makes our students feels like they're in a one-on-one session with the instructor, even if a thousand other students surround them.

I feel we've truly gathered a "dream team" of the digital-imaging industry's best, brightest, most creative, and most gifted instructors and it's an honor and a privilege to have them training for us at the event, and here in the book.

Secondly, I'd like to thank all of our friends at Adobe Systems for all their support, great ideas, enthusiasm, and help along the way. I can't tell you how truly honored we are to have Adobe as our partner, sharing the stage in our opening keynotes, exhibiting on our exhibit floor, and for being the official sponsor of the show. In particular, I'd like to thank our friends Addy Roff, Julieanne Kost, Rye Livingston, Terry White, Russell Brady, Karen Gauthier, Gywn Weisberg, Russell Brown, Bryan Lamkin, Kevin Connor, and a special thanks to our good friend, Photoshop Product Manager John Nack, for writing the Foreword to this book. Also, we'll never forget our friends who've helped us along the way, including three very special people: Barbara Rice, Jill Nakashima, and Teresa Ojeda.

Third, I'd like to thank our own staff at NAPP. We don't hire an outside show management company to run PhotoshopWorld—we literally do it ourselves. From manning the spotlight during the keynote to unloading the trucks, from creating the signage to designing the postcards, from manning the phones when attendees call in to reserve their tickets to shooting the videos you see during our presentations—it's all done by our staff. The person who hands you your workbook might be a copy editor, a customer service rep, our creative director, or even one of the owners of the company—we all chip in to make the whole thing happen and honestly, I think that's part of the magic of Photoshop World—everyone you deal with really cares. They want you to have the best experience possible and they'll go out of their way to make sure that happens. Personally, I love this aspect of PhotoshopWorld, because it's where our entire company gets to come together in one place, at one time, and really see what it is that we do. It's not a concept or a voice on the phone—it's the real deal, live, right in front of you. It's where everyone, from our customer service area to our shipping department to our magazine staff, gets to meet the people "on the other end." It's where they get to shake hands with members, and put a name with a face. Each year this event energizes our entire company and brings out the very best in our team, and their enthusiasm pours right onto the attendees and it creates an electrifying atmosphere throughout the entire show. There's a great feeling of pride that comes from "doing it yourself" and I'm very grateful to our entire staff for coming together the way they do, working as hard as they do working long hours with few (if any) breaks, and with an amazing attitude that transforms PhotoshopWorld from a three-day Photoshop seminar into a very special event. My heartfelt thanks to each and every one of you for taking such great care of our members, and for letting them know how much they matter through your actions and words. You are the very best.

In many ways PhotoshopWorld is the opposite of most other large-scale events because rather than focusing on the exhibit floor, our focus has always been on the training side of things. Maybe that's why we're so delighted that our exhibit area has grown the way it has (in just the past few years it has more than doubled in size), and it now attracts some of the leading developers in the digital imaging industry, including such industry heavyweights as Nikon, Wacom, HP, nikMultimedia, Canon, Epson, Apple Computer, Olympus, B&H Photo, Dell, Peachpit Press, Extensis, Pantone, and dozens more. We're greatly indebted to the companies who, through exhibiting at PhotoshopWorld, give our attendees to the opportunity to get their hands on all the latest gear, to hear directly from industry representatives, and get their questions answered straight from the source. Our Expo has become an important part of the PhotoshopWorld experience and I want to personally thank those companies, whose support, time, and effort mean a lot to us, and certainly to all our PhotoshopWorld attendees.

Lastly, but certainly not least, I want to give my heartfelt thanks to our attendees, without whom there would be no PhotoshopWorld. For me, meeting our members from around the world, face to face, is the most gratifying part of the event. Hearing their stories, learning that we have the same problems and challenges no matter where we're from, laughing and sharing digital imaging nightmares and wild tales—to me, it's just a blast. The fact that we're all in this together, that we have a common bond, that we're all basically trying to do the same thing, coupled with the fact that we're all so passionate about what we do creates a real buzz in the air. It's palpable. You can feel it. You can walk up to anyone and there and strike up a conversation by simply saying, "So what do you use Photoshop for?" It's a place where friends are made, connections are formed—where old friends are found, and new ones are made. When it comes down to it, it's all about the attendees—the students—it's why we're there.

That's why I want to thank all the attendees who have taken their time, a part of their lives, to come and spend three amazing, informative, and inspiring days with us learning about the coolest software program that's ever been made. It's my hope that if you haven't been to PhotoshopWorld, this book, this insider's look behind the scenes, will encourage you to become a part of something very special that you just have to experience to believe. I hope to see you there soon.

All my best,

Scott Kelby
President, National Association
of Photoshop Professionals (NAPP)

FOREWORD

For me, developing the features that go into Photoshop is a bit like a farmer sending food to the grocery store: You make sure everything's clean and ready to cook, and you think you know how it's going to get used, but the real pleasure is seeing what happens when some great chefs get their hands on it.

These are the folks who continually imagine new ways to combine ingredients and create some amazing results. Twice a year, an elite group of these Photoshop chefs come together at PhotoshopWorld, a three-day whirl of non-stop classes, presentations, and parties. If you haven't yet attended a show, you're missing a great chance to learn from and rub elbows with some of the most talented, charismatic instructors ever to touch paintbrush to pixels.

The PhotoshopWorld Dream Team Book, Volume 1 brings together just what it says—a dream team of the very best photographers, painters, retouchers, Web designers, video pros, and more. These practicing artists and trainers have created all-new, never-before-seen tips and tricks that will help you and Photoshop do tricks you never imagined possible. Like the very best chefs, they'll have you taking what you thought were familiar ingredients and combining them into something exquisite. I'm continually amazed by the work these folks do and the clarity with which they bring their techniques to life. I hope you enjoy their work as much as I have.

John Nack
Product Manager
Adobe Photoshop & ImageReady

Opposite: Adobe Senior VP Bryan Lamkin, giving the
2003 PhotoshopWorld West keynote.

ABOUT NAPP

First, a little history. The idea for forming an association for Photoshop users came from a nationwide Photoshop seminar tour we produced starting back in 1993. As we traveled to different cities around the country, users would come to us at the end of the day, and say something like "Hey, this was really great. When you are coming back?" And we'd reply "Next year," and they'd scrunch up their face and say "Well, what do we do to keep learning until then?" and we'd give them a list of books or a Web site or two. We soon realized that there was really no central resource for learning about Adobe Photoshop all year long.

So with Adobe's help we formed the National Association of Photoshop Professionals (NAPP for short). We launched the organization and started signing up members at the 1998 Seybold trade show in New York City. This was also the debut of *Photoshop User* magazine, the "how-to" magazine for Photoshop users. From these humble beginnings, we've grown to nearly 50,000 members in the U.S. and 108 countries around the world, and we have become the world's leading resource for Photoshop training, education, and news.

In 2003, we became the first organization of its kind to become nationally accredited; attendees can elect to receive CEUs for attending both our one-day seminars and PhotoshopWorld.

The focus of NAPP has always been education, so we publish Photoshop training in a variety of formats for our members, including *Photoshop User* magazine (members get an annual subscription as part of their membership), training videos and DVDs, Photoshop books published by NAPP Publishing, Inc., and NAPP's private "members only" Web site. The site is the largest, most comprehensive Photoshop site in the world, with weekly columns and tutorials, weekly video tips, lively forums, discussion groups, and a worldwide community of members helping members.

Besides the educational and networking aspects of NAPP membership, members enjoy a wide range of discounts on everything from AVIS rental cars to hotel room nights to just about any digital imaging product or camera you can imagine.

NAPP membership is open to anyone who wants to learn more about Photoshop, regardless of their level of Photoshop expertise, and the annual membership fee is still the same price it was the day we launched NAPP back in 1998—just $99.

For more information on NAPP, visit the Web site at www.photoshopuser.com.

ABOUT PHOTOSHOPWORLD

PhotoshopWorld has been described as a "three-day Photoshop love fest" and as much as we hate to admit it, that's not far from the truth. It's where Photoshop users from around the world gather each year (one on the East Coast in spring, and once on the West Coast in early fall) to learn all the latest Photoshop techniques, tips, tricks, effects, and shortcuts, from a collection of the world's leading Photoshop gurus—an instructor "dream team" made up of the best, brightest, most talented, and most creative teachers on the planet.

The event kicks off with an opening keynote presentation, but presentation really isn't the right word. It's more of a Photoshop extravaganza. After the keynote, it's off to more than 60 training sessions organized into tracks, including simultaneous tracks for digital photographers, special effects, Web design, productivity, creativity, digital video, prepress, and a host of others.

One of the most important aspects of PhotoshopWorld is getting to make new friends and network with other Photoshop users within the industry; there's plenty of opportunities for that with after-hours parties, hilarious late-night sessions, peer-to-peer discussion groups, and a number of special events that get members mingling.

Although the conference side is the main focus of the event, there's also an Expo floor where the leading names in digital imaging give attendees a chance to get their hands on all the latest gear.

We wrap up PhotoshopWorld with a special general session called Photoshop Wars, (a take-off on the popular TV show "Junkyard Wars") where the instructors are teamed up and forced to create projects live, on the fly, with images chosen by the audience. It's a great way to unwind from a conference where you learn so much your brain hurts.

PHOTOSHOPWORLD LIVE

1 & 6. Russell Brown performs some neat Photoshop tricks on the Show floor. **2.** Jack Davis (right) receives his Photoshop Hall of Fame (education) award from NAPP President, Scott Kelby. **3.** Bryan Lamkin, Adobe's Senior Vice President of Digital Imaging and Video Products gives the Keynote address. **4.** Stephen Johnson thanks the NAPP for his Photoshop Hall of Fame (photographer) award. **5.** At Corel's booth, attendees tried their hands at Painter 8. **7 & 10.** Attendees crowded the Expo Hall floor. **8.** Kevin Ames has a Photoshop Fashion Shoot LIVE! **9.** Nikon's booth on the Expo floor.

PHOTOSHOPWORLD LIVE

11. Photoshop legend Deke McClelland shows his stuff during the opening night Instructor Jam Session. **12.** The "Photoshop All Stars" rocked the house! **13.** *Photoshop User* Creative Director Felix Nelson jammin' with some of his favorite tricks. **14.** The show floor was happening with booths from Nikon, Adobe, Alien Skin, Auto/FX, Epson, Digital Vision, Extensis, Leaf, Wacom, and many more. **15.** Photoshop rocks! **16.** Adobe's info booth was packed the entire show. **17.** (L to R) Guru Awards host Jeff Kelby, Best of Show winner James G. Respess, and Wes Pack of Guru Award sponsor Procreate.

PHOTOSHOPWORLD POSTERS

Each year we create a special PhotoshopWorld commemorative poster and present the attendees with one as they leave the opening keynote. The posters are designed by Felix Nelson, NAPP's own Creative Director (and quite a brilliant illustrator and graphic designer, I might add). The posters always feature the current year's theme and usually the centerpiece of the poster winds up taking a real form. For example, during the keynote we presented Adobe and the winner of the Guru Awards with a real Fender Stratocaster® that matched the one Felix drew from scratch for the poster. It's a great way for our members to remember a very special event.

PHOTOSHOPWORLD 2003 LOS ANGELES

PHOTOSHOPWORLD 2004 SAN FRANCISCO

PHOTOSHOPWORLD 2003 MIAMI

KEYNOTE

From the very beginning, we wanted our opening keynote to be something special. We wanted it to let our attendees know that this wasn't going to be a boring computer conference. This is Photoshop. This is the coolest program on the planet, and PhotoshopWorld should kick off with the coolest opening; that's why we pick a special theme each year. Previous themes have included a real NBA-style opening (complete with a routine from the LA Lakers Girls cheerleaders); our PhotoshopWorld Live theme (based on Saturday Night Live) with videos from the real SNL characters Mr. Bill and the original Father Guido Sarducci; and our Photoshop Built for Speed theme, with a real NASCAR car live on stage. Plus, we had our Photoshop Rocks theme with a full-concert production featuring a live band of Photoshop jammers. People always seem to be amazed at the extravaganza our opening keynote has become, but we feel it's another one of things that transforms PhotoshopWorld from just another conference into a very special event.

PHOTOSHOP MIDNIGHT MADNESS

This late-night session is really designed for just one thing—fun. It's a hilarious, off-the-hook night of laughs, pranks, special surprises, prizes, and giveaways with your hosts Scott Kelby, Felix Nelson, Rod Harlan, and Deke McClelland. Part of the magic of Photoshop Midnight Madness is the exclusivity—although thousands attend PhotoshopWorld, only 150 highly coveted tickets are available and people line up early just to snag a ticket to night of Photoshop mayhem that dare not speak its name. (OK, that's overstating it a bit, but it is, for those lucky 150 people, a night they'll be talking about for a long time.)

Tom Knoll
2001 Inductee
Photoshop Business Development

Russell Brown
2002 Inductee
Photoshop Business Development

*Jack Davis
2003 Inductee
Photoshop Education*

PHOTOSHOP WARS

We wanted a fun way to end each PhotoshopWorld, all of us together as one large group, and Photoshop Wars is it. The idea for Photoshop Wars came from the TV Show "Junkyard Wars" and here's how it works. We split the instructors into three two-person teams. The host, the charming and witty Larry Becker, gives the teams a topic and a 10-minute time limit. Besides this deadline, and having to create projects on the fly in front of thousands of people, what's the catch? The images given to the teams are chosen by the audience right then and there. It makes for an often inspiring, amazing, and sometimes hilarious session of under-the-gun creativity and it's a wonderful way to wrap up the conference and send everybody home with a smile.

THE TECH EXPO

Although the training conference is the main focus, the Tech Expo has grown to become an important part of PhotoshopWorld. This is where the attendees can get their hands on all the latest digital imaging gear including everything from digital cameras to printers, Photoshop plug-ins to calibration software, from flat-panel displays to photographic lighting, from stock photography to graphics tablets—it's all there. And besides exhibits from Adobe (the show's sponsor), the biggest names in the industry have exhibited at the Tech Expo, including Nikon, Epson, Canon, Extensis, Apple Computer, Quark, Wacom, Olympus, Digital Juice, Corel, Macromedia, Xerox, Alien Skin, Pantone, and a host of others.

GURU AWARDS

At every PhotoshopWorld, the NAPP honors the work and creativity of its members through the Guru Awards for Excellence in Photoshop Design. Attendees are elgible to submit pieces in nine different categories:

Photography (digital or traditional scanned images manipulated or collaged in Photoshop) Every Photography entry will be automatically submitted to win the Vincent Versace award for Digital Photography Excellence.

Illustration (original creations drawn or created in Photoshop)

Artistic (artistic creations)

Photo Restoration (Restoring or repairing a damaged images, ie: rips, scratches, etc.)

Web Design (a website whose graphics were designed in Photoshop)

Photo Retouching (Repairing or restoring damaged images, retouching people, landscapes, etc.)

Commercial (brochures, annual report collages, advertising, logos, etc.)

Photo Montage (Collage of images).

***Photoshop User* Challenge** Challenges have included redesign of the Adobe Photoshop product box, mock cover for *Photoshop User*, redesign of the Adobe Photoshop splash screen.

Go to
www.peachpit.com/
dreamteam.html
to download files for
this chapter.

CHAPTER ONE
GHOSTS AND MEMORIES

Kevin Ames

Kevin Ames began his photographic career at the age of 12, when he sold pictures of a class field trip to his schoolmates for a tidy profit. From this entrepreneurial and creative beginning, Kevin has become a recognized leader in the fast-evolving world of commercial digital photography.

"Whenever I'm using a camera, I'm not so much concerned with it as I am with the light," Kevin says of his creative philosophy and process. "I love to control, and model, and make light work on whatever I'm photographing. It's my passion when I'm behind the camera."

His company, Ames Photographic Illustration, Inc., is based in Atlanta, Georgia, and serves clients on location or in the studio. Ames specializes in creating evocative images that promote its customers' products, services, and ideals.

"Making photographs for people, being my own boss…I am doing what I've always wanted to do, since I was a child watching my parents develop photographs in their bathroom darkroom. I always knew I wanted to be a photographer, and so every day that I'm making photographs and creating is a perfect day."

Kevin is much in demand as a teacher and speaker. He is a PhotoshopWorld Dream Team instructor at the semiannual PhotoshopWorld conference. Kevin is also a Software Cinema author and presenter at Dean Collins's Photoshop Training Camp Live! events across the country. His training CDs include *Preserving Pixels—Non-Destructive Editing in Photoshop CS, Managing Digital*

REAL-TIME VISUALIZATION

Creative processes are as different and varying as the artists they serve. They are not formulas or recipes. They are methodologies useful on the journey to an end result.

Ansel Adams would look at a scene he wished to photograph and see the finished print. He named his creative process previsualization.

Jerry Uelsmann's process of making photographs to be assembled later in the darkroom has been called postvisualization. *On his Web site (www.uelsmann.net) Uelsmann says, "If you go into the darkroom with the agenda that you want a specific thing to happen, the anything that happens different from that becomes a mistake. If you're open to accidental or spontaneous events and you can give up your total fixation with the expected result, you may have all kinds of results that might be equally satisfying or even more satisfying."*

Digital capture has given the photographer access to elements of a composition or even the final image that is almost instantaneous. Sometimes the challenge becomes knowing when the photograph is finished.

An image captured digitally is viewed in what is for all practical purposes real time. *The impressions, ideas, and feelings of the moment are available for review right* now *while they are still fresh. Not hours or days into the future when they are at best memories.*

My creative process is an amalgam of pre- and postvisualization, coupled with seeing the result in real time. I call it real-time visualization.

continued on next page

KEVIN AMES, *continued*

Files and Photographs, The Digital Portrait from Many Images to One, and *Retouching Beauty: Digital Makeup and Body Sculpting.* He has taught classes at art schools and conferences around the world, including Fotographia Orvieto in Orvieto, Italy; Arthouse in Dublin; and the Commercial and Industrial Photographers of New England conference in Boston.

"I hope to teach the new way of thinking that digital offers," notes Kevin. "When I'm helping people learn the possibilities of digital, my main concern is to show the problem-solving abilities that are the underlying power of the tips and tricks. I want students to learn how to apply techniques creatively to get the visions in their heads out for others to see."

Kevin writes the "Digital Photographer's Notebook" column for *Photoshop User* magazine. His articles and reviews have appeared in *Studio Photography & Design, Photo>Electronic Imaging,* and *Digital Output* magazines.

He is a Certified Professional Photographer, a Certified Electronic Imager, a Photographic Craftsman, and an Approved Photographic Instructor. He has served as co-chairman of the Digital Imaging and Advanced Imaging Technology Committee and chairman of the Commercial Advertising Group for the Professional Photographers of America.

Kevin's first book is *Adobe Photoshop CS: The Art of Photographing Women* (Wiley Technology Publishing, 2004).

kevin@amesphoto.com

www.amesphoto.com.

REAL-TIME VISUALIZATION, *continued*

I begin with a feeling that evolves into a visual idea. I begin thinking about what the image might be, avoiding what it previously had been forced to be by the literal limitation of the camera's interpretation of a scene. I have learned to see beyond the camera and into the postproduction process. I see how my Photoshop work will tie the elements from ideas into a finished work.

The camera is the tool to capture the parts, pieces, and moments of time that will make up the composition. With stills or landscapes, I shoot with the camera on a tripod, tethered to my PowerBook. I see the images as I make them. I'll change the aperture to vary the depth of field, the exposure to increase the dynamic range, and the shutter to introduce or eliminate motion. I'll wait as the light washes a scene, shooting this variation caused by time alone.

I shoot, see the result, change it, shoot again, observe, follow my intuition, shoot and review some more. In my mind's eye the final image takes shape as the elements appear on the screen.

I work the same way when photographing people. I do take the camera in hand (still shooting to the computer if possible) and interact with my subjects. I move in close for images of eyes or lips. I climb ladders and shoot with a wide-angle lens. I will go across the studio and use an extreme telephoto. Photography with digital cameras gives the feedback to know when I've "got it!" That is important because once I have the shot, I can begin to play, experiment, and go wild. The model sees the results as we make the images and begins to push them further, too. We talk, point at the screen, and discuss what's working and what isn't. We go back on set and play some more. There are no limits. Instead there are possibilities.

New ideas generate from the photographs appearing on the screen. Nothing is left unexplored. Images I never would have attempted with film because I "knew" they wouldn't work or I wouldn't "like" the results now flow into my visual vocabulary. I am free.

Real-time visualization is a creative process that has evolved for me through years of making photographs painstakingly on film. I have learned the procedures that create "proper" exposures, lighting, and compositions. I have studied and applied parts of previsualization and postvisualization to my work. I have evolved my creative processes. Digital photography is another step in my creative journey. The promise that real-time feedback holds is freedom to create with fewer limits. Take your ideas, your camera, your lighting tools, and your photography to a new place.

Create freely.

GHOSTS AND MEMORIES

Birthdays are remembrances of beginnings, events, and moments to dream of future times. Several cool people started their lives on the same date as I did, including actor Maurice Chevalier; Olympic star Jesse Owens; the amazing Barry White; NBA star Yao Ming; and the second *American Idol* winner, Ruben Studdard. In my time, many interesting things have happened on my birthday—among them, John and Jackie Kennedy were married, and Nikita Khrushchev became leader of the Soviet Union. And decades later on that same date, agreements were signed that reunified his wall-divided Germany.

One of my fondest childhood birthday memories is the launch of Gemini 11. Two space shuttle missions have started on my natal date. And it is the only date to have its own *wiki* (a Web site that celebrates a subject).

Figure 1

My birthday is also the last time in recent memory *The Wall Street Journal* ran a 34-point banner headline across its front page (*Figure 1*). That date was the beginning of recovery from the horrific events of the day before. I was born on September 12.

In 2001 my birthday was somber, to say the least. Greetings and good wishes for the day were tinged with sadness and colored with stunned disbelief as clouds of smoke poured from the pyre of the fallen World Trade Center towers.

The events of September 11, 2001, moved everyone on the planet. Around the world, people worked to understand what had happened and why, and struggled to cope with their feelings.

After days of watching the coverage, I remembered that I had photographed some skylines of New York City from the apartment of a friend in Greenwich Village. From 20 floors up, the view included the Twin Towers. I remember pressing the lens of my Nikon F3 tightly to the window to make some photographs on Fuji 400 ISO color

Figure 2

negative film. A quick search through my archives turned up one of the only photographs of the World Trade Center I'd ever made, taken on June 23, 1995 (*Figure 2*).

I put the 4x6 print by my workstation in the Atlanta studio and thought about it for months. The summer of 2002 rolled around, and I found myself in New York again. Once more I was staying in my friend's 20th-floor apartment. I stared out the windows at the towerless scene. I could see the towers in my head. They just weren't there. It was very hard for me to grasp their loss and the loss of all the victims and rescuers who perished when the towers were destroyed that day.

Shortly before dusk, I set up my Kodak DCS 760 (a digital version of the Nikon F3) on a tripod, the lens once again firmly against the glass. With the camera connected to my computer, I used Kodak's Camera Manager software to change shutter, aperture, and ISO settings from the computer. I made a series of photographs as the sun was setting and continued shooting until the sky was dark. The next morning I shot the scene again, making sure that I never touched the camera for fear of moving it ever so slightly. Perfect registration was important for two reasons. Noise reduction was one (check out the sidebar). And the other was the photograph haunting my mind.

Download the Ghosts and Memories folder from www.amesphoto.com/learning. These photographs are copyrighted. You are free to use them only to do the steps in this chapter and to play with the techniques. Please don't make prints, post them on the Internet, or distribute them. Thanks. I appreciate your respect for my work.

NOISE REDUCTION

Digital photographs made in low light can be noisy, noisy—did I mention noisy? Film loves long exposures. Comparatively, digital camera sensors don't. As the exposure time increases, they can generate huge amounts of random electronic "grain," otherwise known as *noise*. The key to reducing noise is that word *random*. No single digital photograph will have the same noise pattern. Hmmm. Here is a simple technique that makes that randomness work for us.

Figure 3

Figure 4

When I shot the skylines, I made five exposures each of the dusk and morning scenes. I processed the Raw files into 16-bit TIF files, opened them all up in Photoshop CS, and dragged them into a single five-layer file (*Figure 3*).

Here's how to use this technique on five long exposures you have made.

1. Select the Move tool from the Toolbox, or press "v."

2. Click one of the open images, and hold down Shift as you drag the file on top of another file. Be sure to keep Shift held down until after you have released the mouse button. This aligns the two images in perfect pixel-to-pixel registration.

3. Close the first file that was dragged onto the base file (it now has two layers in the Layers palette) by pressing Command-W (PC: Control-W).

4. Repeat for the remaining three files. The layer stack will have five layers when you are finished.

5. Double-click the Background layer and rename it 100%. Click OK.

6. Highlight Layer 1. Set the Opacity to 80%. (Tip: With the Move tool selected, press 8. Bingo! The Opacity window reads 80%.) Rename the layer 80%.

7. Highlight Layer 2. Make the Opacity 60% and rename the layer 60%.

8. Highlight Layer 3. Change its Opacity to 40%. Name it 40%.

9. Highlight Layer 4. Set the Opacity to 20% and rename it 20%. Your Layers palette will look like that shown in *Figure 4*.

10. Flatten the image and save your work.

Here's the payoff. The enlarged area shown in *Figure 5* is from the red square in Figure 3. The *Before* image is of a single frame of the dusk scene. The *After* image is the average of the five different dusk photographs, complete with random noise and in perfect registration. Look, Ma, no noise!

Figure 5

Figure 6

> **NOTE**
>
> *In Mac OS X 10.3, the keyboard shortcut for Feather Selection (Command-Option-D) un-hides the Dock instead. Turn this feature off in System Preferences: Open the Keyboard & Mouse pane, click the Keyboard Shortcuts tab, and uncheck the "Automatically hide and show the Dock" box.*

Step 1

Open the 16-bit files 1247-WTC01.tif, 1983-morning.tif, and 1983-dusk.tif in Photoshop CS. Tip: If you are using Photoshop 7.0, change them to 8 bit; use Image>Mode>8Bits/Channel. The noise-reduction steps have already been implemented.

Step 2

Select the Move tool. Click 1983-dusk.tif, hold down Shift, and drag it onto 1983-morning.tif (be sure to keep Shift held down until after you have released the mouse button). Click 1983-dusk.tif again, and press Command-W (PC: Control-W) to close it.

Step 3

Double-click the Background layer and rename it Morning. Rename Layer 1 Dusk (*Figure 6*).

Step 4

Click the title bar of 1247-WTC01.tif to make it the active file. Click the Paths tab to show the Paths palette, and Command-click (PC: Control-click) the path WTC to turn it into a selection. Choose Select>Feather and feather the selection by 0.3 pixels. Hold down Command (PC: Control) and then press "j" to copy the selection into its own layer.

Step 5

Using the Move tool, drag Layer 1 (showing the World Trade Center towers) onto 1983-morning.tif. Close 1247-WTC01.tif without saving it. Rename Layer 1 WTC. Choose File>Save As, and save 1983-morning.tif as a Photoshop document (.psd) file.

The World Trade Center was photographed with a film camera in 1995. The full-frame shot has a slightly different perspective and is much larger than the scene it is going into. The next section deals with sizing and placing the towers in their original position.

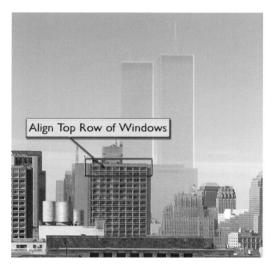

Figure 7

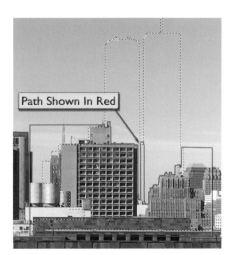

Figure 8

Step 6

Turn off the Eye icon for the Dusk layer. Set the Opacity of the WTC layer to 50%. Choose Edit>Free Transform (Command-T [PC: Control-T]). Click the Maintain Aspect Ratio link icon between the W and H number fields in the Options Bar (it looks like a chain link). Enter 46% in the W field. Drag the Towers layer until the top floor of the apartment building in front of them lines up as closely as possible (*Figure 7*). The foreground buildings of the WTC layer will not exactly match the background buildings of the Morning layer. This is not a problem, as the transformation is for position only. Click the Commit Transform checkbox in the Options Bar, or press Return (PC: Enter). Return the Opacity of the WTC layer to 100%.

Step 7

Hold down Command (PC: Control) and click the WTC layer thumbnail. This makes a selection of the pixels on that layer. Click the layer's Eye icon to hide it. The selection shows where the Twin Towers once stood.

Notice that the area selected is wider than the existing skyline. Buildings that stood in front of the towers in 1995 no longer exist. Hide and reveal the WTC layer to see what I mean. For the next step, leave the WTC layer hidden.

Step 8

Choose the Pen tool from the Toolbox. Draw a path that follows the skyline of the current buildings from the Morning layer inside the selection area that outlines the WTC. The path has to reach up into the space between the towers (*Figure 8*). Extend the path around the outside of the selection down below the section of the NYU library (the rust-colored building bordering Washington Square). Double-click the work path in the Paths palette, and rename it Path 2. (If you want a shortcut on this project, use the predrawn Path 1 that is in the download images when the directions ask you to work with Path 2.)

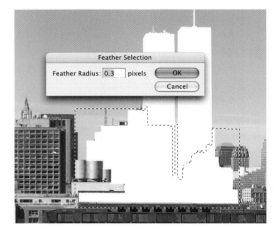

Figure 9

Figure 10

Step 9

Deselect the WTC layer selection (Command-D [PC: Control-D]). Make the Morning layer active, and click the New Layer icon at the bottom of the Layers palette to add a new layer. Drag Layer 1 under the Morning layer. Fill Layer 1 with white: Choose Edit>Fill, and select White from the Contents pop-up menu.

Step 10

Command-click (PC: Control-click) the WTC layer to bring back the selection of that layer. Highlight the Morning layer. Hold down Option (PC: Alt) and click the Add Layer/Vector Mask icon at the bottom of the Layers palette. The outline of the selection from the WTC layer appears as white in the new layer mask.

Step 11

Click the Paths tab. Command-click (PC: Control-click) Path 2 to load it as a selection. Press Command-Option-D (PC: Control-Alt-D) to bring up the Feather Selection dialog. Enter 0.3 pixels (*Figure 9*). Click OK.

Step 12

Click the Layers tab. Highlight the layer mask of Morning by clicking its thumbnail; a layer mask icon appears next to the Eye icon. Fill the selection with white. The keyboard shortcuts are "d" to set the default colors (white is the foreground color) and Option-Delete (PC: Alt-Backspace). The missing skyline reappears. Deselect (*Figure 10*).

Steps 7 and 10 through 12 have to be repeated for the Dusk layer. If only there were a way to copy layer masks. Well, don't tell *anybody*, but there is! Here's how...

Step 13

Click Dusk's thumbnail to make that layer active. Click and hold Morning's layer mask icon, and in one motion (that is, don't release the mouse button) drag it to the Add Layer/Vector Mask icon, and then

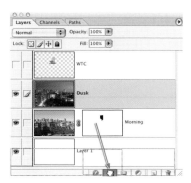

Figure 11

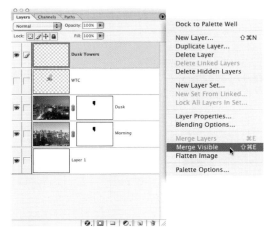

Figure 12

release…BANG! The silhouette of the towers instantly appears in the night sky (*Figure 11*). Copying layer masks is one of many time-saving shortcuts I have learned from Adobe's own Senior Digital Imaging Evangelist, the fabulous Julieanne Kost; kudos and thanks!

Day and Night, Night and Day

My original idea was to portray the faded outlines of the towers against an everyday skyline. Thinking about memories, I began to realize that they truly become painted in our minds as they change through time. The terrorist attacks and their aftermath are marked as time passes. So are the memories of where the towers once stood. The photograph I saw in my mind had to show ghosts and memories *moving in time*, not a frozen reality.

Step 1

Highlight the WTC layer by clicking its thumbnail. Hide it and the Morning layer by clicking off their Eye icons.

Step 2

Make a new layer at the top of the stack, and rename it Dusk Towers. Hold down Option (PC: Alt) and select Merge Visible from the Layers palette menu at the top right (*Figure 12*). This copies the visible layers to the active layer—here, Dusk Towers (for this to work, make sure you keep Option [PC: Alt] held down until you see the new layer thumbnail appear).

Step 3

Hide the Dusk Towers and Dusk layers. Reveal the Morning layer by clicking its Eye icon back on.

Step 4

Using the ultracool shortcut in the Tip, hold down Command-Option-Shift (PC: Control-Alt-Shift), and then press "n" followed by "e." Morning and Layer 1 have been copied onto the new layer. Rename it Morning Towers. Reveal Dusk Towers by clicking on its Eye icon.

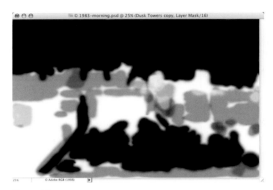

Figure 13

Figure 14

Step 5

Change the blending mode of Morning Towers to Lighten. Turn off the Eye icons for all the layers except Morning Towers and Dusk Towers. Make a new empty layer, and copy Morning Towers and Dusk Towers to it (Command-Option-Shift [PC: Control-Alt-Shift] and "n" and then "e"). Rename the layer Lighten.

Step 6

Click the thumbnail of Dusk Towers to highlight it. Press Command-J (PC: Control-J) to make a copy of it. Drag Dusk Towers Copy to the top of the layer stack.

Step 7

Set the blending mode of Dusk Towers Copy to Pin Light, and then double-click the layer name and rename the layer Pin Light. Click the Add Layer/Vector Mask icon on the Layers palette to add a layer mask to Pin Light.

Step 8

Select the Brush from the Toolbox. Make it a soft-edged 125-pixel 100% Opacity brush. Set black as the foreground color. Paint over the magenta posterized trees. Paint over the sky as well. Set the brush to 50% Opacity. Paint over the tops of the buildings that line the street on the left, the rooftops of the buildings on the right, and the rooftop in the foreground. Your layer mask will resemble *Figure 13*.

To see the mask view shown in Figure 13, hold down Option (PC: Alt) and click the thumbnail of the layer mask. Option-click (PC: Alt-click) the mask thumbnail again to return to the regular view of the image. The layer stack has seven layers at this point (*Figure 14*).

Step 9

Highlight Morning Towers. Duplicate it by pressing Command-J (PC: Control-J). Move it up to the top of the layer stack. Rename the layer Color Burn.

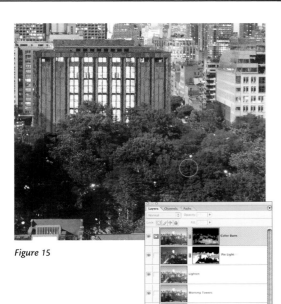

Figure 15

Figure 16

Figure 17

Step 10

Change the blending mode to Color Burn. Ouch! Too much! Lower Color Burn's Opacity to 50%. Much better. This layer is going to add some contrast to selected areas of the composition.

Step 11

Hold down Option (PC: Alt) and click the Add Layer/Vector Mask icon at the bottom of the Layers palette. A new layer mask filled with black appears next to Color Burn's thumbnail. Holding down Option (PC: Alt) when you click the Add Layer/Vector Mask icon creates a layer mask that hides everything on the layer (black), instead of the default, which would be a mask that showed everything (white).

Step 12

Select the Brush from the Toolbox by pressing "b." Make white the foreground color, and set the brush's Opacity to 50%. Paint over the trees. They become darker (*Figure 15*). Change the Brush Opacity to 25%. Work on the edges of the photograph, darkening them slightly. Use the Brush to add contrast to some of the blues in the buildings and the yellow in the windows (*Figure 16*).

Step 13

Duplicate Dusk Towers one more time. Drag it to the top of the layer stack. Rename it Color Burn Inverted.

Step 14

Choose Image>Adjustments>Invert (Command-I [PC: Control-I]). Set the layers blending mode to Color Burn. At this point it might look like way too much contrast. We are going to use only part of this layer.

Step 15

Select the Lasso tool from the Toolbox ("l"). Draw a selection just above the rooftops of the buildings at the front of the skyline and around the entire sky (*Figure 17*).

Figure 18

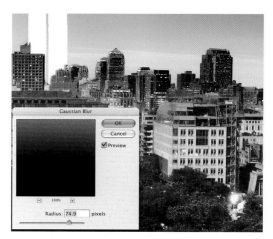

Figure 19

Step 16

Click the Add Layer/Vector Mask icon on the Layers palette. The new layer mask on Color Burn Inverted is white above the roofline and black below it. The transition from the top of the image, with its extra contrast, and the bottom is a sharp line (*Figure 18*). The next step will soften this transition variably *and* interactively.

Step 17

The layer mask on Color Burn Inverted is active. Choose Filter>Blur> Gaussian Blur (*Figure 19*). Set the pixel Radius to around 75 pixels. Click the Preview checkbox on and off to see the effect. What we're looking for is kind of a spotlight edge transition from the sky and the buildings in the background through the rooftops and fading completely in the trees and street. The buildings directly on the skyline still look a bit too cartoonish. In the next step…

Step 18

…we'll knock the effect down a little bit: Choose the Brush tool. Use the 125-pixel soft-edge brush at 25% Opacity. Paint with black over the tallest buildings, and bring their contrast down just a bit. Now lower the layer Opacity to (you guessed it) 50% (*Figure 20*). This enhances the difference between night and day.

Figure 20

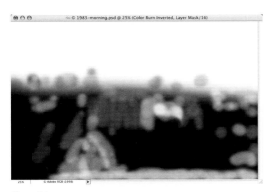

Figure 21

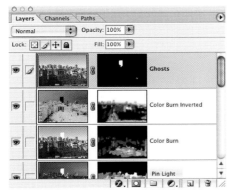

Figure 22

Paint with white on the shadow sides of the buildings on the lighted street to make them slightly darker (Figure 21).

Now it's time to turn the Twin Towers into the ghosts our minds see when we gaze at the places where they used to be.

Step 19

Duplicate the original Morning layer (the one with the layer mask that shows the dark silhouette of the towers). Drag it to the top of the layer stack. Rename it Ghosts.

Step 20

Make the Ghosts layer mask active by clicking it. Press Command-I (PC: Control-I) to invert the mask (*Figure 22*).

Our work here is done (*Figure 23*).

Figure 23

Starting with a simple CLOUDS filter I was able to create the basis for my water effect.

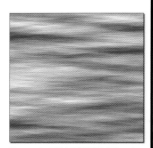

Then I TRANSFORMED the image horizontally and CROPPED to maintain the square dimensions.

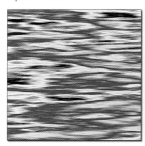

I needed to duplicate the image to create a B&W version. I used CURVES to maximize the lights and darks. I then saved this image to be used as a displacement map.

BIRD'S EYE VIEW

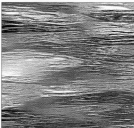

I then ran a DISTORT/GLASS filter using my displacement map to create a very convincing water effect.

Lastly, I placed my seagull image, MASKED out the sky in the image, and ran the DISTORT/DISPLACE filter on the seagull. Using the ADVANCED BLEND modes I was able to make the reflection of the gull more convincing.

CHAPTER TWO

WORKING WITH SPOT-COLOR CHANNELS

Go to
www.peachpit.com/
dreamteam.html
to download files for
this chapter.

Geno Andrews

Geno Andrews is highly respected as a trainer. Jack H. Davis, co-author of *The Photoshop WOW! Book*, says this of Geno: *He's the consummate instructor—extremely knowledgeable, highly practical, and always inspirational. If you want to dramatically improve the quality, speed, and flexibility of your Photoshop work, then Geno is the teacher who will show you the way. I highly recommend him for all your creative training needs.*

Although training has been Geno's focus for the past nine years, his background in television, music, and film took him into the world of interactive CD-ROM game play in the early 1990s.

He started Presto Studios with his partner Jack Davis and a gang of others from San Diego to create the world's first interactive movie on CD-ROM, *The Journeyman Project*. He went on to create one of the first interactive multi-session music compact discs, CD V.I.N.E.L.S, through his L.A.-based record label, The Digital Realm Company. In the latter part of the 1990s, many CD-ROM developers in need of music for their interactive projects turned to Geno's HI REZ AUDIO discs for their royalty-free music needs.

As a singer/songwriter, Geno considers himself first and foremost a storyteller, which has led him to his most recent endeavors: screenwriting, producing, and filmmaking.

His award-winning short film, *Jillian's Vantage*, was recently picked up for distribution through the Spiritual Cinema Circle of Ojai and his most

SPOT COLOR ADVENTURES

Forrest Gump once said, "My mama always said life is like a box of chocolates…you never know what you're gonna get." Minus the goofy accent, most designers (until recently) have had similar sentiments toward the world of spot color.

Before we begin the "How To" section of this project, it helps to give a brief summary of what spot color actually is. Forgive me if this seems too rudimentary, but for those of you who are new to the spot color world, a little background on the print process in general will help to get us all on the same page.

Spot color, or spot channel work, is a print-world issue. If you're doing Web work, or video, or animation, or interactive TV, you don't have to worry about it.

Let's begin with a crash course in offset printing!

Any image you create in Photoshop that you intend to have printed in mass production (on a printing press) has to be color-separated through a program like QuarkXPress, or Adobe PageMaker or InDesign. These programs output four pieces of film. Each piece of film is made up of a series of small and large dots (screens) that represent a given amount of ink to be printed onto a page.

These film outputs (negatives) are then exposed onto metal printing plates, and those plates are attached to rollers on a printing press. The four inks are distributed onto a piece of paper from the rollers,

continued on next page

GENO ANDREWS, *continued*

recent film, *The Visits*, is now in pre-production for a Movie Of The Week.

For more information about Geno's music, movies, design work, and the coveted Geno Andrews Action Figures, please visit him on the Web at www.genoandrews.com.

For information regarding his onsite Photoshop classes, please visit Geno Andrews' Onsite Training Web site (www.genoandrews.com/training).

SPOT COLOR ADVENTURES, *continued*

and the different-size dots form a pattern of colored dots (known as a rosette*) that create the illusion of a color photograph on the printed page. It is not a continuous tone of color. It is simply varying-size dots of cyan, magenta, yellow, and black inks that make up the image. Whew!*

Pop Quiz: How many shades of gray are there in a black-and-white photograph printed in a newspaper?

Answer: None. There are only large and small dots of pure black ink. This is in contrast to a photograph, in which the same image actually has dark and light shades of gray throughout. In a color photograph printed on an offset press, all the colors are made up of varying-size dots of the four process-color inks (cyan, magenta, yellow, and black). If you use a magnifying glass or a loupe and examine any of the illustrations in this very book, for example, you'll see the dot pattern in those colors.

Concept: Think of the detail we could add to a black-and-white image if we could print actual custom gray inks. Now hold that thought …

THE SIMPLE TWO-COLOR JOB: A BLACK-AND-WHITE PHOTO WITH PANTONE (REFLEX BLUE) TYPE

A spot color is simply another color (or custom color besides the CMYK values) added to your offset printing job. To see an example of this in action, take a good look at the cover of *Sports Illustrated*. Usually you'll see a four-color picture of some amazing athlete. But you'll also notice another color—silver! Silver is a custom ink they use for the type, "Sports Illustrated." That fifth color (which cannot be achieved using CMYK values) is what we call a *spot color* or *custom ink*.

Spot colors can be the strange-looking glitter ink on the Barbie packaging. Or the glow in the dark ink on the Lucky Charms cereal box. You've probably seen the reflective silver in the *Terminator 3* one-sheets, or the fluorescent neon colors of a *Wired* magazine cover. Or a spot color can be the glossy surface (spot varnish) that seems to make the shampoo bottle stand out in a print ad.

If you planned on using one of these custom inks, the challenge would be to convey to the client how the finished product would look without actually having these custom inks built into your color palette on the computer. A designer would show the client a comp and say, "Now just imagine"—and show them a silver Pantone swatch—"that this silver color will be running through the type in your logo."

If you couldn't convey it clearly enough, the client might in turn say, "Just imagine that I'm writing a check that you could actually cash." And so has gone the struggle between designer and client in regard to previewing spot color and custom ink work onscreen.

Worse yet was the world of two-color jobs and duotone projects, where instead of creating a fifth spot color, we actually threw away two channels from a four-color file. We'd output two pieces of film and tell the printer to ink the cyan plate with Pantone color X and the black plate with Pantone color Y in hopes of mixing the two colors successfully, and thus avoiding the cost of the four-color printing process.

Two-color disasters sent many young designers back to bartending school.

In the end, the cry from designers to the Adobe team was simple: please give us a better way to more reliably preview our custom color projects onscreen. Adobe's answer: spot channels.

Since the advent of the spot channel in the Channels palette, we now have more control than ever before over viewing our custom color work. But don't think for one second that there's an autopilot function. There are still plenty of ways to crash and burn in a blaze of unwarranted glory. But hopefully this chapter can help you steer clear of some bumpy flying.

There's no way I could create a chapter on spot channels and explain the concept clearly with just one project. So you get two. One is more sophisticated than the other, but both are great for learning the basics of working with spot channels.

Figure 1

Figure 2

Step 1

Let's start with a black-and-white photograph of an old Cadillac (*Figure 1*). (Willie Herath, a very talented photographer friend of mine, created this fine image. Thanks, Willie!) And let's add a layer of white type (*Figure 2*). You'll notice that I have both the Layers palette and the Channels palette in view. If you've ever saved a selection as an alpha channel before, this next step will be very similar.

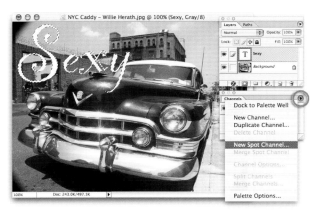

Figure 3

Figure 4

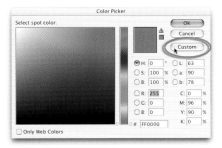

Figure 5

Step 2

You need to load the type as a selection. Any time you Command-click (PC: Control-click) a layer, channel, or path, you will get marching ants based on the shape of the layer, channel, or path. With the ants marching, go to the Channels palette pop-up menu (click the small triangle button in the upper-right corner of the palette) and choose New Spot Channel (*Figure 3*).

In the New Spot Channel dialog, clicking the small Color swatch under the Ink Characteristics (*Figure 4*) brings up the Color Picker.

TIP

Here's a great shortcut: Command-click (PC: Control-click) the Page icon at the bottom of the Channels palette to get the New Spot Channel dialog.

What we want here is the Custom Colors dialog, so in the standard Photoshop Color Picker dialog, just click the Custom button (*Figure 5*) to bring up the Custom Colors dialog (*Figure 6*). From the Book pop-up menu at the top of the dialog choose "PANTONE solid coated." In the vertical color bar, click about a third of the way down from the top in the deep blues (see the circled area in Figure 6) to find PANTONE Reflex Blue (it may take you a few clicks before you see the ink appear in the swatches to the left). Click it to select that ink, and then click OK to leave the Custom Colors dialog.

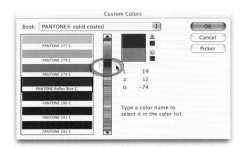

Figure 6

Figure 7

Figure 8

Now pay close attention to the Solidity value. For the purpose of our discussion, go ahead and set it to 100%. If you're not careful, this can cause some turbulence, which you'll want to avoid in the future. Some designers have mistaken this value for some kind of opacity setting. Each ink has a solidity value, which specifies how transparent the ink is. A silver ink, for example, is 100% opaque, meaning that if you print silver anywhere on your page, nothing will show through it. Its Solidity value is 100%. However, in this project, we're using Reflex Blue, which is a very transparent ink. *Figure 7* shows how this image looks onscreen with the Solidity set to 100%. *Figure 8* shows what the image looks like onscreen when the Solidity value is set to 0%. You can see there is a drastic difference.

If your client signed off on the way the blue looked in Figure 7, but the finished job came off the press looking like Figure 8 (which it would have), you would have been one of those designers scratching their heads and wondering what went wrong, somewhere between your third and fourth martinis.

SOLIDITY ROULETTE

Who knows the true Solidity settings for these custom inks? Only your printer knows for sure. If Pantone, Inc., wants a million hits a day, it should post a Web page giving the Solidity amounts for each Pantone ink in its swatch book. My students constantly want to know what the Solidity setting should be for a particular Pantone Ink. But I digress…

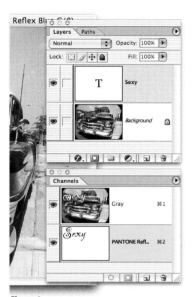

Figure 9

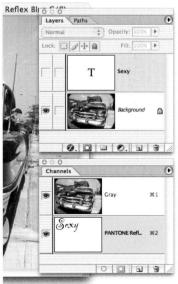

Figure 10

Step 3

If you intend to keep your custom ink (Reflex Blue), regardless of its Solidity value, from mixing with the inks underneath, all you need to do is *knock out* the type from the black plate. This is achieved quite simply by just turning on the white type layer in the Layers palette.

In *Figure 9*, you can see that I've left the visibility for the type layer turned on. In the Gray channel (which represents the black plate in this job) you'll notice the type is white, meaning that no black ink will print inside that area (see Figure 7). In *Figure 10*, however, I've turned off the type layer visibility, and now you can see that the Gray channel (black plate) has no knock-out, so the Pantone plate (Reflex Blue) will print over and blend with the black ink when the image is printed (see Figure 8).

Pop Quiz: How would you "mix" 50% of the black ink with 100% of the Reflex Blue through the type?

Answer: Take the Opacity of the white type layer down to 50%. You're now allowing 50% of the black-and-white image to show through and mix with the 100% of the Reflex Blue ink in the spot channel.

Figure 11

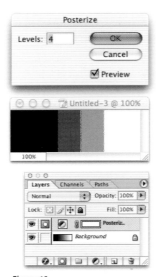

Figure 12

White Flash with Three Spot Colors: Richer Black-and-White Images in Silkscreening

Earlier, I asked you to hold a thought. Now it's time to recall it. I asked, wouldn't it be cool if we could customize a black-and-white image with additional gray inks? If you've ever tried to silkscreen a dynamic black-and-white image onto a shirt, you've probably run into a pretty flat finished product. And after a few washings, those tiny black dots that make up gray areas of the image disappear, causing the photo to fade. But if there were no little black dots to make up the gray areas, just solid custom gray tones, then the job would really pop (not to mention the shirt would last through quite a few more washings).

Here's a spot color concept that makes black-and-white images printed onto T-shirts (or six-color jobs, or any blending of PANTONE colors outside of the four-color process world) really pop.

Step 1

We'll start with a black-and-white photograph (*Figure 11*). You can use any black-and-white photo for the steps in this project.

Step 2

Create a new document that is 3 x 1 inches, and use the Gradient tool to add a gradient blend from black to white. Next, add a Posterize adjustment layer, and set Levels to 4 (*Figure 12*). Now you can flatten the file. This creates a document showing pure black, dark gray, light gray, and pure white. We will use this as a color swatch to sample from.

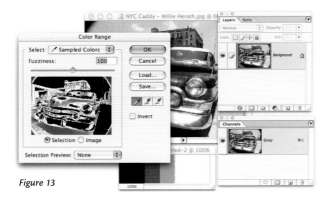

Figure 13

Step 3

With both documents visible, and the Caddy document (or your own black-and-white image) in front, choose Select>Color Range. When the Color Range dialog appears, move your cursor over the dark gray swatch in the posterized gradient document, and click to sample that tone. When you do this, the Color Range tool automatically chooses all of the dark gray values in the image. Click OK, and a selection is created of only the tones that match those dark grays from the swatch document (*Figure 13*).

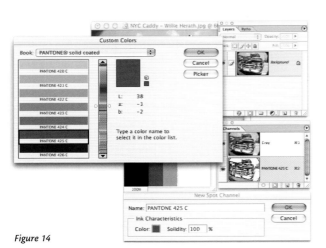

Figure 14

Step 4

With the marching ants still marching, choose New Spot Channel from the Channels palette menu. Then click the Color swatch to bring up the Color Picker dialog, and click Custom to get the Custom Colors dialog. Move the cursor out over the gradient swatch document, and click the dark gray band to sample that color (*Figure 14*). This automatically selects the closest PANTONE ink to that tone and creates a spot color channel representing a seamless selection of the dark gray tones in our image.

TIP

You should turn off the visibility of the spot color channel when you go back to repeat these steps. You want to be picking tones from the original image, *not the image combined with your new spot channel.*

Step 5

Repeat this process to sample the light grays and the blacks in the image.

Step 6

The last step is to create a new spot channel and fill it with 100% black. This channel represents the Flash, or white ink that gets laid down on the shirt as a base for the other tones to be printed on top of. In the end, you can always adjust the values of the gray spot channels by applying a levels adjustment on them for subtle blending.

Cheers!

CHAPTER THREE

HELP DESK LIVE! PHOTOSHOPWORLD'S TOP QUESTIONS

Peter Bauer

Peter Bauer is perhaps best known as the Help Desk director for the National Association of Photoshop Professionals (NAPP). He personally answers more than 20,000 Help Desk questions each year for NAPP and hosts Help Desk Live! at PhotoshopWorld. Pete is a contributing writer for *Photoshop User* and *MacDesign Magazine,* and writes a weekly column for the graphics portal PlanetPhotoshop.com. He is also a regular contributor to IllustratorWorld.com. Pete's books include *Special Edition Using Adobe Photoshop CS and Illustrator CS* (Que Publishing, 2004), *Special Edition Using Adobe Photoshop 7* with Jeff Foster (Que Publishing, 2002), *Special Edition Using Adobe Illustrator 10* (Que Publishing, 2002), *Sams Teach Yourself Adobe Illustrator 10 in 24 Hours* with Mordy Golding (Sams Publishing, 2001), and *Special Edition Using Adobe Illustrator 9* (Que Publishing, 2001).

An Adobe Certified Expert in both Photoshop and Illustrator, Pete also works as a computer-graphics efficiency consultant, helping operations both large and small streamline their workflows. His work includes testing and writing software documentation for a variety of Photoshop- and Illustrator-related products.

Pete and his wife, Professor Mary Ellen O'Connell of the Moritz College of Law at the Ohio State University, live in the historic German Village area of Columbus, Ohio.

THE BREADTH AND DEPTH OF PHOTOSHOP

As the Help Desk director of the National Association of Photoshop Professionals (NAPP), I answer more than 20,000 Photoshop-related emails each year. (Not to mention several hundred face-to-face questions at PhotoshopWorld's Help Desk Live! booth.) NAPP members submit questions about photo retouching, prepress, Web graphics, digital video, illustration, and more. If it can be done in Photoshop, NAPP members are doing it—and asking questions about it. (And, of course, asking questions about things that Photoshop can't do, but the Help Desk can usually handle those, too.)

Photoshop is an incredibly complex program, and most of us use just a fraction of its capabilities.

We're graphic designers or digital photographers or illustrators or prepress specialists or photo retouchers or Web specialists. Some of us work in multiple areas, full time or part time. But very few of us have the need to explore the entire range of Photoshop's capabilities.

I guess I'm one of the lucky ones. As I assist NAPP members working in all areas of Photoshop, I have the opportunity to use every feature the program has to offer.

I've learned more about Photoshop from Help Desk questions than I could ever have imagined. Two of the most important things I've learned are these:

No matter how much you know about Photoshop, there's always more to learn.

The best way to learn more about Photoshop is to experiment.

continued on next page

THE BREADTH AND DEPTH OF PHOTOSHOP *continued*

It's amazing how many great Photoshop techniques involve combining this with that, or doing that before this. But who thinks of doing things that way? The folks who know there's more to learn. The experimenters. Those who aren't afraid to simply play with Photoshop.

Okay, well, sometimes it's the people who aren't on deadline, who don't have a contract pending. Nonetheless, when you have the chance, try something new. See what an unfamiliar filter can do. Use different settings. Combine filters or adjustments or both. Repeat a filter with multiple settings (the new Filter Gallery in Photoshop CS makes it quick and easy to preview various filters and filter settings in combination). Use selections and masks to control the effect of a filter or adjustment. Duplicate a layer and change the blending mode. Work with the Edit>Fade command after applying a filter or adjustment. With experience, you'll have a library of information upon which you can rely. You'll know how the various commands work— and how they can work together.

You're reading a book that contains an incredible collection of information about Photoshop. The authors represented here have produced tens of thousands of pages of Photoshop material, including books, magazine articles, online tutorials, and workshop and conference handouts. Take the information here—and elsewhere— and apply it to your own images. See how you can modify the techniques, forming them to your needs and desires. Build on what you read and see, continuing to grow artistically and productively while you explore the breadth and depth of Photoshop.

TOP HELP DESK QUESTIONS

Throughout the year, the NAPP Help Desk provides answers to Photoshop-related questions via email. During PhotoshopWorld, it's a pleasure to meet NAPP members face-to-face, one-on-one, and discuss questions, problems, techniques, and ideas. Presented here are four of the most common, and most broadly applicable, questions asked at the PhotoshopWorld Help Desk Live! booth.

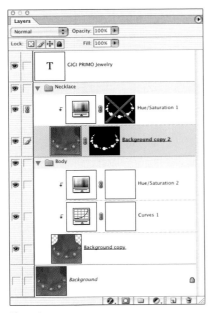

Figure 1
The active layer will always be highlighted in the Layers palette. When the active layer has a layer mask or a vector mask, look for the double box around a thumbnail to see whether the layer itself or the mask is active.

Photoshop is behaving badly: How can I get back to work?

It happens to all of us eventually, and perhaps far too often for some of us. Photoshop suddenly doesn't do what we want it to do. Tools don't work, commands give unexpected results, or the palettes look wrong. Here are the steps to take to get back to work as quickly and easily as possible (of course, you only need to perform those steps necessary to solve the problem).

Step 1: Check the Layers palette

When a tool or a command gives an unexpected result—or doesn't work at all—the first thing to do is to glance at the Layers palette (*Figure 1*). Is the correct layer active? Is the layer itself, rather than a layer mask, active? Is it a type layer that should be rasterized so that a filter can be applied?

The Layers palette indicates the currently active layer by highlighting it. A layer that has a layer mask or a vector mask will have multiple thumbnails in the palette. The thumbnail with a double box around it is the active element for that layer. (If you're trying to paint on the layer and the layer's mask is active, you're actually painting in the mask, not on the layer.)

Certain commands cannot be applied to type layers without rasterization, which converts the type from vector to pixels. Background layers (which are always named *Background*, with the name in italics) do not support transparency and layer masks, and are always locked. To unlock a Background layer, simply double-click it in the Layers palette and click OK in the New Layer dialog that opens. If this doesn't solve the problem, proceed to the next step.

Figure 2

All channels active (top left); just the Blue channel active and visible (top right); the Blue channel active with all channels visible (middle left), the Blue channel active but not visible (middle right); a spot-color channel active and visible (bottom left); and an alpha channel (mask) active and all channels visible (bottom right). An active mask appears in grayscale when it's the only visible channel, and as a red overlay when the other color channels are visible.

Step 2: **Check the Channels palette**

If everything looks correct in the Layers palette, click the Channels palette tab and take a look (*Figure 2*). Is the composite channel (RGB or CMYK) selected, and are all of the color channels active? If you're working on a mask, is the mask's alpha channel active? If you're working on a single channel, is the channel visible (with the Eye icon showing)? If you're working with a spot color, is the spot-color channel active?

If this doesn't solve the problem, proceed to the next step.

Step 3: **Check the Options Bar**

When a tool is not producing the expected results, check the Options Bar. If a Marquee selection tool can't be dragged in the shape you want, make sure it's set to Normal. If a Crop bounding box can't be resized, click the Clear button. Are the Brush's Opacity and Flow sliders at 100%? Which blending mode is the tool using? Remember, too, that no matter which tool is active, you can reset it to its default behavior by Control-clicking (PC: right-clicking) the Tool icon at the far left end of the Options Bar (*Figure 3*). Select the Reset Tool command, and the tool is restored to its default behavior. And while you're up at the top of your screen, try the menu command Select>Deselect—there may be an unnoticed selection active in the image.

If this doesn't solve the problem, proceed to the next step.

Figure 3

Control-click (PC: right-click) the Tool icon at the far left end of the Options Bar and you can reset the tool to its default settings. In this case, the Brush tool is restored to a soft 13-pixel tip and the Normal blending mode, and both the Opacity and Fill sliders will return to 100%.

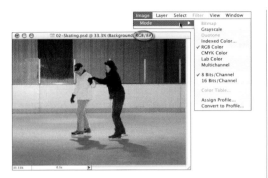

Figure 4

The image window's title bar and the Image>Mode menu show both the color mode and the color depth of the image you're working on. Make sure the image allows you to carry out the command you want to.

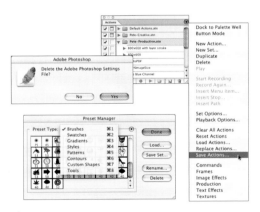

Figure 5

After saving your custom styles, brushes, actions, and other items, restart Photoshop while pressing Command-Option-Shift (PC: Control-Alt-Shift). When prompted, elect to delete the Adobe Photoshop Settings file. After the Adobe Photoshop Preferences file is deleted, Photoshop will start with its default settings and a fresh Prefs file.

Step 4: **Try another file**

Before taking the more radical steps that follow, it's usually a good idea to open another image and see if the problem you're experiencing can be replicated. If the tool, command, or technique works in the second file, take another look at your work file. Is it in a color mode that supports what you're trying to do? Is it a 16-bit or 8-bit image? Remember that you can't apply some color-related adjustments to grayscale images, and not all filters work in CMYK color mode or 16-bit color (*Figure 4*).

If this doesn't solve the problem, proceed to the next step.

Step 5: **Replace the Preferences file**

When Photoshop shows serious problems, or when you can find no other remedy, it's time to replace the Preferences file. This stores the content of certain palettes, the last-used settings for tools and commands, and other such information. Because the Prefs are rewritten every time you quit Photoshop, there's always the chance that the file will become corrupted. If menus, tool icons, or palette content is distorted or missing, it's likely the Prefs. Deleting the file forces Photoshop to re-create it from scratch, using the defaults.

There are a few things you should do before replacing the Preferences file:

• Choose Edit>Preset Manager. Save any custom styles, brushes, gradients, swatches, and the like. (Remember that they aren't saved until you add them to a set and save the set.)

• In the Actions palette menu, select Save Actions to save any custom actions. (You save sets of actions, rather than individual actions.)

• Open Photoshop's Preferences in the Photoshop menu on Mac, in Edit for Windows, and write down your key settings.

When you're ready to replace the Prefs, quit Photoshop. Hold down Command-Option-Shift (PC: Control-Alt-Shift) and restart Photoshop. When asked if you want to delete the Adobe Photoshop Settings file, release the keys, click Yes, and allow Photoshop to finish starting up (*Figure 5*). You'll see Photoshop just as it was when you first installed the program.

If this doesn't solve the problem, proceed to the next step.

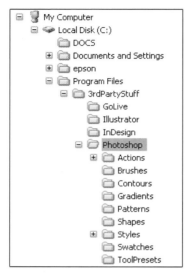

Figure 6

Saving your custom and third-party styles, brushes, actions, and the like outside the Photoshop folder will prevent accidental loss, should you need to reinstall the program. You can create a folder named 3rdPartyStuff and set up separate subfolders inside it for each of your programs.

Step 6: **Reinstall Photoshop**

When nothing else works, it's time to reinstall Photoshop. If you've saved custom styles, brushes, actions, and such, remove them from the Photoshop folder. This is an excellent opportunity to create a folder hierarchy in which you can store all custom bits and pieces for all of your programs. *Figure 6* illustrates one suggested organization for your folders.

Next, uninstall the existing, misbehaving copy of Photoshop:

Macintosh: Go to [Hard drive]>Applications and drag the folder Adobe Photoshop CS to the Trash. Go to [Hard drive]>Users>[user name]>Library >Preferences and drag the folder Adobe Photoshop CS Settings to the Trash. Empty the Trash.

Windows: From the Start menu, select Control Panel. Double-click Add or Remove Programs. Select Adobe Photoshop and click the Change/Remove button. The InstallShield Wizard will walk you through the process. Choose Standard Install so that you won't need to reactivate the software, and remove the user preferences. You'll be prompted to save or delete any files or folders that are shared among Adobe programs. Most can be deleted, but it's worthwhile to uncheck the "Always use this answer" box and look at each, just in case you spot a file or folder you've customized in another Adobe program.

Reinstall Photoshop from the original CD. Reset your Preferences. Reload your custom styles, brushes, actions, and so on. Reinstall any third-party plug-ins. Restart Photoshop and check to make sure the problem is gone. If not, it may be an operating-system or hardware problem, and you may need to call Adobe Tech Support.

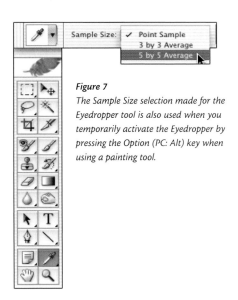

Figure 7
The Sample Size selection made for the Eyedropper tool is also used when you temporarily activate the Eyedropper by pressing the Option (PC: Alt) key when using a painting tool.

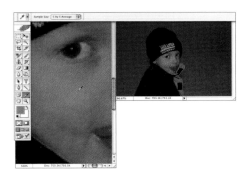

Figure 8
Even when the Eyedropper is set to sample a 5-by-5 average, it's a good idea to take a peek at the foreground color swatch in the Toolbox or the Color palette, just to make sure your new foreground color is what it's supposed to be.

How do I reduce digital noise?

Digital noise refers to the random blue, red, and perhaps green pixels scattered throughout an image taken by a digital camera. It is most common in images taken under low-light conditions or with a high ISO setting. You'll also generally find noise most prominent in the Blue channel. Here's a great way to paint away those colored pixels we call digital noise. (Note that this technique isn't for use with monochromatic luminance noise.)

Step 1: Set the Eyedropper tool

Select the Eyedropper tool from the Toolbox. In the Options Bar, change the Sample Size pop-up menu to 5 by 5 Average. This option controls how many pixels the Eyedropper examines (*Figure 7*). When designating a foreground color for digital-noise reduction (as we will do in the next step), it's best to get an average of the color values in an area rather than a single pixel.

Step 2: Sample an area

Click with the Eyedropper in the noisy image. This takes a look at the 25 pixels surrounding the point on which you clicked, averages their color values, and makes that new, averaged color the foreground color swatch (*Figure 8*). Even in very noisy images, the average is generally the color that should be in that part of the photo. If there is a range of tonal values in that area, click in the midtones.

Step 3: Paint with the Color Replacement tool

Choose the new Color Replacement tool. In the Options Bar, try settings of Mode: Color; Sampling: Continuous; Limits: Find Edges; Tolerance: 30%; and Anti-Aliasing selected. The brush size, of course, depends on the area in which you're working. (For earlier versions of Photoshop than CS, use the Brush or Paintbrush tool with the blending mode Color.)

Paint in the image to change the noisy pixels to the foreground color. As you work, you can change the foreground color by Option-clicking (PC: Alt-clicking). When working with skin tones, for example, you should resample the existing colors as you move from area to area (using a single color for the entire face can produce the appearance of heavy stage makeup).

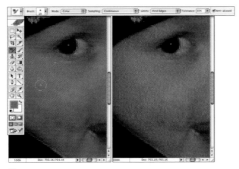

Figure 9

When using the Color Replacement tool to paint away digital noise, Option-click (PC: Alt-click) to reselect the foreground color as you move from area to area. Because the Color Replacement tool doesn't change luminosity, the image's highlights and shadows are maintained.

Figure 11

Command-H (PC: Control-H) hides the type highlighting (visible in the top sample) but leaves the type's baseline visible (middle sample). If you use the View menu to deselect Extras, the type highlighting and the baseline are hidden (bottom sample), but the type remains selected and ready for font previewing.

Reset the foreground color for the cheeks, the nose, the forehead, and other areas (*Figure 9*). When removing digital noise from walls, clothing, and other areas of uniform color, you'll need to select the foreground color only once.

Can I preview fonts in Photoshop?

Photoshop doesn't have a WYSISYG (what-you-see-is-what-you-get) font menu that will display the names of the fonts in the fonts themselves. You can, of course, preview fonts in other programs in order to make design decisions. Microsoft Word and Illustrator CS are two programs with WYSIWYG font menus. And font-management utilities enable you to preview—and even print—font books. But here's how to audition fonts in Photoshop,.

Step 1: Set the type

Add the type to your image. Set it at the size you expect to use, and adjust its other attributes in the Character palette and the Options Bar. (Remember that some fonts you preview may be larger or smaller than the initial font, but you can certainly tweak the attributes after selecting a font.) Add any layer style you anticipate using (*Figure 10*).

Figure 10

Set up your type layer the way you think you'll use it before you begin previewing fonts. You can then better envision the final appearance.

Step 2: Select the type and hide the highlighting

You can preview the font change for all of the type on the type layer, or for selected words or characters only. Ensure that the type layer is active in the Layers palette. If you will be changing only part of the text, drag the Type tool to select it. In order to better see your changes, hide the type's highlighting by pressing Command-H (PC: Control-H). If you find the visible baseline in Photoshop CS distracting, deselect Extras in the View menu (the check mark will be hidden). Deselecting Extras hides both the text highlighting and baseline (*Figure 11*).

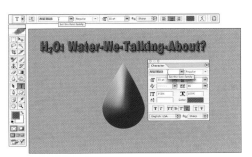

Figure 12
Whether you use the Options Bar or the Character palette, clicking in the Font field highlights the name of the font, enabling you to change fonts from the keyboard.

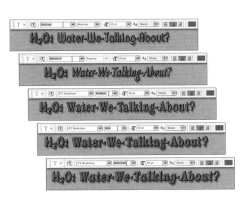

Figure 13
The down arrow and right arrow keys move to the next font alphabetically; the up arrow and left arrow keys switch to the previous font. As you can see in the three lower examples, the Font Style field can also be changed with the arrow keys (when a font has multiple styles).

Step 3: **Activate the Font Field**
In either the Options Bar (with the Type tool active) or the Character palette, click in the Font field to highlight the font family name (*Figure 12*).

Step 4: **Preview the fonts with the arrow keys**
Using the arrow keys on your keyboard, you can now cycle through the available fonts alphabetically. Press any letter on the keyboard to jump to the fonts whose names start with that letter. If the font has multiple styles (Roman, Medium, Italic, Bold, and so on), press Tab and use the arrow keys to cycle through the font styles. With every press of an arrow key, the font changes in your image (*Figure 13*). (Remember that each change of font registers in the History palette—it's a good idea to click the Snapshot button at the bottom of that palette before previewing fonts.)

What scan resolution should I use?

When choosing the proper resolution at which to scan, start at the end and work backward. Determine how many pixels you need in your final image, and scan that number of pixels. If you don't like doing math, you'll find some tips here on how to have Photoshop perform the calculations for you.

Step 1: **Determine the final size and resolution**
If the image will be placed into a page layout document for commercial printing, determine what size the picture will be on the final printed page (*Figure 14*). Also check the line screen frequency at which the job will print.

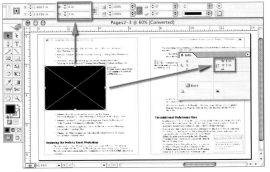

Figure 14
How big does the image need to be in the layout? Typically, a page layout program such as InDesign CS (shown here) gives you the size of an image frame or container in a couple of different places.

For newspapers you may see 85 lpi (lines per inch), while a magazine may be printed at 133 lpi, and a glossy catalog or annual report at 200 lpi. Multiply the line screen frequency by 1.5 or 2 to determine the correct image resolution.

If the image will be output on an inkjet printer, determine how large you'll be printing—will it be 5 x 7, 8 x 10, or perhaps 4 x 6 or even 13 x 19? Because inkjet printers are stochastic printing devices, the optimal image resolution theoretically is one-third the printer's rated resolution. (That provides the optimal balance between image detail and file size.) However, you probably don't need an image resolution higher than 300 ppi (pixels per inch) for any standard inkjet printer. A few sample prints on your printer with your paper will determine the best resolution for your needs.

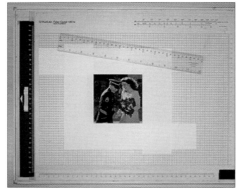

Figure 16
Ensure that you take steps to protect the original image before placing a ruler on it—for example, using a protective sleeve. You can use paper or cardboard to help compose an image prior to measuring.

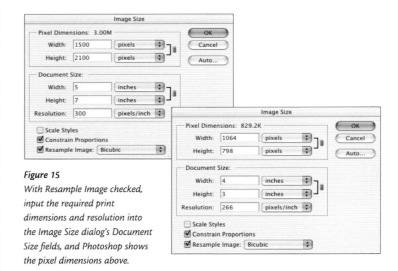

Figure 15
With Resample Image checked, input the required print dimensions and resolution into the Image Size dialog's Document Size fields, and Photoshop shows the pixel dimensions above.

Step 2: Calculate the final pixel dimensions

To get the final pixel dimensions, multiply the final print size in inches (or centimeters) by the output resolution. An image that will be placed into a page layout program at 4 inches by 3 inches at 200 ppi measures 800 pixels by 600 pixels. An image of the same dimensions with a resolution of 266 ppi measures 1064 pixels by 798 pixels (*Figure 15*). A 5 x 7 image at 300 ppi measures 1500 pixels by 2100 pixels. Photoshop's Image Size dialog can do the math for you.

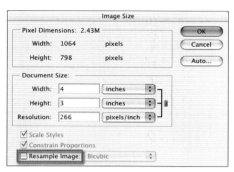

Figure 17

When the Image Size dialog's Resample option is not selected, Photoshop preserves the image's pixel dimensions. Entering a new figure in any of the three available fields (Width, Height, and Resolution) results in a recalculation of the other two fields.

Step 3: Measure the original

If you know the size of the original you have the dimensions already (consider a 35mm slide or negative to be 1.4" by 0.95"). If not, or if you'll be using only a portion of the image, measure the width and height (*Figure 16*). If you're measuring a portion of a slide or negative, it's a good idea to use a loupe or magnifying glass.

Step 4: Divide the original's measurements into the pixel dimensions

You know the size of the original in inches (or centimeters). You know the required pixel dimensions for the final image. Divide the pixel dimensions by the original's measurements to get the required scan resolution in pixels per inch (or centimeters).

The original image might not have the same *aspect ratio* (relationship between width and height) that you require for the final image. If so, you'll get different results when you divide the original's width and height into the required pixel dimensions. In this case you'll have to crop the image after scanning. If the calculations produce different resolutions, scan using the higher figure.

If you don't want to do the math, let Photoshop's Image Size dialog perform the calculations. Create a new document using the pixel dimensions you require for your final image. Choose Image>Image Size. With the Resample option unchecked, enter either the width or height of your original image (*Figure 17*). Photoshop will show you the required scan resolution in the Resolution field. (If you enter the correct width, but the height field changes to a figure other than that required, you have an aspect ratio difference.) Click Cancel and close the empty document without saving. Some scanners can also do the math for you. Input the print dimensions and print resolution, and the scan resolution will be calculated automatically.

CHAPTER FOUR

PUSHING PIXELS: USING PHOTOSHOP TO CREATE A PRODUCT MAKEOVER

Daniel Brown

Everything from database integration to digital image editing has held equal fascination for Daniel Brown as he has attempted a balance between left- and right-brain endeavors. With a background in traditional design, he went on to found the core Web Development team at Metagraphics in Palo Alto, CA (now artmachine.com). He served such clients as Apple, Netscape, Sun, Silicon Graphics, and Hewlett-Packard. Daniel joined Adobe Systems in 1998, taking on the role of Evangelist, lending a hand in product development, marketing, interface design, and customer education. Daniel is a frequent speaker at industry events worldwide.

RETOUCHING AND BEYOND WITH PHOTOSHOP

In product photography, Photoshop work can be the subtle removal of blemishes or scratches; other times it is making a prototype look like a finished product. I learned to value Photoshop, not just as a retouching tool, but as a key production machine that could work together with cameras and lights to achieve a result. In this chapter, we look at not just "correcting" an image in terms of exposure and color balance, but at synthesizing an identity for a product from very raw ingredients. We also look at ways of planning your entire project knowing Photoshop is in your arsenal of tools.

Special thanks to Jeff Kalt of Resolution Audio for allowing us to use his images.

PUSHING PIXELS

I was a serious pixel pusher, big-time. I did pixels, on a Macintosh, out to Scitex equipment when other people were still shaking their fists at Linotronics because their halftones looked like the herringbone pattern found on late-60s sport coats. I remember rotating a document 15 degrees that measured 18x30" at 300 dpi, and going to a rather lengthy lunch while my thoroughly souped-up Macintosh IIci hammered away at line after line of errantly oriented pixels at a whopping 40 MHz. Ah, those were the days!

And I learned a few things along the way. While each project had its own set of challenges (hence my love of the job), a few things remained constant. Routinely, we'd assure clients that their job was doable in the impossibly short 48-hour deadline they'd given us. Meanwhile, in my head I'd estimate that it would be 48 hours before I would know if the project was even possible. Sure enough, in the span of about 45 minutes, I'd have a plan. The project would be completed in 6 hours, but we'd bill them for the rest, anyway. So, you ask, how does a project go from impossible to complete in 6 hours? Therein lies the first lesson.

Lesson 1

Learn when to put down the mouse and step away from the keyboard.

I always come back to a single core truth about all creative tools. There is only one you need bother mastering, whether you are a graphic designer, photographer, Web designer, movie director, or architect—pencil and paper. They give you something few other media can: a plan. A pencil doesn't require a great deal of expensive training or hardware resources. If it crashes, you sharpen it. While technology certainly has the capacity to accelerate an idea to its ultimate form, unless the idea is clear in your head in the first place, you're driving a very fast car with no steering wheel.

Understanding and truly being able to use Photoshop require that you not only work with it on a regular basis, but that you also simply play with it. But if you're having trouble getting through a project or you're not quite sure how to achieve the results you're after, though, by all means *get away from the computer*. Stop asking Photoshop to finish your idea for you (or to create one for you in the first place). This methodology, by the way, applies to just about everything creative you can do on a computer. People often have unrealistic expectations of technology simply because it's cutting-edge. One wouldn't, for example, ever expect a piano to compose the music on its own. Photoshop won't help you with the vision. It can distract you for a while, and you may learn something during that time, but ultimately it'll just drag you down into blending mode puzzles and channel madness. A hammer won't help you decide what kind of house to build, so put it down until you finish the blueprint.

Lesson 2

Photoshop is not the punctuation mark on the process; it's an integral part of it.

Clients wasted money. They would pay us too much, and, human nature being what it is, we took it. They were well-meaning, perfectly nice people who simply didn't understand the potential of what we were offering them. More specifically, they didn't understand the overall process. Let me give you an example.

I once worked on an ad for a computer device that could connect to all kinds of other devices. To brag about this fact, the client envisioned an advertisement displaying their incredibly unattractive device and, above it, a shower of cords with various connectors raining down from the sky. Their boast was that this device could connect to "any port in a storm." Get it? Okay, it was pretty clever.

The cords were photographed straight up and down in front of a storm cloud backdrop. The client wanted them falling at more of an angle—20 degrees, as I recall. All I had to do was rotate the cords and fade the ends a little to make them look as if they were moving. Piece of cake. Probably a 4-hour job.

Two days later, the proof came back. Our client's clients had changed their minds. (Isn't that the *definition* of client?) It seemed the clouds looked a bit more than stormy; they were downright menacing.

In came a 35mm transparency of some kinder, gentler storm clouds, and, armed with the Pen tool, I began outlining every single cable in the shot. One by one, point by point, I traced them and isolated them into their own layer. It took me about half a day ($800 in billable time), and it required another proof (at $125), courier charges, another meeting with their clients to show the new proof, courier charges to send it back, and so on.

The problem? Our client did not understand the entire process. If they had called me first, I could have explained to them that they needed to shoot the cords on a solid background and shoot the clouds separately. A 10-minute conversation could have saved them about $4,000. To them, Photoshop was still a finishing touch.

It was relatively easy work, and fortunately I had great music to carry me through. But now I see how advising the client about how to shoot the project correctly in the first place is much more valuable than any Photoshop skill by itself. Here's the lesson: When you're getting ready to produce a project with Photoshop, *think* about how it will be assembled in the first place. Follow the path that the image will need to take, and anticipate what is likely to change about an image. Get involved early.

Good Photoshop users focus on mastering the tools. Although details are certainly important, great Photoshop users focus on the whole process.

Figure 1
The original product shot.

The Resolution Audio Project

To illustrate both lessons, I'm going to take you through a real-life project and explain not what filter I used at what level in what order, but what I did *before* I even started the project, what was involved in the project itself, and ultimately what the client gained from it.

Someone who knows Photoshop only in passing (as these clients did) might assume that it primarily *corrects* images or gets rid of unwanted elements. While that's all true, this assumption overlooks Photoshop's ability to solve much bigger problems.

Resolution Audio makes high-end audio equipment, and the appearance of that equipment is a consideration to customers making a purchase. In this case, their CD transport and external DAC (a very sophisticated version of what we mortals call a CD player) are offered in four color combinations of black and silver.

They needed a photograph of each of the color combinations. This was a problem from several angles. First, it meant paying someone to shoot all four combinations of what is essentially the same thing. Second, it meant building all four variations of the devices immediately. The company wanted to send some "teaser" materials out before committing to build all the units (prototypes cost about $8,000 apiece). And finally, it meant paying to scan four photographs, and paying me to fix all four of them.

I placed my hands on my hips and laughed at them heartily. "You need to understand, I can create all four variations of the units from a single photograph."

This was not only cheaper and far easier for them; it was also much simpler for me. Every tweak, levels change, color modification, and logo nudge would apply to all four variations at once. A single document contained all four variations of the product. Sad to say, I created this document three years before layer comps, a feature new in Photoshop CS, was available. It would have made the whole process much easier.

Figure 2

Figure 3
After initial tonal and color adjustments.

Step 1

The first problem was that the product shot was a rather dull scan of a rather dull photograph (*Figure 1*). It showed the product, all right, but the display was washed out; the paint was a bit glossy, which washed out the top; and it just wasn't very contrasty overall. As a special bonus, it was also a tiny bit green.

So I adjusted the tonal range a bit (*Figure 2*) and darkened the top with a levels adjustment layer (*Figure 3*). Better, but still bland.

Step 2

I turned to the display. All the levels commands in the world couldn't make it look better. It's one thing to master what you can correct in Photoshop, but it's a whole other skill to know when you're beaten and start from scratch. And that's just what I did. Rather than try to restore the LED display lights and button icons, I redrew them. I re-created the dots for the display element in Adobe Illustrator (*Figure 4*). Photoshop has some fairly powerful vector functionality, but Illustrator takes it to a

Figure 4
The rebuilt LED display.

Figure 5
A background from another photograph in the series was used for the product shot.

Figure 6
Noise was added to the table surface to give it some texture.

whole other dimension. We certainly don't have time to get into Illustrator tricks here, but let's just say this would have been really tough to do entirely in Photoshop.

Step 3

Next came the background. The original wasn't very exciting. Some previous shots the client had done were much more dramatic and kept with the company's blue theme. So I borrowed the background from one of those shots and used it here. I probably could have re-created it entirely with gradients, but it takes four or five gradients to simulate what the real world can do in a single frame. I grabbed a bit from the real world and placed it behind them (*Figure 5*).

Step 4

The "ground" that the units were sitting on didn't "feel" as if it was really there, so I added some noise to it to give it some texture (*Figure 6*).

Figure 7
The unit appeared to be floating above the table.

Figure 8
A drop shadow was added to eliminate the floating effect and ground the product.

Step 5

The units still seemed to be floating (*Figure 7*). A drop shadow drawn around the edges grounded them a bit more. For the record, I've found that a good drop shadow actually has two or three parts (see the sidebar "Drop Shadows and Reality Shadows"). Placing the darkest, sharpest stroke closest to the object and then adding a lighter, broader, softer stroke makes for a much more convincing effect (*Figure 8*).

DROP SHADOWS AND REALITY SHADOWS

Figure 9

Figure 10

Figure 11

While it pays to practice skills in Photoshop, it also pays to look carefully at things outside of Photoshop—specifically, the things we are trying to emulate. In this case, we're after a shadow that "anchors" the player to the table. A real shadow is much more than a simple blurred shape of the object. Light does some amazing things, and while it's pretty tough to simulate all of them, knowing a few basic characteristics of light will help a lot.

In *Figure 9* we see the player with no shadow. It doesn't appear to be sitting on anything. This is where the shadow comes into play.

Rather than relying on one layer to display a drop shadow, I used two different layers, of different sizes and opacities, to achieve the effect. Starting with the darker and smaller of the two, I drew a path based on the shape of the player, filled the inside with black, and then blurred it just slightly. This was the primary shadow (*Figure 10*).

Separately, I created another layer from the same path used to create the small shadow and filled that with black, but I blurred it a bit more by using a larger Radius setting. This gave it a somewhat different dimension but wouldn't be believable by itself (*Figure 11*).

When the two shadow layers were combined, they achieved a different effect than either could alone (*Figure 12*).

Figure 12

Figure 13

Step 6

Like the display, the logos and button icons had gotten lost in the product shot, so restoring them was next to impossible. New icons were born, and since they were fairly simple shapes, they were easily drawn in Photoshop (*Figure 13*).

Step 7

So far, so good. I had one great-looking product. Now I needed three more of them. I had silver on black, thanks to the original photo; I needed to create black on silver, silver on silver, and black on black.

Levels adjustment layers did most of the work, but the texture in the brushed-metal areas was once again a bit of an issue. I went back to one of the oldest Photoshop tricks in the world: brushed aluminum. That's right, boys and girls, the fronts of these units never existed. They're entirely faked (see the sidebar "Pixels of Steel").

PIXELS OF STEEL

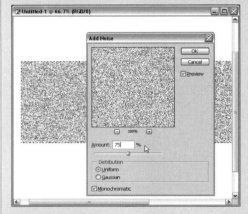

Figure 14

Figure 15

Reproducing brushed metal is one of the first tricks I remember learning in Photoshop, and it's funny that it *still* comes in handy. The other great thing about this technique is that it shows how three seemingly unrelated tools—Noise, Blur, and Levels—can be combined in interesting ways.

First, there's some noise—in this case, with a value of 75%—but this technique is very forgiving about settings. Do make sure that you choose Monochromatic, although I have seen brushed metal take on a slightly prismatic appearance. You could leave Monochromatic turned off and reduce the saturation later, but I chose to keep it at black and white in this instance (*Figure 14*).

Now the other key to the whole effect—Motion Blur. A Distance setting of 80 pixels gave it a nice look, and the angle should be kept horizontal. You can always distort it later (which I did, in fact). We've taken noise and stretched it sideways. We're almost there (*Figure 15*).

Now, we just need to crank up the saturation a tad. Again, the exact settings depend heavily on your project, but the goal here was to darken down the shadows a bit. I used Levels for this (*Figure 16*). What you're left with is the basic ingredient for the entire faceplate.

From here, it was just a matter of transforming the faceplate into perspective and attempting to match the shading of the original shot (via adjustment layers). Voilà! Something from nothing.

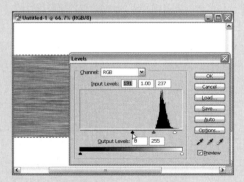

Figure 16

Figure 17

Figure 18

Figure 19

Step 8

Once I had the texture back, I added adjustment layers to create the different variations of the product (*Figures 17–20*).

The important question is: How long does a process like this take? If you know the tool (in this case, Photoshop), about 3 hours. Jeff at Resolution Audio estimated that that's how long it would have taken them to package up the units to ship them to the photographer.

Any questions?

Figure 20
The final four treatments, all created from a single product photograph.

CHAPTER FIVE
PANORAMAS GONE BAD!

Russell Preston Brown

As Senior Creative Director at Adobe Systems Inc., Russell Preston Brown facilitates the exchange between digital designers and software developers that is so vital to Adobe's product development.

Russell's wacky and whimsical design work has been published in *Design Graphics* magazine, in *Photoshop User* magazine, and on the Web at Adobe's Web site (www.adobe.com) and at his own site (www.russellbrown.com). He is also the author of *The Photoshop Show Starring Russell Brown* (Peachpit Press, 2003). Always delighting in testing the creative limits of his tools, Russell is the prolific creator of an entertaining collection of Photoshop tips and tricks. His double treat of great information presented in a bold, zany style has won him a regular following among beginning, intermediate, and advanced users alike.

Go to www.peachpit.com/ dreamteam.html to download files for this chapter.

GO WHERE NO PHOTOSHOP USER HAS GONE BEFORE!

I have discovered the secret to life itself, and it's not in this book—and possibly not on this planet!

What?! Is Russell Brown out of his mind?! Yes he is, but that's another story for another day.

The truth is that the answer to all life's secrets lies in your own creativity. (Deep, yes. Think about it.) The creative energies constellated in this book are simply catalysts to spark and stoke your own ideas. Travel through the pages, like a starship exploring the galaxy, and seek out bold, new concepts with open eyes and open mind.

I know you were drawn, as if in a gravity well, to my chapter of cosmic perfection, but do take the time to explore the others. Remember, just because you think you may never do a Photomerge doesn't mean you should zoom past my chapter. As a great mind once said, "That would not be logical." What if an idea I gave you, combined with an idea from Bert Monroy's chapter, for example, were to ignite the solution to your quest for the perfect image? Don't miss the obvious connections in this book, or you could be forever Lost in Space. Bend the linear continuum; be sure to go forward and backward in time as you travel through the seemingly two-dimensional pages.

Connections, connections. Think of this book as a solar system, not just a single planet. Hopefully, as you transport among the creative supernovas arrayed here, you will discover new ways of taking the normal and making it special. Then you will bring those ideas back to Earth and make it so. In the end, you will discover a wonderful satisfaction in sitting back, looking at an image you've just created, and knowing it is good. (Some experience a euphoric sense of weightlessness!) You will say to yourself, "I did that, and it's really out of this world."

And now, as we prepare to embark on our voyage, I would like to leave you with a closing thought: Herein lies the wisdom of the few, to enrich the minds of the many.

WHEN PANORAMAS GO BAD: A TRUE STORY

In your search for the perfect Photomerge panorama, do you have problems such as blue skies in different images not matching each other (*Figure 1*)? Or do you suffer consternation and dismay when images overlap and you get annoying ghosting effects or broken parts where image detail doesn't line up properly (*Figure 2*)? If so, then you have experienced the strange phenomenon of a panorama gone bad! Well, take heart, dear reader, because we're going to solve these and many other problems associated with panoramic images in this very tutorial (brought to you by the same creative powerhouse team behind the classic tutorial hits "When Small, Cute Dogs Attack!" and "Sharks on Parade").

Figure 1
Mismatched skies are a classic hallmark of a panorama that's gone bad...

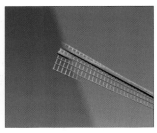

Figure 2
...as are edges that do not align properly.

Figure 3

> **TIP**
>
> *Check your camera manual to see if your camera offers an Exposure Lock feature that allows you to lock the exposure for all the images in your panorama. This will help you avoid problems like those seen here. If your camera offers a Manual Exposure mode, you can take a general meter reading of the entire scene, adjust aperture and shutter speed to the recommended exposure, and then leave the camera set that way for all the shots in your panorama.*

The Strange Case of the Mismatched Skies

Our story begins innocently enough with the three individual images that will make up our panorama: a pastoral scene of the Queen Wilhelmina Tulip Garden in San Francisco's Golden Gate Park (*Figure 3*). Though the images are bright, colorful, and well exposed, there is a sinister problem lurking in the tulip garden! When viewing the three images side by side, the keen-eyed observer will see that the sky in all three is different. This is because these images were created with a digital camera set to the automatic-exposure mode. Thus, as the camera panned across the scene to capture these images for a panorama, the exposure changed just enough to render the brightness and color of the sky a bit differently for each shot.

We need to fix this problem of the mismatched skies before we even start the panoramic merging procedure. To do this, we're going to use a new feature in Photoshop CS called Match Color. Match Color will allow us to choose one of these images as the blue sky that we prefer to use (the source) and match the other two images to that sky. I have chosen the center image, Image Two, as the source for my "good" sky.

Figure 4
A Magic Wand selection of the sky in the source image.

Figure 5
Repeat the procedure from step 1 on Image One and Image Three to create selections of the sky areas in each image.

Step 1

The first step in solving the strange case of the mismatched skies is to select the Magic Wand tool from the Toolbox. In the Options Bar, set the Tolerance to the default value of 32, and make sure the Contiguous box is not checked. Leaving Contiguous unchecked will ensure that when we click with the Magic Wand in the sky area, the selection will jump over the borders and include the blue sky within the matrix inside the windmill blades.

Click once in the upper part of the sky in Image Two to start the selection. Then hold down Shift and click in the lower, lighter part of the sky to add to the selection. Shift-click as many times as necessary to create a selection that includes all of the sky (*Figure 4*). This will create a sampling of all the colors in the blue sky that we will use as our source for the Match Color command.

Step 2

Move over to Image One and repeat the Magic Wand selection process. Shift-click to add to your initial selection until you get all the blue sky tones selected. Then move over to Image Three and do the same thing, making sure that all of the sky is selected (*Figure 5*).

Note: Yes, it's true that you could have chosen Select>Color Range (*Figure 6*) to make a wonderful selection of the blue sky region in each of these images. But I felt that the Magic Wand tool was being neglected; thus I used it for this project.

Figure 6
The Color Range command is another way to make precise selections based on color.

Step 3

With Image Three active, direct your mouse to the main menu and choose Image>Adjustments>Match Color. Take a look at the lower portion of the Match Color dialog. The image in the preview is the same image that we currently have selected and targeted. To the left of this preview image is a Source menu. Open the menu, and choose Image Two, our master source

Figure 8
Image Three matched to Image Two: before (top) and after (bottom). The selection edges have been hidden to better show the match.

Figure 9
Image One matched to Image Two: Before (top) and after (bottom). The selection edges have been hidden to better show the match.

image (the middle one), for this panoramic scene. As you do this, watch the main document window and you'll see the image update to reflect that the sky has been matched to the source image. In that same part of the dialog, make sure that the Use Selection in Source to Calculate Colors and Use Selection in Target to Calculate Adjustment boxes are both checked (*Figure 7*).

Figure 7
With Image Three active, these are the settings to use in the lower part of the Match Color dialog.

With this image the color match is very good, so there is no need to adjust the Luminance or Color Intensity; go ahead and click OK when you're finished (*Figure 8*).

Step 4
Move over to Image One and click its title bar. Clicking the title bar activates the image but does not disturb the selection of the sky that we made back in step 2. Open the Match Color dialog (Image>Adjustments>Match Color) and repeat the procedures from step 3 to match the color to the source image (Image Two) (*Figure 9*).

With Match Color applied to the left- and right-hand images of the windmill panorama, you can see that even though they are not merged yet, we will have no problem with the skies' not matching each other. Match Color is a great way to take an isolated selection of colors and match them. It works very well with a small selection of colors and when you use a selection tool.

Incredible Secrets of the Photomerge
Onward! It's time to delve deeper into the treasures of Photoshop CS and discover some truly incredible secrets for working with Photomerge. Yes, you've seen it on TV; you've heard about it in myth, legend, and lore; and now you have it on your own computer. Better living through Photoshop technology is yours, with Photomerge!

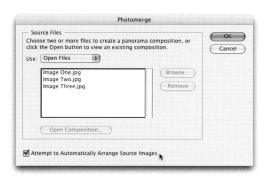

Figure 10

The initial Photomerge dialog, where you choose which images will be used.

Figure 11

For some panoramic series, Photomerge may have trouble automatically aligning all of the images.

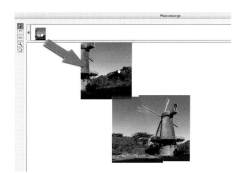

Figure 12

Drag the images that were not automatically aligned from the top of the window down into the main image-assembly area.

Step 5

From the File menu, choose Automate>Photomerge. In the Photomerge dialog that appears, we need to choose which images will be merged. Here, we are going to choose Open Files (*Figure 10*). If you have other files open as you are working through this tutorial, you will need to select their names from the list of open documents and click the Remove button until the only files left are the three windmill images we are using for our project.

Note that I am also checking the box at the bottom of the dialog that tells Photomerge to Attempt to Automatically Arrange Source Images. Click OK when you're done with this dialog to initiate the merging process.

Step 6

Next you'll find yourself in a very large and impressive dialog that is the main Photomerge mission control area. And, if you're like me, you'll find yourself confronted with a message telling you that Photomerge could not automatically arrange all the images into a single panorama (*Figure 11*). This may happen if you are merging a particularly complex series of images.

But all is not lost, as we can manually drag the problem image from the "waiting room" area at the top down into the main assembly area. Go ahead and do this now (*Figure 12*). As you drag the image in, try to place it in the approximate position where it needs to be (*Figure 13*).

Figure 13

Try to place the image in the approximate position where it needs to go.

Step 7

Use the navigator slider on the right side of the dialog to zoom in for a closer view. As you can see from the version that I worked on, although Photomerge has done a pretty good job of aligning the three images, there are still problems, especially with the windmill blade on the left side and the circular

Figure 14

When we zoom in for a closer look, problems with the initial merging become apparent.

Figure 16

Clicking on the center image and applying a perspective correction will often fix most of the alignment problems, though sometimes new ones will show up, as seen here in the image on the right side.

Figure 17

Image Three is removed from the merged group in order to select a new perspective origin point.

platform around the middle of the structure (*Figure 14*). But notice how well the skies are blending together because we used Match Color to correct that initial problem.

Step 8

Click on the center image to select it (a red line should appear around the image), and then, over on the right side controls click the Perspective radio button to select it (*Figure 15*).

Why am I doing this? Because I happen to know that the advanced mathematics that operate under the hood of Photomerge will often do a very good job of correcting problems just like the ones we see here.

The perspective correction has indeed done a better job of aligning the images on the left side, but there are now some new problems in the wheel on the top of the windmill, the blade on the right, and the alignment of the

Figure 15

The Perspective option in the Photomerge dialog.

platform (*Figure 16*). Remember that Photomerge is a very individualistic tool, and the merging issues you see here may not be the same as the ones you run into when doing this exercise on your own, even if you are using the same images. It's that very element of chance and unpredictability that makes this chapter so exciting!

Step 9

Click to select the image where most of the problems are occurring. A red line should appear around the edge. For my panorama project here, that is the image on the right side, Image Three. Drag it away from the other two merged photos (*Figure 17*).

I happen to know that if you align the correct points within two of these images, you can get a better distortion and merging of the two images. Through careful research and experimentation, I have found that if you select a point within the center edge of the image rather than the top or the bottom, you can get improved results...in some cases.

Figure 18
The center window on the windmill tower is a good point to use for applying a perspective correction to the right-hand image.

Figure 19
Here you can see how Image Three was dragged over the other two images and the center window was lined up with the same window in the center image. Photomerge automatically reduces the opacity of the image you're dragging to allow for easier positioning.

Figure 20
Applying the perspective correction to Image Three has fixed the problems in that image.

Here, I clicked on the edge of the center window in the middle of the windmill tower in Image Three (*Figure 18*). Next, I dragged Image Three over the other two images so that the center window lined up as closely as possible with the same window in the center image. Photomerge reduces the opacity of the image you are dragging so that you can see where to position it (*Figure 19*). Before releasing the mouse button, I held down Command (PC: Control) to ensure that Photomerge would use this point as it distorted the perspective of this image into position (*Figure 20*).

Step 10

If you still see any minor alignment problems, you can also try this: Click on the image in question to activate it, and use the arrow keys to nudge it up, down, left, or right one pixel at a time. If you are still having merge issues, then you can try the Rotate tool. Upon closer inspection, for example, I found that I had to slightly rotate the left-hand photo (Image One) in a clockwise direction in order to straighten a faint bump in the windmill blade and also to line up the platform below (*Figure 21*). After the rotation, I selected the Arrow tool and nudged the photo a few pixels to the right with the arrow keys (*Figure 22*).

Note: The Rotate tool can be tricky to use and often introduces additional problems if used incorrectly. That's why I saved it as a last resort in trying to get these images to line up. I always say, "Look for the simplest tool to solve the simplest problems." In many cases the Perspective option combined with the arrow keys can provide exceptional results.

Figure 21
By rotating the left-hand image (Image One) a bit, I was able to correct a slight bump that was visible in the left windmill blade.

Step 11

Click on the white area around your merged photos to clear the red line around the image you've just adjusted. In the right-hand controls click the Advanced Blending check box (*Figure 23*). I recommend that you use the

Figure 22
The merged result after applying a slight rotation to the left-hand image.

Figure 24
The Photomerge preview of the Advanced Blending results.

Figure 25
For difficult panoramas, you may need to check the Keep as Layers box and finish your merging using Layer Masks in Photoshop.

Advanced Blending option to create a better blend between the merged images. In this case, since I used the Match Color feature like a True Professional, there seems to be no problem with the skies. Using Advanced Blending, however, never hurts.

After selecting Advanced Blending, click Preview to see how this feature will affect the merged result. In my version I noticed that it improved a merged edge in the sky on the left side of the image (*Figure 24*). Click Exit Preview to return to the editing mode of Photomerge. If you're satisfied with the Photomerge preview, go ahead and click OK.

Figure 23
Using the Advanced Blending option will generally give you the best results with Photomerge.

Keep as Layers

The very last option in the Photomerge dialog is a check box called Keep as Layers (*Figure 25*). While Advanced Blending generally gives the best results, it delivers the merged photos as a single layer. In some cases, even with Advanced Blending turned on, you may run into...a Panorama that's Gone Bad!

Yes, it's true that some panoramas are so difficult to merge that not even the highly evolved mathematics in Photomerge, combined with the fact that you are, at heart, a good person, can create a decent result. In such cases, you would check the Keep as Layers option and then finish the panoramic compositing using Layer Masks in Photoshop to manually blend the images together. When you use Keep as Layers, the Advanced Blending feature is not available.

Trouble in the Tulip Garden: Using the Healing Brush, Patch Tool, and Perspective Crop for Final Touch-ups

After the merging process is complete, we can see that Photomerge has done an excellent job of merging these three images together (*Figure 26*). If we look closer, however, we can see that all is not well in Queen Wilhelmina's Tulip Garden. I must admit that this was a difficult task and we still need to address a few problems. And as we all know, if there were no problems, then I would have

Figure 26
After we've clicked OK and processed the merged panorama, it appears that Photomerge has done an excellent job of merging the images together...

Figure 27
...but upon closer inspection we see that a few glitches remain to challenge our Photoshop skills.

Figure 29
Sampling good sky detail with the Healing Brush and repairing the sky glitch on the right.

nothing to tell you and I would be out of a job! So here are some cool things you need to know about correcting images that might have gone bad.

In this panorama you can see some strange discoloring and distortion at the top of the image. I'd like to make that go away. Also, down at the tip of the windmill blade on the right side, the edges of the two images do not line up (*Figure 27*). I'd like that to be fixed. Read on and you'll see some amazing tips and techniques that will correct both of these problems. Let's get started!

Step 12

We'll tackle the problem in the sky first. The Healing Brush can easily fix this. Select the Healing Brush in the Toolbox. Go to the Layers palette and Command-click (PC: Control-click) the layer thumbnail to load the transparency mask as a selection (*Figure 28*). Then click on the flyout arrow in the upper-right corner of the Layers palette to open the palette

Figure 28
Preparing to fix the sky with the Healing Brush: Load the transparency mask of the layer as a selection and flatten the image.

menu, and choose Flatten Image. The reason we are doing this is that the Healing Brush behaves differently on a flattened image and also when there is a selection active.

Step 13

Before we begin with the Healing Brush, make sure that you are using a brush size that is appropriate to the task at hand. I used an 80-pixel brush to retouch the skies. The selection should still be active. Now, hold down Option (PC: Alt) and click on a good area of the sky to sample that tone and texture (*Figure 29*). Move over the discolored and distorted areas, and click to brush over them. When you release the mouse button, the Healing Brush will consider the color and luminosity of the area you are trying to fix, and blend those together with the texture and detail from the area you sampled. Amazing!

You may need to make a second or third pass over the area to further smooth out and soften some of the edges as they blend together. Repeat the

Figure 30
The sky glitches are easily fixed with the Healing Brush.

Figure 32
Selecting along the meeting edge of the two misaligned blade images with the Patch tool.

Figure 34
The Options Bar for the Patch tool.

procedure to fix the sky on the other side of the windmill (*Figure 30*). Choose Select>Deselect when you are finished fixing the sky.

Step 14

Now we'll zoom in for a closer look at where the windmill blade does not line up (*Figure 31*). As mentioned earlier, your own Photomerge result may be different from mine, so in this part of the chapter I will tell you how I fixed this problem in my image, rather than give you step-by-step directions to use on your own image.

I'm going to solve this problem in a very special way. Among the many ways I could choose to fix the problem, this one is very nice. In the Toolbox, I 'm going to click the Healing Brush and hold down the mouse button until the tool pop-out menu appears and then I will choose the Patch tool. With the Patch tool, I'll start in the sky above the blade, bring the tool down, and cut through the edge of the blade where it doesn't align with the main image. As I do this, I will avoid the soft edges where the two images blend together (*Figure 32*). I will also make sure that I have a good chunk of the sky on the right side of the blade selected (*Figure 33*). The sky selection is important, as it will help me patch the two images together.

Figure 31
A serious alignment problem with the blade of the windmill.

Figure 33
The finished Patch tool selection with a generous portion of the sky included.

Step 15

In the Options Bar for the Patch tool I have selected Destination as the source for the patch. I find that I get my best results when I use the Destination option (*Figure 34*).

With the Patch tool cursor inside the selection, I moved it into position and lined up the two parts of the windmill blade. But then I noticed a new

Figure 35
The two parts of the windmill blade are different sizes. Drat!

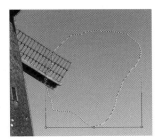

Figure 37
Scaling the size of the floating selection using the Free Transform command.

Figure 38
The windmill blade after patching.

problem: The two blade images seemed to be of different sizes (*Figure 35*). This was indeed a tricky situation! How could I correct for this unexpected turn of events?

First I needed to cancel the patch in progress that I had already started, so I moved the patch selection away from the blade, and then from the Edit menu I chose Undo Patch Selection.

Step 16

OK, let's try this again. What I want to do is adjust the size of the windmill blade inside my selection so that it matches the size of the blade outside the selection. To do this, I will hold down Command-Option (PC: Control-Alt) until the cursor changes into double black and white arrows, indicating that I am about to make a copy of this selection (*Figure 36*). Clicking and dragging the selection away from the blade will create a floating copy of that portion of the image.

Figure 36
Clicking inside the selection with the double-arrow cursor to turn it into a temporary "floating" selection that could be moved around and resized.

Step 17

While the selection is floating, I still have access to the Patch tool. More important for this next step, I also have access to the Free Transform command. Choosing Edit>Free Transform brings up a bounding box around the floating selection; I can click in the box and drag it into position, and then begin to line it up with the blade in the main part of the image. Clicking the corner and side handles of the Free Transform bounding box and dragging inward allows me to scale the selection so that it matches in size the rest of the windmill blade (*Figure 37*). Pretty cool!

Once I was satisfied that I had accurately scaled the selected part of the blade to the correct size, I pressed Return (PC: Enter) to apply the transformation. The selection was still floating at this point and ready for the final merging using the Patch tool.

Figure 39
The panorama after all the glitches have been fixed.

Figure 40
The initial crop box.

Figure 41
After the Perspective option is selected, the corners of the crop box are aligned with their corresponding corners in the image.

Step 18

With the Patch tool active, I click inside the selection and align it with the rest of the image. Releasing the mouse button finalizes the patch and merges the two images (*Figure 38*). I choose Select>Deselect and then double-click the Hand tool to see the entire image onscreen. I now have what appears to be a perfect panorama (*Figure 39*).

Putting It All in Perspective: The Final Crop

Step 19

For the final step in this project we need to crop the image. But this is not just any old crop; this is a special crop. For in this last part of the tutorial I will show you a technique that is sure to amaze you as I myself was amazed when I first saw it.

First, select the Crop tool from the Toolbox, and click and drag in your image to create a crop box. At first this appears to be a normal, everyday crop box (*Figure 40*). As you do this, however, you'll notice that there is image detail on the left and right sides of the image that would be cropped off if we used this crop box. Plus, it seems to be distorted a bit near the edges.

To address both of these issues, check the Perspective box in the Options Bar. Then grab the corner handles of the crop box and drag them until you have aligned the corners of the crop box with the corresponding corners of the actual panorama (*Figure 41*). The goal here is to have the left and right sides of the crop box align with the angles of the actual edges of the image. How interesting…

Step 20

Finally, click the top middle handle and drag toward the center of the box until there is no white background inside the box. Repeat this step with the bottom middle handle (*Figure 42*). Notice that the sides of the crop box

Figure 42
After aligning the corners of the crop box to the corners of the image, click the top and bottom center handles and drag inward to exclude any white areas of the background. The sides remain aligned with the left and right edges.

remain aligned with the edges of the image. How cool is that?

Double-click inside the crop box or press Enter to apply the final crop. If you cannot see the entire image, double-click the Hand tool (*Figure 43*). To fully appreciate just how amazing this feature is, use the Command-Z (PC: Control-Z) shortcut to toggle back and forth between the cropped version of the image and the way it looked before you cropped it. Repeat to yourself: "Mr. Brown is right. That is truly amazing!"

So now you know several cool tricks and techniques that will help you keep your composure and be calm, cool, and collected under pressure when you find yourself faced with a panorama that's gone bad!

Figure 43
After the Perspective crop.

CHAPTER SIX

STOP WORKING SO HARD MAKING SELECTIONS!

Dave Cross

Dave Cross is Senior Developer, Education and Curriculum for the National Association of Photoshop Professionals. In that role he is involved in all aspects of the training that is provided to NAPP members, including the content of seminars, conferences, and workbooks. He also creates the very popular weekly QuickTime-based tutorials that appear on the members' Web sites.

Prior to joining the NAPP, Dave spent many years as a trainer and author, training thousands of users across North America. A Photoshop user since version 1, he has progressed from scanning images on a 3-pass 300 dpi scanner to working with multiple layered, highly adjustable files that are so big his old Mac IIci would have exploded. Dave is the co-author of two very difficult-to-find books: *Photoshop 7 & Illustrator 10: Create Great Advanced Graphics* and *Photoshop 7 Trade Secrets* (both from Friends of ED), and is the author of the soon-to-be-published *Illustrator CS Killer Tips* (Peachpit Press). Dave writes the Classic Effects, Beginners Workshop, and Q&A columns for *Photoshop User* magazine, teaches at PhotoshopWorld, and is the Lead Instructor for the Photoshop Seminar Tour. He is also featured on a series of instructional DVDs such as *Best of Photoshop User*, *Photoshop CS for Beginners*, *Photoshop Selection Secrets*, and *Photoshop CS Layer Techniques*.

In his spare time Dave is the Graphics Editor for *MacDesign* magazine and dedicates the remainder of his time freaking out his Florida co-workers by wearing shorts to work every day, simply "because he can."

THERE YOU HAVE IT

Well, as we often say at the end of a PhotoshopWorld class, "There you have it": some ammunition to help you make better selections. As you approach a selection "challenge," take a moment before you jump in and start using the Lasso or the Magic Wand or the Pen. Look at the area you're trying to select to see if it has very well-defined edges that might call for the Pen tool, or perhaps it has solid areas of color that are ideal for the Color Range command. Each situation is different but one thing remains the same: aim to end up with a great selection, using the entire toolkit of selection methods. Be prepared to try a variety of tools and techniques—and stop working so hard!

SELECTIONS: THERE IS AN EASIER WAY

One of the best parts of teaching at PhotoshopWorld is the personal contact I get with attendees throughout the event. It is particularly rewarding to hear from students how I've solved a long-time problem, answered a burning question, or how one of my suggestions will save them time.

Of all the classes I've taught at PhotoshopWorld, I've probably received the most feedback from my class on selection techniques. I think the reason is that everyone has to make selections—and most people are admittedly working too hard when they are selecting.

I usually start my selections class with a tongue-in-cheek demonstration of the "typical beginning Photoshop user" trying to make a selection with the Lasso tool. I painstakingly move my mouse around the object, with a look on my face somewhere between concentration and absolute fear. Then I announce that, much to my frustration, I've run out of mouse pad and will have to start again. My performance is exaggerated, of course, but even though I mention this fact, a lot of people chuckle, perhaps recognizing themselves in my demo. The point of the demonstration of course is to suggest that many people work way too hard trying to make accurate selections.

Part of the challenge is that many Photoshop users are "self-taught." And the problem with being self-taught is… the teacher! In reality, when we say we're self-taught, what we really mean is that we discovered a way to do something that seems to work, but we can't help but wonder if there's an easier way. Right? Making selections is a prime example of this. Most people make a decent selection, but they're probably putting in more time and effort than they need to. So let's take a look at some of the keys to not working so hard when you are making selections.

Figure 1

The Overall Approach

This is more of a philosophy or a plan of attack than a trick or technique (a philosophy of selecting? Who am I trying to impress?). Maybe it's just semantics, but all the time I hear people say, "I need to select that area of the image." What if, instead, they said, "I need to end up with that area selected"? Would that change their approach? For many people it does seem to make a difference. Rather than sticking with one tool, they use multiple tools together, using less time and effort to *end up* with a great selection.

I want to select the cyclist in this photo—or rather, I want to end up with a great selection of this cyclist (*Figure 1*). Instead of painstakingly trying to select around the cyclist with the Lasso tool, I select the area

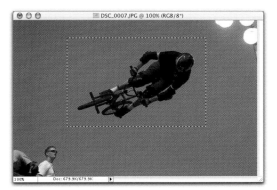

Figure 2

Figure 3

Figure 4

around him, using the Marquee tool (*Figure 2*). Then I switch to the Magic Wand and uncheck the Contiguous box in the Options Bar. Holding down Option (PC: Alt), I click in the blue sky to remove the areas that shouldn't be selected. One click and all of the sky around the cyclist will be removed from the selection. Voilà! I end up with a great selection of the cyclist, much easier and more quickly that trying to manually select around him (*Figure 3*).

This is a somewhat oversimplified example, but that "philosophy" can easily be applied to any image: aim to "end up" with a great selection.

Toolkit

One important aspect of that example was the fact that more than one selection tool was used to make the selection. In many (if not most) cases, you'll need to use the unique advantages of several selection tools. I want to highlight this extremely important technique:

- *Use Shift to add to an existing selection.*
- *Use Option (PC: Alt) to remove from an existing selection.*

With those two keys it is easy to use more than one selection tool to fine-tune your selection. No matter which selection tool you start with, one of these two keys will let you switch tools and improve your selection.

Another key to success in selecting is feathering

When you make a selection you must decide if it should be feathered, and if so, how much. Feathering "softens" the edge of your selection—the higher the number the more gradual the edge of the selection will be. It is important to remember that feathering is cumulative: You cannot reduce feathering, only add to it. In other words, if you have created a selection with the feather amount set to 10 pixels, you cannot "reduce" the feathering to 6. Instead, you'd have to start over, making a new selection with the lower feather setting. Before using the Marquee or Lasso tools you need to think about the feather amount; specifically, you need to check the Options Bar to see if feathering has been set to some number (*Figure 4*). The Options Bar has a long memory, so if you previously entered a value for the Feather amount, that value will remain there, almost like a default setting, until you change it.

Figure 5

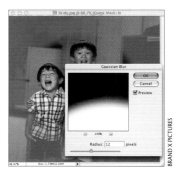

Figure 6

Figure 7

Figure 8

Option 1: Use a contextual menu to add feathering

One of the worst feelings in the world is to finish a challenging selection with the Lasso tool, only to discover that the Feather amount was set to 8, and you wanted zero. Unfortunately, there is no "remove feathering" command, so you're basically out of luck. Here's a simple solution: always leave the Feather setting on the Options Bar at zero. Make your selection, then Control-click (PC: right-click) to open a contextual menu that includes Feather (*Figure 5*). In the Feather dialog, choose the feather amount and click OK. This way, you are always adding the feathering you want, without changing the default setting in the Options Bar. (If you're into keyboard shortcuts, press Command-Option-D [PC: Control-Alt-D] to open the Feather dialog.)

Option 2: Use Quick Mask to preview feathering

It can be a challenge to determine how much feathering is the right amount for a selection. It helps to take advantage of Quick Mask mode to preview the amount of feathering. Here's how you do it: Make a selection with no feathering. Press "q" to switch to Quick Mask mode, and then use the Gaussian Blur filter to blur the mask (*Figure 6*). This is the equivalent of feathering, and you can preview the end result. Once you're happy with the amount of blurring (feathering), press "q" again to return to normal mode and your feathered selection.

Option 3: Blur a filled selection

If you are using a selection tool to create a filled object and you want a feathered edge, try making a normal selection (with a feather setting of 0) on a separate layer and filling it (*Figure 7*). Then use the Gaussian Blur filter to blur the edges of the pixels—again, the equivalent of feathering (*Figure 8*).

Figure 9

Marquee Tools

You can use both the Rectangular and Elliptical Marquee tools to create a selection in a number of ways, based on the choices in the Options Bar: Normal, Fixed Aspect Ratio, or Fixed Size. As always with the Options Bar, remember to check this setting each time before you use the Marquee tools.

Tip 1: Enter a fixed size of any measurement

You've got your preferences set to inches, but when you change the Marquee tool options to Fixed Size, the measurement defaults to pixels. Rather than figure out the pixel equivalent of your desired measurement, use this method. Enter the size you want and then type "in" for inches—this will override the default measurement of pixels (*Figure 9*). You can also use "cm" for centimeters, "pt" for points and "px" if you want to measure in pixels again.

Tip 2: Use the spacebar to reposition as you create

Here's a trick that can be of great help in creating marquee selections that are the size you want in the location you want: As you are dragging to create a marquee selection, keep pressing the mouse button while you press the spacebar. This will suspend the creation of the marquee and let you drag to reposition it. Then let go of the spacebar to continue dragging to create the marquee selection.

Tip 3: Draw from the center outwards

Sometimes it's easier to create a marquee selection by drawing from the center outward, as opposed to diagonally. To do this, hold down Option (PC: Alt) as you drag with either Marquee tool (Rectangular or Elliptical), and the marquee will be created from the center outward. (Use Shift with Option [PC: Alt] to keep the selection proportional and draw from the center outward.)

STREAMLINE SELECTION TOOL SETTINGS WITH TOOL PRESETS

If you find that you are switching between various tolerances in the Magic Wand tool or creating certain fixed Marquee sizes on a regular basis, consider creating and using Tool Presets. To do this, set the tool the way you want to use it. Then, in the Options Bar, click and hold the tool icon (or the arrow next to it) to open the Tool Presets palette. Click the New Tool Preset button at the bottom of the palette. Name the

preset, and from then on, choose it from the Tool Preset palette any time you need it (*Figure 10*).

Figure 10

Lasso Tools

There are three Lasso tools: Lasso, Magnetic Lasso, and Polygonal Lasso. Of the three, the Lasso tool is the most manual since it creates selections where you click and drag (it's all up to you and your mousing skills!). The Magnetic Lasso attempts to find edges of contrast and snap to those edges, while the Polygonal Lasso creates straight-sided selections. It is unlikely that any one of these will create the exact selection you want, so once again you should expect to do some fine-tuning.

Tip 1: Use the spacebar to scroll as you create

It is quite common to zoom in a bit to get a closer view of the area that you are trying to select. However, as you get closer to the edge of your document window, you may need to scroll your view to continue with your selection. Here's the dilemma: how to scroll the window without losing the selection you're in the middle of creating. The solution is the spacebar. With any of the Lasso tools, hold down the spacebar to "interrupt" the Lasso and get the Hand tool. Click and drag to scroll to the view you want, and then let go of the spacebar to continue with your selection. Just make sure you return your cursor to the place where you interrupted your selection before letting go of the spacebar (this is especially important when using the Magnetic Lasso!).

Tip 2: Always hold down Option (PC: Alt)

As a general rule, when using any of the Lasso tools, always hold down Option (PC: Alt) when you are creating a new selection. There are two reasons for doing this. First, if you let go of the mouse button without any key being held down, the Lasso tool thinks you're finished and closes off the selection. By holding down Option (PC: Alt), you can let go of the mouse, reposition it, and so on, and the selection will not close off. Second, if you are using the Magnetic Lasso tool and want to switch on the fly to the Lasso or Polygonal Lasso tool, pressing Option (PC: Alt) does this, too. With this key held down, click and drag to make the Magnetic Lasso behave like the Lasso; single-click and it will act like the Polygonal Lasso. Release the Option key (PC: Alt) to use the Magnetic Lasso.

Figure 11

Figure 12

Magic Wand

The Magic Wand is often a good starting point in the process of making an accurate selection. It is unlikely that the Magic Wand will make a perfect selection with one click—in fact, many people spend way too much time trying it over and over with different tolerance settings, trying to get the perfect selection. Instead, consider this technique: Use a lower tolerance setting and use the Shift key to add to the existing selection. If you add a little too much to the selection, fix it later using a different tool and the fine-tuning methods described earlier.

Tip: The settings for the Eyedropper affect the performance of the Magic Wand

Believe it or not, the sample size setting for the Eyedropper tool plays an important role in the performance of the Magic Wand. In this first example, the Eyedropper tool option was set to Point sample. With a tolerance of 15, a large area of the sky was selected (*Figure 11*). Then, the Eyedropper setting was changed to 5 by 5 average. Using the same tolerance setting of 15 and clicking on the same spot (using the guides), a larger area was selected (*Figure 12*). Bottom line? If you're not getting the results you want, try changing the Eyedropper sample settings before using the Magic Wand.

Pen Tools

The Pen tools can also act as selection tools, offering a couple of important advantages. First, compared with selection edges, it is very easy to adjust the path that is created by the Pen tool using the Direct Selection tool. Second, the path can be saved as part of the document, adding very little to the file size, yet saving the selection information in the document.

Tip 1: Use shortcuts, don't switch tools, part one

Rather than switching between the Pen tool and the Add Anchor Point or Delete Anchor Point tools, just stick with the Pen tool. To add an anchor point, position your pointer on the path where no anchor point exists (look for a plus sign next to the Pen icon). Click to add a point. To delete an anchor, position the pointer over an existing anchor point (look for a minus sign next to the Pen icon). Click to remove the point.

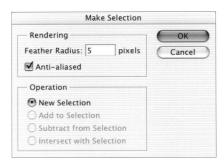

Figure 13

Tip 2: Use shortcuts, don't switch tools, part two

The same concept applies to the Convert Point tool. Keep the Pen tool and hold down Option (PC: Alt). Click a curved anchor point to convert it to a straight point. To convert a straight point to a curved point, hold down Option (PC: Alt) and then drag outward to create handles for the Bézier curve.

Tip 3: Use shortcuts, don't switch tools, part three

To use the Direct Selection tool to move and edit anchor points, keep the Pen tool as the active tool and hold down Command (PC: Control). When you want to use the Pen tool again, just let go of Command (PC: Control).

Tip 4: Scaling a path

If you've created a path and you need to slightly change the overall size, don't edit the individual anchor points. Instead, to scale the overall path, choose the Selection tool, and in the Options Bar, check Use bounding Box. Then use the handles to scale the path. Press Return (PC: Enter) to finalize the transformation.

Tip 5: Making a selection from a path

To make a selection based on the path press Enter (on the numeric keypad) or Command-Return (PC: Control-Enter). Or Control-click (PC: right-click) on the path name and choose Make Selection from the pop-up menu (*Figure 13*). To add options such as feathering, hold down Option (PC: Alt), and in the Paths palette click the Load Path as Selection button.

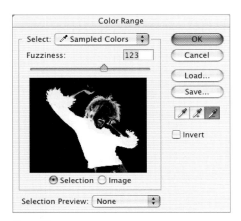

Figure 14

Select>Color Range

The Color Range command is somewhat like an interactive Magic Wand: In the Color Range dialog you can preview the selection as you experiment with the numbers. After clicking with the Eyedropper to choose the color you want to select, use the Fuzziness slider to expand or reduce the selection. In the preview window, white represents the areas that will be selected, and black shows the portions that will not be selected (*Figure 14*).

Tip 1: Add or remove colors with the Eyedropper

To change the colors being selected, position the Eyedropper on the image and press Shift to add to the selection; press Option (PC: Alt) to remove a color from the selection.

Tip 2: Narrow the choice

To focus the results of Color Range, make a loose selection around the area where you need to select a range of colors before using the Color Range command (*Figures 15 and 16*).

Figure 15

Figure 16

BRAND X PICTURES

Figure 17

Figure 18

Quick Mask

Quick Mask is a great way to fine-tune and finalize an existing selection. To adjust a selection in Quick Mask, just remember that black is the masking color, meaning that you paint with black any areas that should not be selected. Those areas will be represented by the colored overlay (the default color for the overlay is red). To add areas to the selection, paint with white, which will show up as clear (with no red overlay) in the image (*Figures 17, 18, and 19*).

The brush you use has an important impact in Quick Mask: a soft-edged brush will create feathered selections, while hard-edged brushes will create a selection with no feathering.

Figure 19

BRAND X PICTURES

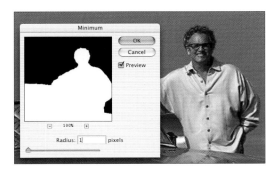

Figure 20

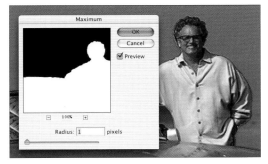

Figure 21

Tip 1: Use keyboard shortcuts in Quick Mask

Use these shortcuts to speed up your work in Quick Mask:

- Press "q" to switch between Quick Mask mode and Standard Selection mode.
- Press "x" to swap between black and white as the foreground color.
- Press [(left bracket) to make the brush size smaller, press] (right bracket) to make the brush size larger.
- Press Shift-[to make the brush softer, press Shift-] to make the brush have a harder edge.
- To change the opacity of the brush, press the first number of the percentage you want (1 for 10, 4 for 40, and so on). Note: If you have the Airbrush option turned on in the Options Bar, the number will affect the flow of the Paintbrush rather than the opacity of the brush. To change the brush opacity while the Airbrush option is turned on, hold down Shift as you enter the number for opacity.

Tip 2: Apply Filters to Quick Mask

It's not unusual to create a selection that is almost perfect, but not quite tight enough. Or perhaps you've created a good selection, but you want to expand the selection to include a slight border. Theoretically, you could use the Select>Modify command and expand or contract the selection. Unfortunately, you may not know exactly what number to enter to get the desired result. Here's how Quick Mask can help once again. In Quick Mask mode, choose Filter>Other, and pick Minimum to make the selection smaller or Maximum to make the selection larger. Check the filter preview to determine the appropriate amount to enter to get the result you want (*Figures 20 and 21*).

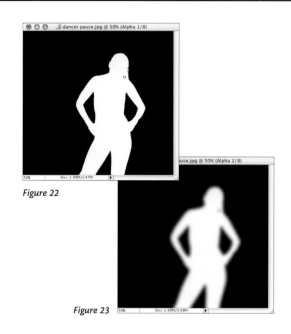

Figure 22

Figure 23

Figure 24

BRAND X PICTURES

Save Selection

To avoid having to make a complex selection more than once, you can save a selection as an Alpha channel. To create a channel, make a selection and then from the Select menu, choose Save Selection—you can name the channel if you wish. Click on the channel in the Channels palette, and you'll see your selection represented by shades of gray: white pixels represent the selected area, black pixels are the areas that are not selected, and gray areas represent partial (feathered) selections (*Figures 22 and 23*). Once you've created one or more Alpha channels for your selections, save the document to include these channels for later use.

Here are some Save options:

- To load the channel as a selection, choose Load Selection from the Select menu, or Command-click (PC: Control-click) the channel.
- To load the channel and add to an existing selection, hold down Command (PC: Control) and Shift, and click the channel.
- To load the channel and subtract from an existing selection, hold down Command-Option (PC: Control-Alt) and click the channel.
- To load the channel and have it intersect with an existing selection, hold down Command-Shift-Option (PC: Control-Shift-Alt) and click the channel.

Tip: Viewing channels as Quick Mask

To assist in editing an Alpha channel, it might help to look at it as if you are in Quick Mask mode. To do this, in the Channels palette, click on the Alpha channel to view it and make it active, and then click in the left-hand column of the Channels palette beside the RGB channel to turn on its Eye icon so you can view the Alpha channel and the image at the same time (*Figure 24*).

Figure 25

BRAND X PICTURES

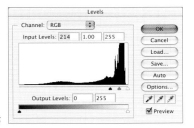

Figure 26

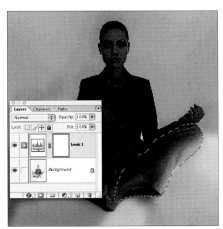

Figure 27

Selecting the hard to select

In some cases you'll encounter images in which the area you need to select is difficult to see. Needless to say, it's pretty challenging to make a selection when you can't even see what you're trying to select. Often this is due to over- or underexposure (in *Figure 25*, it's very difficult to see the edge of the pant leg on the right side). Here's a simple but extremely effective way to deal with this problem.

Step 1

Add an Adjustment layer—try Levels or Curves.

Step 2

Deliberately overadjust the image until you can see the problem area. Don't worry that the rest of your image looks horrible—remember, this is an adjustment layer, so it is not permanent (*Figure 26*).

Step 3

Use whatever selection tools you want to make the selection of the problem area (*Figure 27*). Concentrate just on the problem area for now.

Step 4

Throw away the adjustment layer and select whatever other areas you need.

Go to
www.peachpit.com/
dreamteam.html
to download files for
this chapter.

CHAPTER SEVEN
CREATIVE FOCUS WITH THE LENS BLUR FILTER

Jack Davis

Jack Davis has been an internationally recognized creative spokesperson for almost 20 years, teaching on computer graphics and creativity at conferences and universities around the world. He is co-author, with Linnea Dayton, of *The Photoshop CS Wow! Book* (Peachpit Press, 2004) and *Adobe Photoshop 7 One-Click Wow!* (Peachpit Press, 2002). Jack and Linnea also have a column in *Photoshop User* magazine called "The Wow! Factor." Jack is the author of *Adobe Photoshop Elements 2: One-Click Wow!* (Peachpit Press, 2003), and his latest book, co-authored with Ben Willmore, is *How to Wow: Photoshop for Photography,* (Peachpit Press, 2004). He has been a contributing editor to numerous other books and magazines on digital imagery, design, and online communication; and he created the training CDs *Wow! Photo Retouching Techniques, Wow! Photo Optimizing Techniques*, and *Wow! Photo Enhancing Techniques* (Software Cinema; www.software-cinema.com/wow).

Jack has degrees in traditional Commercial Art and Graphic Design and an MA and MFA in Digital Imagery, Art and Design. An award-winning designer, illustrator, and photographer, he routinely teaches as part of the PhotoshopWorld Dream Team and the Photoshop Wow Tour. When he's not in front of his Apple Cinema Display in San Diego, he's usually on the beach somewhere in Polynesia with digital camera and analog paints soaking up the local color.

RAMBLINGS OF AN ELATED MIND

Yup, elated, jazzed, stoked, over the top, dance-up-and-down giddy with glee! You may not believe it, but that's really the feeling I get when I scroll through our beloved File Browser after another round of experiments with my (now surgically attached) digital camera (a Nikon, to be exact). If you have to ask "How can pressing a button on a little black box stuck to your nose bring about so much uninhibited joy?" Well, you obviously haven't caught the bug…yet.

If you are an explorer (and since you're reading a Photoshop book, odds are ten to one that you are), then by definition you love to learn—how things work, why they work, and what you can do with them to make your friends say "Ohhhhhh!!" (I'd say Wow!, but some would think that a shameless plug.) That's where the digital component of the new cameras comes in. Among other things they're fast (at least in terms how long it takes to get a photo from the camera into Photoshop), they are forgiving (ya gotta love the Delete button). They are flexible (changing your ISO sensitivity from shot to shot, or even automatically, is pretty darn cool), and they give you instant feedback in the field (if God is the ultimate source of all good gifts, then He obviously created Histogram Reviews and Blinking Highlights).

And it's this instant feedback of these electronic tools (not only cameras, but also software like Photoshop, new

continued on next page

RAMBLINGS OF AN ELATED MIND, *continued*

desktop Giclée printers…golly, just about everything with a little blinking light) that makes mad little creative scientists like us so giddy. We can experiment 'til we're blue in the face, winnow through the chaff of the "what was I thinking?" failures, and dig down to those situations where our intuition and our gleaned experience (limited or vast—we all got some) intersect and we find that we have hit paydirt with results that say: Now that photograph tells a story. That logo personifies the client. That painting expresses my heart.

    I warned you that these would be ramblings. My point is that we've been gifted with living in a time of almost unlimited creative potential—so take advantage of these new-fangled tools. And when you get to the end of your day of doing what you need *to do, take an hour with your digital friends (Photoshop, camera, tablet…whatever) and do something that you* want *to do. And make sure that you "fail" on your first few adventures, because that's the only way that you'll really loosen up; give yourself permission to play, and be sure that you are pushing the tools,* and *yourself, to where that elation with the creative life resides.*

CREATING A DEPTH MASK FOR THE LENS BLUR FILTER

The Lens Blur filter in Photoshop CS is a wonderful addition to the collection of blurring filters. The one thing that sets this filter apart from the other blur filters, however, is that it re-creates the effects produced by the optical blurring of a scene photographed with a camera and a lens. The quality of the blurring effect is much more natural and nuanced than that produced by the old standby, the Gaussian Blur. When used in combination with a mask, Lens Blur can be used to effectively simulate a shallow depth of field where one part of an image is in focus and the rest is out of focus. That is what we'll be focusing on (pun intended!) in this tutorial.

Figure 1
Drag the Background layer to the New Layer icon to make a copy of it. Duplicating the Background layer before running the Lens Blur filter ensures that the original image is protected.

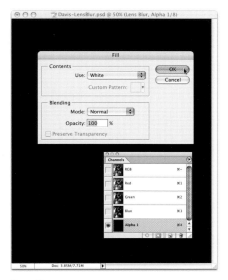

Figure 2
Using the Fill command to fill the new alpha channel with white.

Step 1

Our first step whenever using one of the filters, of course, is to duplicate the Background layer so that we do not affect the original image. This creates a flexible structure for our file in case we change our mind or decide to apply the filter differently. To make a copy of the Background layer, just drag it down to the New Layer icon at the bottom of the Layers palette (*Figure 1*). Double-click the layer name and rename it Lens Blur.

Step 2

Next, we need to create an alpha channel that will allow us to target specific parts of the image with the Lens Blur filter. In this image, we're going to protect the happy Buddha's face from the effects of the blur filter by painting dark tone or black into an alpha channel in those parts of the photo. In the filter dialog we'll be able to instruct the filter to use this alpha channel for the application of the blurring effect.

Click the New Channel icon at the bottom of the Channels palette. The default behavior when you add a new channel is for the channel to be all black. In this case, we want the channel to be white, so we're going to go to the Edit menu and choose Fill. In the Fill dialog, choose White from the Use menu. Make sure that the Opacity is 100% and the Blending Mode is set to Normal (*Figure 2*). Another way to accomplish this would be to use the Invert command; choose Image>Adjustments>Invert or press Command-I (PC: Control-I).

Figure 3
Preparing to paint on the alpha channel: The alpha channel is active, and the Eye icon is turned on for the RGB color information in the image.

Figure 5
Painting on the alpha channel with black shows up as a semitransparent red when viewing the image and the alpha channel at the same time.

Step 3

In order to see our work, we need to view the alpha channel and the image at the same time. To do this, click in the empty column next to the word *RGB* at the top of the Channels palette to turn on the Eye icon for the full-color image. Initially you won't see any difference, but once you start painting in the alpha channel, you will. Make sure that the alpha channel is still the active element in the Channels palette; this is indicated by highlighting of the channel in the Channels palette and also of the image's title bar, which indicates the currently active layer (Lens Blur) and the active channel (Alpha 1) (*Figure 3*).

In the Toolbox choose the Brush tool, and click the Brush arrow at the left side of the Options Bar to select a 45- to 100-pixel brush (the actual size of the brush you use will vary depending on the size of your image and the area you are masking). Move the Hardness slider to set an edge hardness value of about 50% (*Figure 4*).

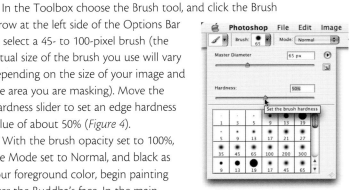

Figure 4
Selecting a brush size and changing the brush's hardness.

With the brush opacity set to 100%, the Mode set to Normal, and black as your foreground color, begin painting over the Buddha's face. In the main image window this will show up as a semitransparent red color, but if you look at the thumbnail of the alpha channel, you'll see that it is actually black. Photoshop is using the transparent red color to represent the areas where we are painting with black in the alpha channel so that we can see both the masked areas and the image at the same time (*Figure 5*).

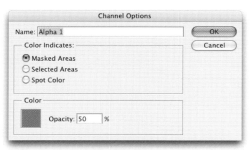

Figure 6
If you want to change the color or the transparency of the mask overlay, double-click the alpha channel in the Channels palette to bring up the Channel Options dialog.

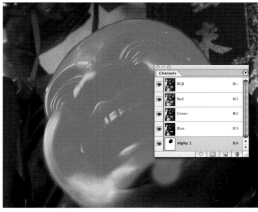

Figure 8
Zoom in close and use a smaller brush with a Hardness value of 50% to fill in the mask along the edges of the Buddha's head and face.

The default color for the overlay is red, but you can change the color and the transparency of the overlay by double-clicking the channel in the Channels palette and using the Channel Options dialog (*Figure 6*).

TIP

Here's a cool trick to speed up some of the painting of the mask, particularly as you trace around the edges of the Buddha's head. You can draw a straight line between two points by clicking once to set down a dab of paint and then moving your cursor to a point where you want to continue the initial paint stroke and holding down Shift as you click again (Figure 7). Using this method of clicking once, moving the cursor, and then Shift-clicking, I was able to very quickly trace around the edges of the statue's head.

Figure 7
Click once to establish the start of a brushstroke (A), and then move the cursor to where you want the stroke to end and Shift-click to paint a straight line between the two points (B).

Step 4

Zoom in to 100% (View>Actual Pixels) so that you can see the edges of the Buddha's head and face clearly, and carefully paint along this edge with a smaller brush; I used a 45-pixel brush set to 50% hardness for this area. It's important that this part of the mask be accurate, since the statue's head will be in focus, but the background behind will be blurred (*Figure 8*). If you make a mistake and paint over the edge and onto the background areas, just exchange your colors by pressing "x" to make white the foreground color, and paint with white to remove the red overlay (the black areas in the alpha channel).

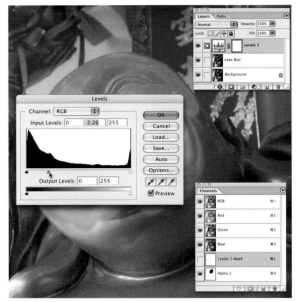

Figure 9
Adding a temporary adjustment layer can help you better see an object's edge in darker areas of an image.

Figure 10
With the image lightened by the temporary levels adjustment layer, the edge of the statue on the right side of the image can be easily outlined. After this has been done, the adjustment layer can be thrown away.

If you're having trouble seeing the edge of the statue in the areas by the ear on the right side of the image, you can add a temporary adjustment layer to lighten the photo so that you can see where the edge really is. Click the Add Adjustment Layer icon at the bottom of the Layers palette, and add a levels adjustment layer. In the Levels dialog move the middle slider to the left to lighten the image until you can clearly see the edge (*Figure 9*). Click OK and then click back on the Alpha 1 channel to make it active again (adding the adjustment layer makes the adjustment layer's mask active). Continue painting along the edges until you are finished with those areas (*Figure 10*). Once you are done with this, you can discard the levels adjustment layer by dragging it to the trash icon at the bottom of the Layers palette.

Step 5

Once the head, the face, and the top edge of the shoulders have been painted over in the alpha channel, it's time to move on and cover up the top part of the chest. This time I switched to a larger 300-pixel brush and set the Hardness to 0% to cover more area in each stroke and also to have a soft, faded quality to the edge. For the areas in the middle part of the chest, try lowering the brush Opacity to about 45%. This will create a portion of the mask where the blur effect will be only partially applied. At the top of the head, the smaller, harder brush that was used will result in a more abrupt transition between areas that are in focus (the Buddha's head) and the background behind them.

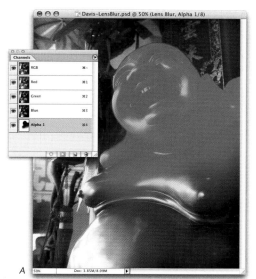

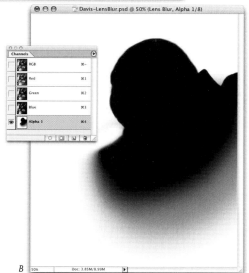

Turn off the Eye icon for the RGB composite channel, and you can view just the grayscale version of the alpha channel. Wherever it is white will be blurred completely by the filter, where it is black will not be blurred at all, and the gray areas will create a subtle transition from areas that are in focus to those that are out of focus (*Figure 11*).

Step 6

Click back on the word *RGB* in the Channels palette to make the main image active again. If your alpha channel is still visible as a red overlay, click its Eye icon to turn it off. In the Layers palette, make sure that the copy layer (ours is named Lens Blur) is the active layer. From the Filter menu choose Blur>Lens Blur (*Figure 12*).

Figure 11
The combined view of the alpha channel and the main image (A); the alpha channel by itself (B).

Figure 12
With the copy layer active in the Layers palette, choose Lens Blur from the Filter menu.

Figure 13
In the Lens Blur dialog choose Alpha 1 as the source for the Depth Map.

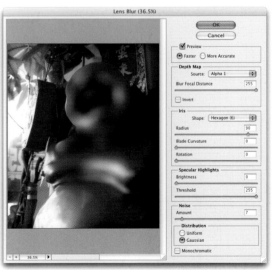

Figure 14
Clicking different parts of the image preview sets the gray values in those areas of the Depth Map to be protected from any blurring effects.

Initially, the Lens Blur filter will apply a blurring effect to the entire image because we haven't told it to do anything otherwise. We need to tell it to use the alpha channel we created as a Depth Map that will control what is in focus, what is blurred, and what is a transition between the two. In the top part of the Lens Blur dialog where the Depth Map controls are, open the Source menu and choose Alpha 1 (*Figure 13*).

> **NOTE**
>
> *At the top of the Lens Blur dialog there are two options for the type of preview that is generated: Faster and More Accurate. Lens Blur is a processor-intensive filter, and when working with large images on slower machines, it can take several seconds for Lens Blur to create a preview. Since it creates a new preview after each little adjustment you make to the sliders, you'll notice this when working on large files. Unless you have a super-screaming-fast machine (and a lot of patience), it's probably best to leave the preview set to Faster.*

Step 7

The Depth Map feature is using the gray values in the alpha channel to determine where the blur is applied in the main image. You can control what gray levels in the mask receive a blur by adjusting the Blur Focal Distance slider. The default setting is 0, which means that areas of the mask that are level 0 (black) will be protected from the blur effect. To change this, you can move the slider, enter a new value, or simply click in different areas of the preview window. The areas where you click, and any corresponding areas in the mask that have the same gray level, will be protected from the blur effect. Click the background behind the Buddha's head, and you'll see it come into focus while the face becomes blurred. This is essentially reversing the mask's default behavior so that white areas of the mask are protected (*Figure 14*).

When you're finished experimenting with this feature, click back on the face or set the Blur Focal Distance to 0.

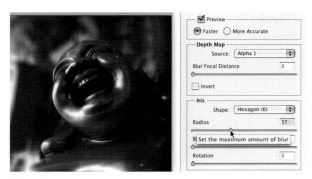

Figure 15
The Radius slider controls the amount of the blur.

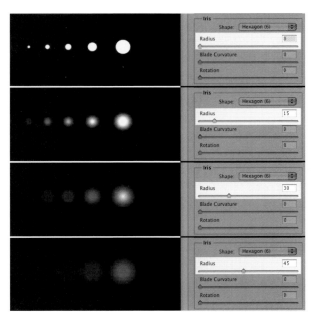

Figure 16
Radius settings of 0, 15, 30, and 45.

Step 8

To adjust the amount of blurring that is being applied, use the Radius slider in the Iris section of the dialog. Higher numbers yield a blurrier image (*Figures 15 and 16*).

For the final setting in this part of the tutorial, direct your pointer to the bottom part of the dialog and increase the Noise amount to about 15. This adds a little noise to the areas that have been blurred so that they blend in better with the rest of the image.

That covers the basic steps you need to know to create an alpha channel for use as a Depth Mask, as well as the primary controls of the Lens Blur filter. For a closer look at the other settings that this filter offers, read on.

Exploring the Lens Blur Dialog

The Lens Blur filter creates a more natural blur than the Gaussian Blur filter, which is what we've all had to use until this gem came along. Where the Gaussian Blur tends to simply mush image detail together to create its blurring effect, the results from the Lens Blur filter are much closer to what you would get from a scene that had been optically blurred through a combination of lens focal length and aperture settings.

> **NOTE**
>
> *If you really want to get a sense of how these settings work, make a file such as that shown in Figure 16, with a black background and several small, hard-edged white circles of varying sizes. The circles in these images were made with the hard-edged brushes at the top of the Brush picker and they range in size from 5 to 45 pixels. You can also download the Lens Blur test file from the book's companion Web site.*

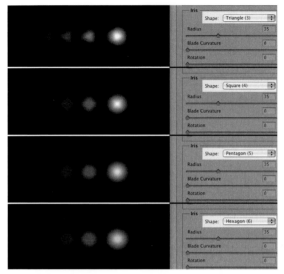

Figure 17
The Iris Shape choices determine the shape of the "virtual" lens iris that can sometimes be seen in very bright highlight points. From top to bottom are Triangle, Square, Pentagon, and Hexagon.

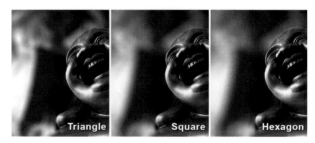

Figure 18
The Iris Shape choices can also create subtle differences in the blur. From left to right, this image shows how Triangle, Square, and Hexagon iris shapes all result in slightly different blurring effects. All other filter settings are identical.

Iris Settings

The aperture in a camera lens is a bladed iris that can be opened and closed to control the amount of light that enters the lens. One of the hallmarks of a blur that has been created with a camera lens is that the very bright highlights take on the shape of the lens aperture. In the Iris section of the Lens Blur filter dialog there are three settings for controlling the shape of your virtual lens iris.

Shape

The Shape menu lets you decide how many blades the iris has, ranging from Triangle (3) to Octagon (8); the default setting is Hexagon (6) (*Figure 17*). Even if you are not interested in crafting highlights that reflect the shape of a lens aperture, or if you're working on an image with no bright highlight points, try out the different shape settings, as each one can subtly influence the character (for want of a better word) of the blurred areas (*Figure 18*).

Blade Curvature and Rotation

These two settings are for when you really need to "get tiny" with the details. As is evident from their names, they control the curvature of the iris blades (whether they are straight-sided or somewhat curved), as well as the overall rotation of the iris shape. The differences here can be subtle and are sometimes hard to see. Try setting the shape to a triangle to check out how these work. When you think about it, this amount of control for tweaking the fine details is pretty mind-boggling, but that's what makes Photoshop such a thing of beauty!

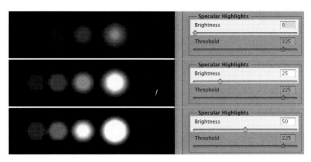

Figure 19
With the Specular Highlights settings, you can control which highlights in your image flare out to reveal the shape of the lens iris. In this illustration, the Threshold has been set to 225, and the Brightness amount has been set at 0, 25, and 50 (from top to bottom).

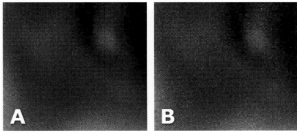

Figure 20
A 300% detail view of the default colored noise (A) and monochromatic noise (B). Both examples are set to an Amount of 30 and Gaussian Distribution.

Specular Highlights

The Specular Highlights settings work hand in hand with the Iris settings in controlling how the Lens Blur filter treats the bright highlights in an image. The Threshold setting determines how bright a pixel needs to be before it is brightened, and the Brightness setting controls the amount of brightening that is applied (*Figure 19*). You can use these controls to play around with the character of the "lens flare" that is produced by bright highlight points in your image.

Noise

As mentioned previously, this setting adds noise to the image areas affected by the blurring. This is useful for reducing the smoothing quality that is sometimes introduced by blurring an image. If your photograph is from a film original, then adding noise becomes even more important and will help blend the blurred areas with the unblurred portions where the film grain may still be visible. Uniform and Gaussian just control how the noise is distributed, with Gaussian being a little more random and often a little more pronounced. Checking Monochromatic adds gray noise, in contrast to the randomly colored noise that is the default (*Figure 20*).

A

Quest for Blur

By selectively blurring portions of a photo, by either a little or a lot, you can mute and de-emphasize certain areas of an image while bringing other portions to the forefront. This helps to focus the viewer's attention. The precise controls and photographic qualities of Lens Blur make it a wonderful addition to Photoshop's blurring filters. By mimicking the real-world qualities of optical blurring created in camera lenses, Lens Blur gives photographers yet another tool to use in the quest to get their images looking just right (*Figure 21*).

B

Figure 21
The happy Buddha, before (A) and after (B) enhancement with the Lens Blur filter.

Go to
www.peachpit.com/
dreamteam.html
to download files for
this chapter.

CHAPTER EIGHT

COLLABORATING ON DIGITAL IMAGE CREATION

Jim DiVitale

Jim DiVitale, M.Photog, MEI, Cr, API, F-ASP, is based in Atlanta, GA and has been a commercial advertising photographer and instructor for over 25 years. For the past ten years, Jim has specialized in digital photography and computer photo illustration for ad agencies, design firms, and corporations nationwide. His award-winning digital photography has been featured in *Graphis Photo*, *Print*, *Archive Magazine*, *Creativity*, *Professional Photographer*, *Photo Electronic Imaging*, *Digital Output Magazine*, *Digital Imaging*, and *Photo District News*. Jim has lectured at Seybold, Photo Plus, PhotoshopWorld, Imaging USA, HOW Design, and the World Council of Professional Photographers.

He has made presentations to students and facility at art schools nationwide including Brooks Institute of Photography, San Francisco's Academy of Art College, and The Portfolio Center. As a member of NAPP's Instructor Dream Team, Jim writes a bi-monthly column for *Photoshop User.* For the last two years, Jim has been creating Photoshop Training CDs for Dean Collins' *Software Cinema* that are shown at Photoshop Training Expos across the US and Europe. As a member of the Professional Photographers of America, he has earned Master of Photography, Master of Electronic Imaging, and Photographic Craftsman degrees, and has earned the Fellowship of the American Society of Photographers. His clients include IBM, BP Amoco, MizunoUSA, Carter's, Genuine Parts Company, AT&T, Doc Marten, Brother, Witness Systems, JP Morgan Financial, TEC America, Coca-Cola USA, and Scientific Atlanta. You can see more of Jim's work at www.DiVitalePhoto.com.

THE DIGITAL ADVANTAGE FOR PHOTOGRAPHERS & DESIGNERS

I remember sitting in a digital system demonstration at a prepress house about 15 years ago watching a technician move part of an image with the Cloning tool. After years of assembling images on 8 x 10 transparency film, I could see the computer changing everything—my mind raced with the future possibilities. This particular computer was a refrigerator-sized machine that cost millions of dollars. I had to wait a few years until I could afford to get a computer capable of handling images. That first 64MB of RAM I purchased cost almost $3000 and I thought I had all the power I would ever need!

As I began to work more and more on the computer and less in the darkroom I began to notice my shooting techniques changing. I started to approach the assignments differently from the point of view of assembly. The ability to shoot the elements separately and assemble them individually with perfect masking was a photographer's dream come true. When doing assembly in the darkroom, I had always gotten a slight black or white edge where two elements were masked together. I could work for hours on an image, and then have to wait for hours to see the results. I am glad I learned masking the traditional way first because it allows me to appreciate the power and depth of Photoshop's masking abilities. When Photoshop 3 came

continued on next page

out with savable layers, I knew that I would never work in a conventional darkroom again. Along the way I began shooting digitally and have never looked back.

After ten film-free years, I have realized that I have been creating digital clients along the way. In the beginning the designers would ask "Can you digitally change this to that?" Now they just ask me to do it because they know I can do it. Designers have learned along the way to watch the photographer work and learn the workflow in the process. They've started to incorporate the digital capture process into their designs so that the designer and photographer can work together as a team. A good designer and photographer working together can create images that might not have happened without their collaboration; the way designers use Photoshop might be different than the ways photographers use it. There are many ways to approach a job—when you work as a team you combine your strengths. When you add the Internet and Photoshop's Web Gallery feature into the mix, the possibilities are wide open. Designer and photographer combinations are not held back by physical location, either. In my studio, we now use the Mac iSight video conferencing cameras to art-direct face to face over the Internet. With the compressed schedule of many commercial jobs today, you need to get answers fast. Digital photography gets us the results fast and we can post them to clients anywhere they might be. The best part is that we are still in our infancy in terms of working with digital imagery—it's only going to get better from here. This is a client-driven technology; it is up to us to keep up with the changes.

DIGITAL PHOTOGRAPHY: CONTROL OVER THE CREATIVE PROCESS

Digital photography is about getting high degree of quality control in your image making. Commercial, wedding, portrait, editorial, and fine art photographers all have the same goals in digital photography: to create professional images with precision tonal control, and to simplify the production workflow in order to obtain predictable results. It's now the job of digital photographers to make sure that the perfect color they are capturing follows the image through the entire production process. Digital cameras allow you to adjust the tonal range, resolution, file type, and bit depth for maximum control over the images. If you want the best results, however, you still have to get the exposure right. Get it in the camera first!

An 8-bit RGB file can have up to 256 levels of information in the red, green, and blue color channels. Zero is pure black with no detail, and 255 is pure white with no detail. That's like a black-and-white Zone System gray scale chart with 256 steps of gray. Creating the perfect blend of these 256 tones is the challenge. The most important numbers to know in digital capture are where the highlight with detail and shadow with detail fall on that final 256-level scale. I have found that 240–245 is a good range for highlight detail in offset printing, Web use, and film and print output. Pixels that have a higher exposure value than 245 tend to start becoming pure white without pixel detail. On the shadow side, a range of about 20–25 is a good place for darkest shadow detail (*Figure 1*). Try to always expose for the proper highlight exposure, and adjust the histogram or curves to bring the shadow information into the proper exposure tone rather than expose for the shadows and try to bring back the highlights with tone adjustment. Just remember: *Expose for the highlights, develop for the shadows.*

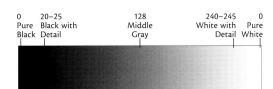

0   20–25   128   240–245   0
Pure   Black with   Middle   White with   Pure
Black Detail   Gray   Detail White

Figure 1

WORKING WITH HIGH-BIT DIGITAL CAPTURES

Most digital SLR cameras can presently capture 12-bit RAW files that have 4,096 tones per color channel. Higher end digital camera backs capture 14-bit and 16-bit files which can contain 16,384 and 65,536 tones respectively. The reason to capture more tonal values is that it gives you much more editing overhead to adjust the file in Photoshop without any data loss. Many high-bit camera files can be adjusted in their own proprietary software to get their best highlight and shadow information. You can then export the file into Photoshop as a 16- or 8-bit file to continue modifying it.

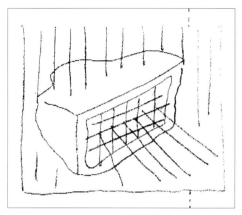

Figure 2
The original illustration concept sketch from the art director.

Figure 3
The basic photograph of the monitor.

Digital capture means that clients can now art-direct over the Internet with more speed than ever before. A photographer can capture a photograph, reduce it to a 72-ppi JPEG, and quickly send it as an attachment to an email message. Thereafter, the client can view the image, place it into a page layout program, make alterations, and return it to the photographer with corrections before the studio set is taken down. For multiple-shot assignments, a folder of images can be batch-processed in Photoshop's Web Photo Gallery and loaded to a Web site for viewing. When the photos have been approved, the photographer can burn the high-res images to a CD-ROM and send it overnight to the client. This new way of working has allowed art buyers to work with the right photographers for the job long distance without leaving their offices when their schedule or budget doesn't allow for traveling to a different city. Some commercial jobs call for approval from many levels. A single art director can travel to the shoot, while the account executive, creative director and clients are back at the home office, waiting to view the results. This doesn't work as well with film capture due to the time delay in processing the film and then scanning it before being able to send it off. Art directors who want to come on the shoot find it very efficient to be able to shoot, retouch, and then place the photo in their layouts, all in one simple session. It's a good idea to have a computer set aside just for the art directors, loaded with everything they need for their jobs. Then they only need to bring their page layout files and fonts in order to place everything the photographer is shooting right into the finished job.

For the tutorial featured in this chapter, the assignment was to create an image to illustrate an article for *DV Magazine* on the transfer of analog color space to digital color space in video. The art director had seen an image of mine that had very colorful grids and wanted an effect like that for his article illustration. I received a sketch of his idea showing beams of light coming into and going out of the monitor (*Figure 2*). The rest was open to interpretation and left a lot of room to have fun with the image.

After establishing a budget and deadline for the project, we discussed how we would work together to review versions of the image as it progressed. As the client was in California and I am in Georgia, posting the images online using Photoshop's Web Photo Gallery dialog was the best solution. The key to making an image this complex work without the designer present is to use "the way of the fast retreat." Photographers generally don't like doing things over, so every step in the creation of this image has to be able to be easily

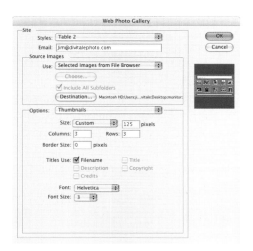

Figure 4
Photoshop's Web Photo Gallery dialog.

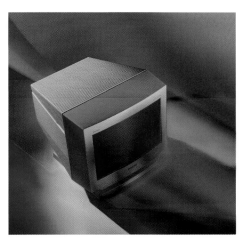

Figure 5
The multicolored background created by the "kaleidochrome" lighting technique.

undone at any time. This allows me to work knowing that if a change is going to be made on the image, I don't to have to start over from scratch to fix it. Art directors can change their minds at any time after seeing a version of the image. It is the close collaboration between the digital photographer and the designer that can make the image really work.

Step 1

I started by shooting a photograph of a monitor to get the position approved. This was a two-part image—one was the monitor and the other was the multicolored background that was to be the anchor image for the illustration. For this to work correctly, they had to be in perfect registration. I set the monitor up on a white background, locked down the camera on its stand, and recorded the first image. I used a Leaf DCB II digital camera back mounted on a Fuji GX680 camera with an 80 mm lens to create this image (*Figure 3*).

To create a Web gallery with the Web Photo Gallery dialog, I chose Web Photo Gallery from the Automate menu in Photoshop's File Browser (*Figure 4*). I prefer posting a site online rather than attaching an image to email, so the designer can easily click a link from any computer to view an image, or to send the link to anyone else who might need to see the image as it progresses. The set had to stay locked down until the designer approved the monitor's overall position. Once it was approved, I could create the background image

Step 2

To create the multicolored background image, I used a single strobe light shining through a piece of rippled glass. The Leaf is a three-shot camera back that takes three separate pictures through a red, green, and blue filter wheel mounted on the lens, and combines them in the camera software. It was designed to work so that everything stays in the same place during the three exposures. If the white light moves during the exposures, a different amount of light is striking the three channels of the image, creating a rainbow of colors. This is a technique I developed over ten years ago and it has been an important part of my lighting style. My clients call it "that weird color thing you do," and a PhotoshopWorld attendee once suggested that I call it "kaleidochrome." While the lighting effect is being produced during the camera's 3-pass exposure, it was important that nothing moved on the set so that this multicolored background image would be in perfect registration with the original monitor image (*Figure 5*).

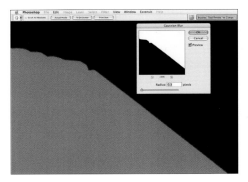

Figure 6
Adding a soft edge to the Quick Mask by using Gaussian Blur.

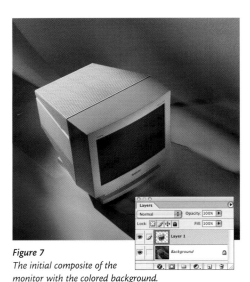

Figure 7
The initial composite of the monitor with the colored background.

Step 3

After the two images of the monitor had been photographed, I outlined the original monitor image with the Pen tool, which I prefer to the Lasso tool because I can save the path without adding any additional weight to the file. Plus, the bezier points and handles can be adjusted afterward to create a very accurate path that fits the subject perfectly I turned the path into a selection by clicking it while pressing Command (PC: Control). The monitor's edge needed to be slightly feathered so that it had an aliased transition. You can feather such a selection using the Feather command in the Select menu, but I prefer to press Q and go into Quick Mask mode, which makes a temporary mask from the selection, and then use Gaussian Blur to blur the Quick Mask and create the soft, feathered edge. In the main menu choose Filter>Blur>Gaussian Blur and type in .03 in the dialog (*Figure 6*). This is the same as pressing Command-Option-D (PC: Control-Alt-D) to open the Feather Selection dialog and typing in .03, except you can see how the feather/blur will look. I prefer to see the edge as a Quick Mask rather than guessing how it will look by feathering the selection. To return back to the regular selection mode, I pressed Q again.

Step 4

Next, I dragged the monitor image over to the colorful background using the Move tool ("v") and pressing Shift. Since the two images were shot without moving the camera, they were in perfect registration. Pressing Shift while dragging and dropping is what makes them line up exactly (be sure to release the mouse button first, and then Shift in order to preserve the image alignment). The normal monitor image was placed as a new layer right over the colorful monitor. I added a layer mask to the layer by clicking the Add Layer Mask button at the bottom of the Layers palette. Painting on the mask with black using a soft, low-opacity brush brought a little color into a few selected areas to make it look more natural (*Figure 7*). At this point I saved the file and set it up in another Web gallery to get approved. This was a critical step because I needed to move the camera to shoot the next part. If a change had been made to the overall position at this time, I would have had to re-create the image from the beginning.

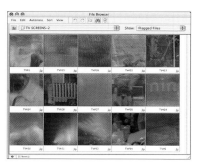

Figure 8
Close-up views of TV screens will be used as collage elements in the final illustration.

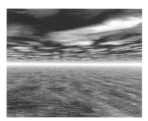

Figure 9

Figure 10 *Using Free Transform to fit the sky/water image onto the monitor screen.*

Step 5

Once the basic image of the monitor and colored background were approved, I set the camera up in front of a TV set and macro-focused so that one square inch of the screen filled the entire viewfinder. I took several different shots of the TV set. Changing the TV stations between the red, green, and blue exposures created many different colorful versions of the close-up TV screen (*Figure 8*). These screens would be randomly added later as overlapping layers all over the image.

Step 6

I then opened a 3D image of a sky and water that had been created earlier in Corel Bryce (*Figure 9*). I dragged the Bryce image with the Move tool ("v") to the colorful monitor image. I reduced the opacity to 50% by pressing 5. Command-T (PC: Control-T) brought up the Free Transform bounding box. To distort the sky-and-water image to make it appear to be on the monitor screen, I pressed Command (PC: Control) while dragging the image's corners to the corners of the monitor screen (*Figure 10*).

Figure 11
A TV screen close-up.

Figure 12
A full spectrum gradient applied using the Color blend mode.

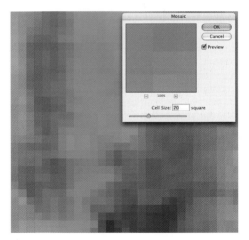

Figure 13
The effect of the Mosaic filter to suggest a pixelated, digital look.

Step 7

I opened one of the TV-screen images (*Figure 11*). Double-clicking on the background layer in the Layers palette turned this into a regular layer. I applied a rainbow-colored gradient using the Gradient tool ("g") set to Color Blend mode. This left the original luminosity values of the TV screen and replaced the color with a full spectrum of color (*Figure 12*). Although this was a good effect, it wasn't enough to suggest the transition of color space that was the main point of the illustration. I duplicated the layer by dragging it to the New Layer button at the bottom of the Layers palette. I tried different filters one at a time. The Mosaic Tiles filter did the trick—it made the screen look very digital (*Figure 13*). The plan for the illustration was to have the screen blend from the original rainbow TV screen to the pixelated Mosaic Tiles version to suggest the idea of transition from analog to digital.

Step 8

With the mosaic TV screen layer active, I linked it to the other layer by clicking in the Layers palette in the middle column between the Eye icon and the layer thumbnail of the unfiltered layer. Using the Move tool, I dragged the two layers from the open file (not the Layers palette) to the monitor image. I dragged the two TV-screen layers in again to create a second set: one to represent input color and the other to represent output color. Using the Free-Transform Tool, I transformed each pair of linked layers into the desired position. Since the layers are linked together, I will transform both with a single application of the Free Transform tool.

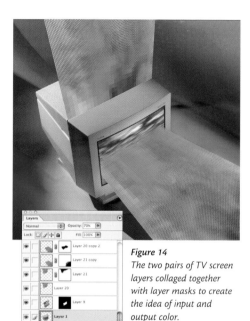

Figure 14
The two pairs of TV screen layers collaged together with layer masks to create the idea of input and output color.

Pressing Command (PC: Control) distorted the corner points to the correct positions. I forced the perspective by dragging the outer points wider. I added a Layer mask to the top layer and painted with black to reveal the lower layer. Having the image's texture change from that of the original TV screen into the more digital, mosaic version really gave the image a transitional feel (*Figure 14*). At this point in the evolution of the image, I created another Web Photo Gallery for client approval.

Step 9

Next was the fun part. I opened up the additional TV-screen files and added them one at a time to the illustration. As each file was brought in, I used Free Transform to move and scale each screen image into position. After the TV screen layers were transformed and scaled, I tried out different blend modes by pressing Shift-+ and Shift-− to cycle through the blend modes without having to use the drop-down menu in the Layers palette. Pressing the numbers on the keypad reduces the opacity. I used lots of different blend modes to get the desired effect. Many of the layers were positioned on top of each other at very low opacities to give the image depth (*Figure 15*).

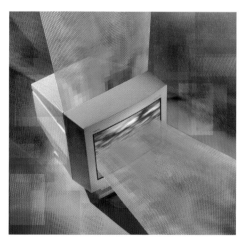

Figure 15
Other TV screen images are added to create additional depth and texture.

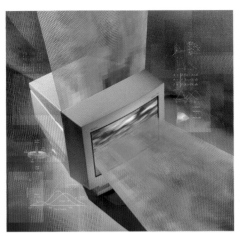

Figure 16
Scientific diagrams added a nice touch to the illustration that further integrated it with the subject matter of the article.

Step 10

After studying the image for a while I realized that it still needed something. I called the designer and asked if he had any charts or diagrams that explained some of the video color space technology. He emailed me a PDF file of some cool scientific formulas and charts that were part of the article. This is exactly what the image needed. The PDF charts were very low resolution, so I tried to keep them small in the illustration. I brought the charts in one at a time and sized them into position. I cycled through the blend modes until it looked good—some were Lighten Mode and some were Screen Mode. I lowered the opacities to about 25% (*Figure 16*).

Step 11

For the final addition, I enlarged two of the charts. They started out with black type on a white background; I inverted the files by pressing Command-I (PC: Control-I) so the charts had white type on a black background. I was going to add a drop shadow, so the black background needed to be cut off rather than

Figure 17
The final illustration.

made invisible with a blend mode. To select the black background, first I chose Select>Color Range. Then, using a tolerance of 50, I clicked the black with the Eyedropper tool and clicked OK. The black background was now selected. I used Command-X (PC: Control-X) to cut the black away, leaving only white letters. I dragged the files over to the illustration and transformed them into place over the mosaic screens going into and coming out of the monitor. To make the shadow of the charts, I duplicated the layer and inverted it to black (Command-I/Control-I). I placed the inverted black layers under the white chart layers and blurred them a little to soften the edges. I blurred them both a little, and reduced the opacity to 25%. To create the feeling of the type floating over the screen, I moved the shadow layer away from the white type (*Figure 17*).

I set the final file up on another Web gallery for the final approval. I archived the file to a CD with all its layers and masks; then flattened it and put it on a CD to send to the client.

This way of working is great because it lets designers work with photographers who are not in their area. They can make critical decisions at points along the way and keep working in their offices at the same time.

CHAPTER NINE
EXPLORATIONS IN ORGANIC SYMMETRY

Daniel Giordan

Daniel Giordan is an artist, photographer, and creative professional based in Columbus, Ohio, who divides his time between art and image making, Web development, and writing and teaching on Photoshop and design aesthetics.

Giordan began his career in the fine art sector as a painter. After receiving his bachelor's and master's degrees in fine arts, Dan showed his work in numerous one-person and group shows throughout the East Coast and New York City. He made the shift to digital art in 1995 and has worked to translate his organic, hands-on aesthetic into the digital realm.

When he's not pushing pixels, Dan works as the Creative Director for AOL Web Properties, directing the design efforts for some of the Web's largest properties, such as Netscape, CompuServe, AIM, and many others.

In addition to all this, Dan finds time to write and teach, sharing his passion for digital design. He writes a column on photo retouching for *Photoshop User* magazine, and he lectures on digital art and design for corporate and academic venues as well as at the PhotoshopWorld and Mac Design conferences. He has also worked as a writer and contributing editor for numerous graphics periodicals, including *Adobe Magazine, Publish, Digital Camera,* and *Dynamic Graphics.*

For more on Daniel Giordan and his work, visit his Web site at www.artofphotoshop.com.

IS IT EVER "DONE"?

"When they take it away from me."
PABLO PICASSO - On how he knows when a painting is finished.

Although this tutorial has shown four variations on a thematic design, there is really no limit to how far you can push the digital design process. As you explore and create variations, it's important to understand that this process involves more than just changing a color and calling it a new piece. Three general areas of exploration involve the refinement of a central message, the addition of new design variables and subjects, and a shift in emphasis from one design variable to another. The key is to do something different with each variation rather than making small, incremental tweaks that don't show anything new.

The Beatles did that; when they began their careers, their work wasn't stylistically different from what other bands were playing, steeped as it was in skiffle, blues, and Chuck Berry. But with each release they moved in a different direction, exploring new ideas, and they never repeated themselves.

In graduate school I studied with a prominent New York painter who constantly pushed me, saying, "It's not what it is, it's how it feels." The idea was that the most innocuous flower, pebble, or even paper clip could become powerful and evocative in the hands of a sensitive artist. This can be overtly expressed as metaphor, and the surrealists immediately come to mind, although normative painters such as Manet, Guston, and Chardin

continued on next page

BOOKS BY DANIEL GIORDAN

Current:

The Art of Photoshop (Sams, 2002)

How to Use Photoshop CS, 2nd edition (Que, 2003)

How to Use Photoshop 7 (Que, 2002)

Out of print but available online:

Kai's Magic Toolbox (1996, ASIN 1568302231)

The Whole Mac (1996, ASIN 1568302983)

Dynamic Photoshop (1997, ASIN 1558515623)

Using Adobe Photoshop 5 (1998, ASIN 0789716569)

How to Use Adobe Photoshop 5.5 (1999, ISBN 0672317192)

How to Use Adobe Photoshop 6.0 (2000, ASIN 0672319543)

IS IT EVER DONE? *continued*

also worked wonders with objects that transcend their literal depiction and represent other things.

In his last paintings before his death, Manet painted an amazing series of flower arrangements that were imbued with passion, reflection, and the irresistible undertow of his own mortality. These works are not the overt ominous "funeral" paintings that most of us would probably start with. They are beautiful, thoughtful, and irresistibly powerful in their understatement.

Philip Guston created an amazing world that was populated with shoes, cigarettes, and one-eyed heads. Even as I type these words, they sound silly to me—shoes and one-eyed heads? What is this, something from the Sci-Fi Channel? And yet as you look at the work, you get it—you cross a bridge and understand on a visual and emotional level the things that words fall short in expressing. Meaning lies in the space between the subject matter and its execution.

So what is the space between the digital subject and the pixels used to express it? On my bad days I wake up and fear that we've just found better ways of rendering the chrome spheres and checkerboards we were doing back in the late 80s, when we were still working on 8-bit monitors and our first copy of PixelPaint or Digital Darkroom. The technology was more important, and the art was almost secondary.

In the end we all have to find our own way. Picasso, Manet, and Guston could not have been more divergent in terms of their approach and execution, and yet they all succeeded in imbuing their work with an emotional quality that transcended the subject itself. Can we do that? Can we push past the photograph and the chrome spheres and create digital art that takes its place with other art masterworks?

Ask more of digital art—demand greatness from it, and continue to push the limits of what's possible.

EXPLORATIONS IN ORGANIC SYMMETRY

I'd like to start out by thanking those of you who pushed past the dry, academic-sounding name of this chapter to see what was in store. I suppose I could have dumbed down the title a bit, but in the end I just decided that "Explorations in Organic Symmetry" was the most descriptive. If anyone suffers from an irrational fear of organic chemistry, my advice for you is to get over it and overlook the phonetic similarity.

This tutorial encompasses much of my philosophy and approach to creating digital art, while showing how I go about developing a finished design. My work has always had strong ties to organic shapes and marks, whether they were abstract or naturalistic. As I began to focus more on the image components of photography, the landscape also began to assert itself in my work, along with a strong desire for the visual narrative. My goal is to use photographic images like a painter, not like a photographer. I'm not making photographs; I'm making digital art.

The challenge is that this approach tends to run counter to the primary characteristics of digital tools and technology. Digital art is about pixels—tiny squares arranged in a predictable grid, with colors that correspond to numeric lookup values. How do you create naturalistic and organic accidents in such an analytical and programmatic world? How do you interject chaos or randomness in a meaningful way when everything has to pass through the precisely defined grid of the software and operating system?

One of the things you'll see me doing in this tutorial is flipping image layers to create pattern and texture effects, and then modifying and wiping out areas to break up the formal symmetry. The goal is to keep the design open and fluid, and to resist the pull to become easily satisfied by the seductive effects of mirrored repetition.

In keeping with the spirit of exploration, remember that the goal of this lesson is *not* to create a single image effect in a linear progression from start to finish. This tutorial produced four separate compositions that I would consider completed works. Don't focus too intently on the finished works, though; try to look between the lines and grasp the process.

Figure 1

Step 1: **The original image**

The original image is of a farmer's field after a light Connecticut snowfall (*Figure 1*). I drove past this field every day on my way to work. I must have driven past it 500 times before I finally pulled the car over and set up my gear.

Figure 2

Step 2: **Duplicate the Background layer**

In the Layers palette, highlight the Background layer and select Duplicate Layer from the palette menu (*Figure 2*). In the dialog that appears, name the new layer, if you want to, and click OK.

Step 3: **Flip and blend**

With the new layer highlighted in the Layers palette, select Edit Transform>Flip Vertical to flip the top layer. Choose Darken from the Layers palette Blending Modes menu to combine the two layers (*Figure 3*).

Figure 3

Step 4: **Copy and paste composite**

Choose Select>All to select the entire image, and then choose Edit>Copy Merged to duplicate the entire composite (*Figure 4*). Choose Edit>Paste to have the copied composite added as a new layer.

Figure 4

Step 5: **Flip and blend again**

Select Edit>Transform>Flip Horizontal to flip the new layer. Choose Darken from the Layers palette Blending Mode menu to combine the layers again (*Figure 5*).

Figure 5

Figure 6

Figure 7

Step 6: **Duplicate and offset**

To offset the repetition, I duplicated the layer created in step 4 by selecting it in the Layers palette and dragging it to the New Layer icon. Select the Move tool from the Toolbox and drag it to the right. The result is an interesting symmetrical pattern, but one that is still just a little too perfect in its repetition (*Figure 6*).

Step 7: **Add a Lens flare; complete first version**

To complete the first stage of this exploration, with the offset layer still active, I applied a Lens flare to the center tree. To do this, select Filter>Render>Lens Flare, and choose 50-300mm Zoom, adjusting the Brightness slider to 68%. You can click and drag in the Lens Flare preview to reposition the flare effect (*Figure 7*). The result (*Figure 8*) is an elegant high-contrast image that illustrates how a few simple moves and adjustments can create a finished piece (of course, having just the right photo is also a requisite).

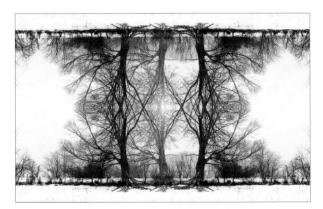

Figure 8 Variation 1: The first finished version of the collage.

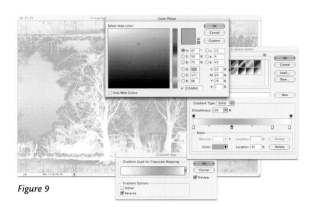

Figure 9

Figure 10

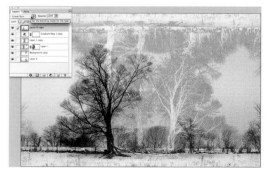

Figure 11

Step 8: **Add a Gradient Map**

To push the exploration further, we'll create a Gradient Map adjustment layer by selecting Gradient Map from the New Fill/Adjustment Layer pop-up menu in the Layers palette. A Gradient Map changes the normal tonal ramp in an image (black on the left, midtones in the middle, and white on the right) to match the colors in the same locations on the chosen gradient. In the Gradient Map dialog click the gradient preview bar to launch the Gradient Editor. Click twice beneath the gradient to add two color stops and then double-click each color stop to launch the Color Picker. Set the end stops to white, the lighter midtones and highlights to a light ocher, and the shadow-area stop to a slightly darker ocher. This creates a custom effect where the shadows are inverted but the highlights are normalized (*Figure 9*).

Step 9: **Duplicate the original image layer**

To reemphasize the dark end of the tonal range, duplicate the original image by selecting the layer in the Layers palette and dragging it to the New Layer icon. When the new layer appears, select it in the Layers palette and drag it to the top of the layer stack (*Figure 10*).

Step 10: **Invert and burn**

With the duplicate layer at the top of the stack still selected, choose Edit>Transform>Flip Horizontal to flip the tree to the left side of the image. To complete this layer application, select Linear Burn from the Layers palette Blending Modes menu (*Figure 11*).

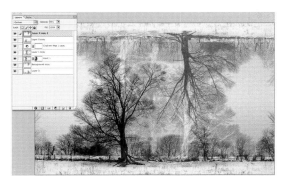

Figure 12

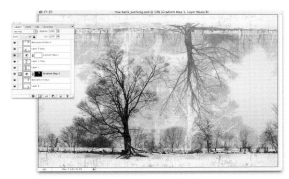

Figure 13

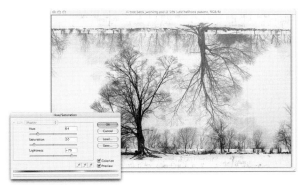

Figure 14

Step 11: **Invert and darken**

Drag the duplicate layer to the New Layer icon to create another copy, which will appear at the top of the layer stack. From the Edit menu choose Transform>Flip Horizontal, and then choose Edit>Transform>Flip Vertical. Set the layer Opacity slider to 56% and the Blending mode to Darken (*Figure 12*).

Step 12: **Duplicate Gradient Map layer**

To add more contrast to the inverted tree on the right, I duplicated the Gradient Map layer by dragging it to the New Layer icon at the bottom of the Layers palette. I then dragged this copied adjustment layer to the layer stack to the position third from the bottom, just above the inverted-tree layer named Background Copy. To isolate the effect to the tree, highlight the mask thumbnail for the duplicate Gradient Map layer and select Image>Adjustments>Invert to turn the mask black. With the Gradient Map effect hidden from view, select the Brush tool with white as the foreground color, and paint the layer effect into the inverted tree trunk at the right of the image (*Figure 13*).

Step 13: **Create a Hue/Saturation layer**

Next I wanted to add an organic, modulated color texture. With the original, unmasked Gradient Map layer selected, add a Hue/Saturation adjustment layer above it by selecting it from the New Fill/Adjustment Layer pop-up menu in the Layers palette. In the Hue/Saturation dialog set the sliders for Hue to 64, Saturation to 10, and Lightness to +79, and click OK to create the layer (*Figure 14*).

Figure 15

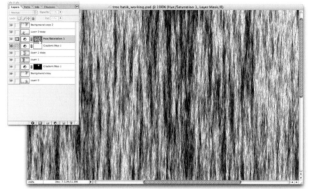

Figure 16

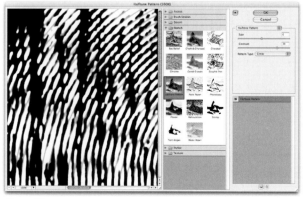

Figure 17

Step 14: Create the mask

Next select the mask thumbnail for the Hue/Saturation adjustment layer in the Layers palette and fill it with black, using the Paint Bucket tool. Press "d" to set the default colors to white and black, and then press "x" to make black the foreground color. With the layer mask as the active element, click anywhere in the image to fill the mask with black (*Figure 15*). This will temporarily hide the effects of the Hue/Saturation layer.

Step 15: Modify the mask with the Fibers filter

To add an organic pattern to the color shift created by the Hue/Saturation layer, select Filter>Render>Fibers to open the Fibers filter dialog. I set the sliders for Variance to 16 and Strength to 4, and applied the filter. *Figure 16* shows the mask by itself. To view the mask this way, hold down Option (PC: Alt) as you click the mask thumbnail in the Layers palette. Remember that the color shift will show through the white and lighter areas and will be hidden by the dark tones.

Step 16: Modify the mask with the Halftone Pattern filter

Click the Eye icon for the Hue/Saturation layer to exit the mask view and return to the composite view of the image. With the mask thumbnail still highlighted, select Filter>Sketch>Halftone Pattern. Set the Size slider to 6 and the Contrast to 38, and select Circle as the Pattern type (*Figure 17*). Click OK to exit the dialog and apply the filter.

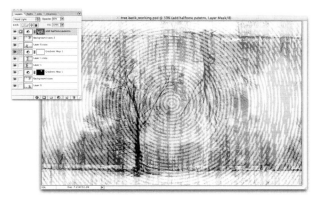

Figure 18

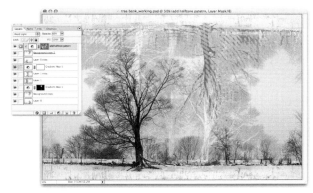

Figure 19

Step 17: **Reposition the Hue/Saturation layer**

In the Layers palette, drag the Hue/Saturation layer to the top of the layer stack, set its blending mode to Hard Light, and set the Opacity slider to 83%. The result is that the lighten effect of the Hue/Sat layer is applied through a circular mask pattern (*Figure 18*).

Step 18: **Create a clipping mask**

To apply the textured pattern a bit more selectively, restrict its application so that it affects only the inverted tree layer beneath it. To do this we'll create a clipping mask by positioning the cursor between the Adjustment layer and the target layer (the layer beneath it), holding down Option (PC: Alt) as we click. The cursor changes to show two circles merging together as the Option (PC: Alt) key is pressed, and after you click, an indented arrow appears on the masked layer to show that its contents are masked to the layer beneath it. The name of the layer that forms the base of the clipping group is underlined (*Figure 19*). This same command is available from the main menu under Layer>Create Clipping Mask (Command-G [PC: Control-G])

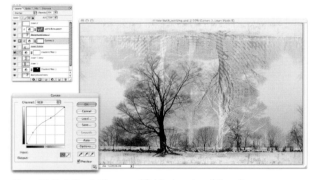

Figure 20

Figure 21 *Variation 2: The second finished version of the collage.*

Step 19: **Paint to lighten corners**

At this point I felt that the corners were a bit too dark and heavy, and that they pulled attention away from the center of the image and the dark tree. As a simple fix we can create a new layer at the top of the layer stack by clicking the New Layer icon in the Layers palette, and then select a large feathered brush. With white as the foreground color, I painted over the upper corners, varying the Brush Opacity slider in the Options Bar as I worked to create a light, semitransparent wash (*Figure 20*).

Step 20: **Add a Curves adjustment layer; complete a second version**

To increase the sharpness in the black tree branches, we'll add a Curves adjustment layer in the seventh position from the bottom, above the layer named "Layer 0 copy." To do this, select it from the Adjustment Layer pop-up in the Layers palette. After setting the Curve points to input 44 = output 78, and input 162 = output 179, I applied it only to the black tree layer with a layer clipping mask, as described in step 18 (*Figure 21*).

Figure 22

Figure 23

Step 21: **Adding another component**

In looking at the second version, I decided that I had pushed the one landscape image as far as it could go. To continue the exploration I needed to introduce another variable or subject. After considering a wide range of images, I selected an image of seedpods that I had shot in my studio. The pods were similar to the tree branch structure, and the light falloff resembled a landscape horizon. They also added a sense of mystery and ambiguity (*Figure 22*).

Step 22: **Combining the images**

Another reason for using the pods image was the way the images aligned when superimposed. Starting with the original tree file from step 1, I dragged in the pods image to create a new layer, selected Edit>Free Transform, and scaled down the pods image to match the size of the original tree file. I set the layer blend mode to Multiply to complete the effect (*Figure 23*).

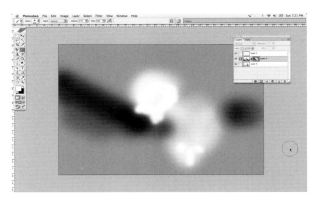

Figure 24 *The layer mask for the seedpods.*

Figure 25 *Variation 3: The third finished version of the collage.*

Figure 26

Step 23: **Adding a mask**

To integrate these images further, I clicked the Layer Mask icon in the Layers palette to add a mask, selected a middle gray foreground color, and clicked in the image with the Paint Bucket tool to fill the entire mask with gray. This made the entire pod image translucent. I then selected the Brush tool and painted with white and black to complete the mask and integrate the images (*Figure 24*).

Step 24: **Lighten the sky; complete third version**

To complete this side-trip exploration, I added a new layer to the top of the layer stack and painted in the sky with the Brush tool, adding the warm ocher color from the pods layer. The effect is very subtle and doesn't really show up in these illustrations, but it was visible in the large iris prints I made from this image (*Figure 25*).

Step 25: **Another variation**

I brought the pods image into the previous version created in step 20 by dragging the layer from one document window to the other (*Figure 26*). Since the layer mask and blending modes follow the layer as it's dragged in, the images combine immediately with the same layer mask and blending mode. This is also a solid variation, and some would say that it works well on its own, although I did push things a bit further.

Figure 27

Step 26: **Turn off some layers**

Specifically, I thought things were a bit dark and muddy. To address that, I simply started turning off layers to lighten and simplify things. I turned off the Curves layer, the layer with the dark dominant tree, and one of the inverted tree layers from the background sequence (*Figure 27*).

Figure 28

Step 27: **Crop the image**

To continue the refinement process, we'll crop the image in order to focus on the central subjects. Draw a marquee with the Crop tool to define the crop area and double-click inside it to complete the crop (*Figure 28*).

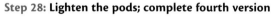

Step 28: **Lighten the pods; complete fourth version**

The pods still felt dark to me, so I selected the pod layer to lighten it. I selected Image>Adjustment>Curves to launch the Curves dialog and set a single curve point to Input 167, Output 200. *Figure 29* shows the final result.

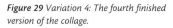

Figure 29 *Variation 4: The fourth finished version of the collage.*

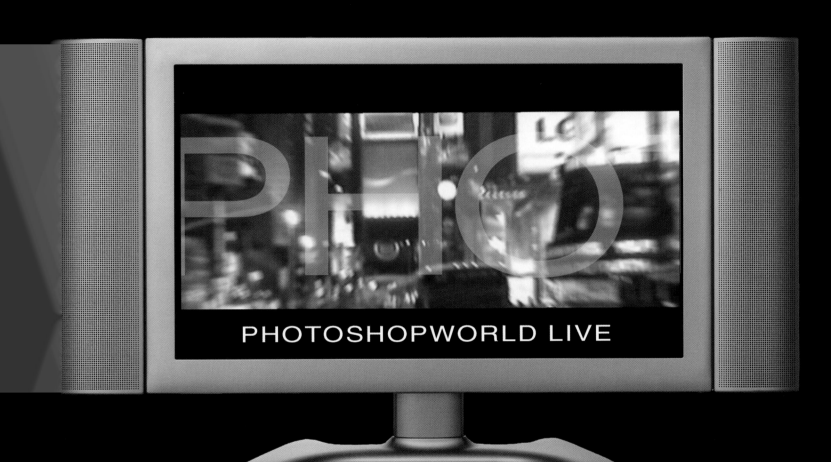

PHOTOSHOPWORLD LIVE

CHAPTER TEN
USING PHOTOSHOP FOR VIDEO WORK

Rod Harlan

Rod Harlan is Executive Director of the Digital Video Professionals Association (DVPA) and Multimedia Editor for *Mac Design Magazine*. The author of numerous books and countless magazine articles, he is a frequent speaker and trainer at many of the largest conferences and expos. Rod is also the Audio-Visual Director for both the Adobe PhotoshopWorld Conferences and the Mac Design Conference, and he works in all things related to digital video, including digital editing, animation, and special effects for television, video, CD-ROM, DVD, and the Web.

Rod runs the Digital Video Professionals Association (DVPA), which has the world's largest online training university, with more than 30,000 full-screen streaming-video files. This training covers all major software applications, including Adobe Photoshop, Premiere, After Effects, GoLive, and Illustrator; Apple Final Cut Pro and DVD Studio Pro; Macromedia Director MX, Flash MX, and Dreamweaver; ProTools; 3ds max; Mac OS X; Unix; Oracle; PHP; Microsoft Office; and many more.

Besides the DVPA Online Training University, Rod is also in charge of the DVPA Buyers' Club, where members pay only 3% above cost for all of their purchases. Rod is constantly working on adding new vendors and special deals to the Buyers' Club. He is also working on adding to the DVPA's vast array of services a royalty-free Stock Club and free Web hosting for members in 2004. Rod lives in the Tampa Bay area of Florida.

AN INTERVIEW WITH ROD HARLAN

The Digital Video Professionals Association (DVPA) is an international community of new media professionals open to all those who are involved as visual communicators using digital media. This includes, but is not limited to, producers, directors, educators, animators, videographers, editors, motion graphic artists, film groups, video game developers, advertising agencies, television stations, and design studios.

The purpose of the DVPA is to provide members with technical resources, training, and discounts on hardware and software, to further expand their understanding and appreciation for the field of digital video. Members of the association have joined together to share their resources and expertise and to further the advancement of the DV industry. By providing affordable access to new media tools and training, the DVPA encourages its members to try new forms of communication, which benefit members, their clients, and the visual medium as a whole. The DVPA is the largest organization devoted exclusively to meeting the needs of those who use DV technology.

No person, on the basis of gender, race, color, national origin, or physical disability, is excluded from participation in, denied the benefits of, or subjected to discrimination, under any DVPA program or activity.

continued on next page

AN INTERVIEW WITH ROD HARLAN *continued*

Q. What is the DVPA doing to contribute to the success of its members?

A. The DVPA expands the technical and creative knowledge of its members by providing access to the latest information and promoting the sharing of techniques. This interactive sharing of knowledge is one of the key ingredients to the DVPA's success. Some of the many topics of interest shared by DVPA members include special effects, DV editing, animation, HDTV, DVD equipment and authoring, QuickTime, MPEG, color correction in film and video, video and audio streaming, analysis of new production tools, among many others.

The DVPA also has set up the Buyers' Club, which is the ultimate resource for digital video professionals to save money on all their purchases. Buyers' Club members pay just 3% above cost for most all of their hardware, software, video gear, and peripheral purchases.

Members are given special access to custom-built extranets with some of the leading international reseller groups. Members can research and purchase items 24 hours a day, seven days a week, from anywhere in the world. Two major international resellers that have already been approved are CDW and PCMall/MacMall. It is amazing to see how easy it is to research products and pricing and still save hundreds of dollars on just one order. Both CDW and PCMall/MacMall have also dedicated specific sales associates who are trained to help DV professionals to working with DVPA members.

Q. Does the DVPA offer any educational programs for its members?

A. The DVPA holds several regional conferences throughout the country each year. These conferences bring in the top trainers for the hardware and software products that DVPA members use every day. Conference attendees get world-class training at a fraction of the cost it would take to bring even one of these individuals to their studio for a single day. The DVPA also produced the Digital Video Production Workshop for the National Association of Broadcasters (NAB) in 2002 and 2003. DVPA conferences and seminars take place all across the United States and in countries around the world.

Besides the conferences, the DVPA offers the DVPA Online University, the ultimate resource for learning DV applications without going into educational debt. This service covers all major software applications with full-screen streaming-video clips of step-by-step tutorial-based training available on your desktop 24 hours a day, seven days a week.

For years, members of the DVPA have been asking association management to come up with a way that they can learn all the creative applications that they use in their daily course of business, without having to fly to a special seminar for training or pay outrageous fees for in-house training. This request was finally granted in April 2003 when the Online University was launched. This service contains more than 30,000 streaming-video training files, making quality DV education available for less than $3 a week.

Members have access to Web-based software training for DV, graphics, and animation programs such as Final Cut Pro, Premiere, After Effects, Photoshop, Illustrator, Carrara Studio, ProTools, Director, 3ds max, alias Systems' Maya, QuickTime, Acid Pro, Flash MX, Macromedia Fireworks MX, Cleaner, and many more. The association has also made the decision to invest in training resources outside of the DV domain for those members who need to interface their skills with others. Some of these video training lessons cover topics and applications including Dreamweaver MX, GoLive, Microsoft SQL Server, Mac OS X Jaguar, Adobe PageMaker, FileMaker Pro, Perl Fundamentals, Oracle9i SQL, Microsoft Windows, PHP Programming, Visual Basic, and many more. The DVPA is committed to the continuing growth of its library of training for the benefit of its members.

The organization's training services have been greatly expanded with the addition of the DVPA Online University. However, the system also functions as a fantastic video-on-demand technical help and resource center. Should a member ever become stuck in the middle of a creative session, say while color-correcting an image in Photoshop, all they need to do is launch the viewing application from their desktop, click through the table of contents for the right clip, watch the brief tutorial, and return to work without interrupting their creative workflow. Technical and creative help has never been easier!

Q. What kind of future do you envision for the DVPA?

A. I definitely envision a future of growth for the DVPA. We are already seeing a convergence of other industries coming to the world of digital video. Graphic designers for print are becoming motion graphic artists and joining the DVPA. Programmers are becoming DVD authors and joining the DVPA. Even broadcast engineers are becoming HDTV editors and joining the DVPA.

As the future becomes the present, I believe we will see all industries using digital video as their visual communication medium of choice. This means that the Digital Video Professionals Association needs to be ready to support them when they get here. We are working toward that goal now.

For more information on the DVPA and the services it offers, please visit www.dvpa.com.

BROADCASTING PHOTOSHOP

Photoshop is an integral part of the print and publishing world. It is also an integral part of Web design. What many people don't realize is that Photoshop is a basic ingredient of the digital video, motion graphics, and multimedia markets as well. This tutorial chapter focuses on how to use Photoshop in these dynamic media environments.

Most graphic designers using Photoshop started by developing graphics for print. Designers who want to apply their training and expertise to the world of digital video (DV) usually find that they continue to create graphics as they did for print and then convert them for use in video applications. However, a designer can encounter a number of problems when converting print graphics to video, such as the following:

• Images that are "too big" for video

• Thin lines, particularly horizontal lines, that cause interlace flicker

• Colors that are "out of range" for video

• Images without alpha channels (for proper keying)

• Colored backgrounds (especially white) that should be transparent

• Graphics that fade out to white (instead of to transparent)

Most designers use Photoshop for bitmap images and either Adobe Illustrator or Macromedia Freehand for vector graphics. Motion graphics programs, like Adobe After Effects, and 3D animation applications can use vector-based artwork. Most DV editing applications cannot. If you have vector-based artwork, you may need to convert the image to the bitmap format your editing software will accept (usually PICT on the Macintosh and TIFF or Targa on Wintel computers).

When rasterizing (converting vector art to bitmap), it is worth considering the size you will rasterize to. You need to be careful not to change the shape of the image if the image was not created in a 4:3 aspect ratio (this is the aspect ratio for standard TV and video uses). Never change the proportions (aspect ratio) of an image when rasterizing. It is better to leave some empty space on the sides or at the top and bottom than to reshape the image.

Bitmap images for print are usually in the range of 200–400 dpi (dots per inch), while video only needs 72 dpi. When the bitmap image is larger than the video image, you can scale it in your video editing software, but that will create larger-than-necessary file sizes and, probably, more work for the editing software. I would recommend scaling the image closer to the final size in Photoshop rather than in your DV editing software. Photoshop will do a better job.

This chapter is a study in graphics and document preparation more than it is a cool design project with lots of eye candy. Consider it your crash course in Video 101 and more of a trouble shooting lesson than a design class. It is intended to show you how to prepare graphics for video use and to solve some of the problems mentioned earlier relating to repurposing print graphics for video use.

Specifically, this chapter will look at the following:

• Making your graphics look correct on a TV screen

• Preparing your graphics for television using Photoshop CS

• Preparing your graphics for television using Photoshop 7 or earlier

• Preparing your Photoshop documents with the appropriate NTSC safe areas

• Using Photoshop's De-Interlace filter to repair video images and prepare them for print

• Computer screen versus television screen (square pixels versus non-square pixels)

Have you ever created artwork that looked great on your computer screen but appeared squished on a video monitor? This problem affects every video editor and motion graphic designer when they first get started in DV. Fortunately, there is a fairly simple solution for this problem, and all it takes is a little understanding.

Figure 1

The example on the left shows how the basketball graphic looks on a computer monitor (square pixels). The example on the right demonstrates what the graphic would look like on a video monitor (with non-square pixels) if no conversion process were applied.

Back in the Day...

Before computers, most graphics that were used for the screen were shot with a camera and recorded directly to tape or film. When computers came along, they were able to scan images and dissect them into tiny picture elements called pixels. These pixels, as shown on computer monitors, were perfectly square and still hold that attribute today. However, when the first digital tape format came along (called D1), it used non-square pixels (tall and rectangular) to represent images. Thus was born a world of confusion that stands to this day—two completely different standards to represent the exact same image.

So what does this mean in plain English? If you are looking at a graphic on your computer monitor, then it is broken up into square pixels. If you are looking at the graphic on your video monitor, TV, and so on, then it is chopped up into rectangular pieces. For the average video editor/designer, this means that moving any images between these two distinct systems will cause some degree of aggravation because what you see on one screen is not what you get on another.

An example of this can be seen with a picture of a basketball. Any object that appears to be round on your computer display will appear to be squished on your TV monitor (*Figure 1*). More precisely, it will look as if the ball is held

IF YOU WANT TO MAKE STANDARD 4:3 NTSC DV VIDEO	
…and your video output is…	…then your graphic should be…
720x486	720x540
720x480	720x534

IF YOU WANT TO MAKE THAT COOL 16:9 LETTERBOX NTSC VIDEO	
…and your video output is…	…then your graphic should be…
720x486	864x540
720x480	864x534

IF YOU WANT TO MAKE STANDARD PAL DV VIDEO*	
…and your video output is…	…then your graphic should be…
720x546	768x576

PAL is the other main video standard used throughout the world.

Figure 2

Figure 3

in an invisible vise. Therefore, any graphics that are created on a computer but are destined to be seen on a video display need to go through a conversion process to compensate for the changes in pixel shape. This conversion process will "pre-squish" your graphic on your computer monitor so that it appears correctly when you transfer it to your video monitor.

The Conversion Process

Unfortunately, the conversion process isn't the same for everyone. The differences depend on your system and capture settings. For example, D1 (the first digital tape format) defined the scan lines for NTSC television (what is used in the United States) as having 720 horizontal pixels and 486 vertical pixels. This defined the "size" of an image that could be displayed. When the DV format came along, it defined the scan lines for NTSC as having 720 horizontal pixels and 480 vertical pixels (6 fewer pixels than D1). This is why some systems work and capture footage at 720x486 (the Targa cards, for example), and others use 720x480 (Apple FireWire).

Luckily, the whole process of creating graphics on your computer monitor and preparing them for use on a television monitor is a simple one, especially if you have Photoshop CS. It allows you to create a graphic at a square-pixel size and then resize the graphic to match the aspect ratio of your final video image. To find out the correct graphic pixel size for your appropriate video output, refer to the table in *Figure 2*.

Preparing Graphics for Television Using Photoshop 7 and Earlier

The following takes you step-by-step through creating a graphic and converting it for a 720x480 editing system.

Step 1

In Photoshop, create a new document with a width of 720 pixels, a height of 534 pixels, a resolution of 72 pixels, and your color mode set to RGB Color. The Contents setting can be whatever suits your project best (*Figure 3*).

Figure 4

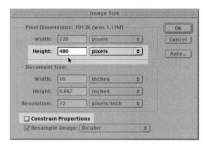

Figure 5

Figure 6

Note: You may want to change your Resolution setting to 300 pixels if you plan to use the graphic with the "pan and scan" video editing method.

Step 2
Add your artwork to the document, type in your text, blend in photographs, and finish the graphic (*Figure 4*). It would be a good idea to save the document at this time.

Step 3
Now for the conversion process. From the Image menu choose Image Size. Uncheck the Constrain Proportions box at the bottom of the dialog, and in the Pixel Dimensions section at the top, change the Height setting from 534 to 480. Leave the Width setting as is (set to 720). Click OK and save your document (*Figure 5*).

Your image should look a bit distorted (flattened) (*Figure 6*). This is a good thing. It means that your graphic will now look correct when the square pixels get converted to rectangular pixels on a video monitor.

Preparing Graphics for Television Using Photoshop CS

Photoshop CS is different from previous versions in that it scales the pixels to the video format you'll be working with and allows you to skip the step of resizing your images. It actually makes it possible to work on non-square pixels while viewing them on a square-pixel computer monitor!

When you set up a new document in Photoshop CS, for example, you can choose a video resolution from the presets in the New dialog. By default, non-square-pixel documents open with the Pixel Aspect Ratio Correction enabled. This automatically scales the image so that you can preview it as it will appear (correctly) on the output device (usually a video monitor).

For an example of how Photoshop CS allows you to work natively on non-square-pixel documents while still viewing them correctly on your square-pixel monitor, follow these steps.

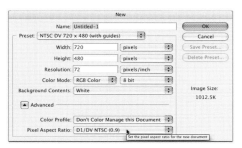

Figure 7

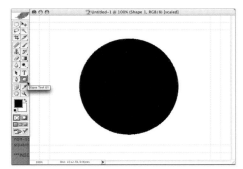

Figure 8

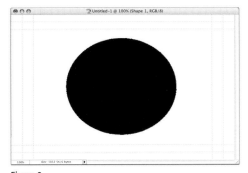

Figure 9

Step 1

Create a new document, and choose the NTSC 720x480 preset. Notice how the Pixel Aspect Ratio automatically sets itself correctly to 0.9 in the Advanced settings at the bottom of the dialog (*Figure 7*).

Step 2

Choose the Ellipse tool from the Toolbox palette, and hold down Shift as you draw a perfect circle in your document (*Figure 8*).

Step 3

Now select Image>Pixel Aspect Ratio, and choose Square. Notice how your image stretches out (*Figure 9*).

Tips for Working with Video Graphics in Photoshop CS

- When making a new image for use in a video project, create a non-square-pixel document in the New dialog. Do not work with a regular square-pixel document.

- After creating a non-square-pixel document, you can choose View>Pixel Aspect Ratio Correction to turn off the scaling correction and view the image as it looks on a computer monitor (square pixel).

- You can simultaneously view an image with Pixel Aspect Ratio Correction turned on and with the correction turned off. With the non-square-pixel image open and Pixel Aspect Ratio Correction enabled, choose Window>Arrange>New Window for [name of document]. With the new window active, choose View>Pixel Aspect Ratio Correction to turn the correction off.

- When bringing in a picture that was saved from your nonlinear editor (a video still), tell Photoshop CS that this image is built from non-square pixels by choosing Image>Pixel Aspect Ratio.

- If you are going to transfer your non-square-pixel video artwork to print or to the Web, copy and paste (or drag) your layers into a regular square-pixel document. Do not simply change the aspect ratio of your existing document to square pixels, as that will stretch your image (*Figure 9*).

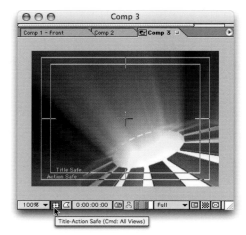

Figure 10

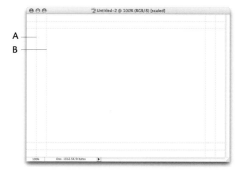

Figure 11

Video Safe Areas

When designing for television or video for the first time, many graphic artists are shocked to see their artwork chopped off at the sides. This occurs because television sets have an overscan area, and each make and model scans differently. For this reason, the industry has adopted safe areas where text and images are guaranteed to be visible onscreen.

There are two types of safe areas for NTSC television: Action Safe and Title Safe. The Action Safe area ensures that all action on camera or flying graphics onscreen can be seen on any television set. The Title Safe area ensures that all text can be seen, without distortion, on television sets. The Action Safe area is defined by a bounding box that is set inside from the edge by 10%. The Title Safe area is set inside from the edge by 20%.

Most professional video applications, like Adobe After Effects, have a button you can click to turn these areas on and off so that you can check the positioning of your work (*Figure 10*).

Photoshop, however, has no such button. Instead, Photoshop CS has preset file sizes in the New dialog for video resolutions with guides for safe areas. These presets create a document with nonprinting guides that specify the Action Safe and Title Safe areas of the image. Using the preset file sizes, you can produce images for specific video systems, including NTSC, PAL (what is used overseas), or even HDTV.

Figure 11 shows the video preset file size guides: A indicates the Action Safe area (outer rectangle), and B indicates the Title Safe area (inner rectangle).

Using Photoshop's De-Interlace Filter to Repair Video Images

In Photoshop's Filter menu there are two plug-ins built specifically for use with DV images. These filters are found at the bottom of the menu in the Video submenu and are called NTSC Colors and De-Interlace. The NTSC Colors filter simply scans your image to make sure that all your colors are NTSC-compliant. The De-Interlace filter can fix an image that has been captured from a video source, and that is the focus of this tutorial.

Video and television signals use interlaced images. In these images, every frame is divided into two fields, and each field shows half of the horizontal lines that make up the frame. Field 1 (also known as the upper or odd field) has

Figure 12

Figure 13

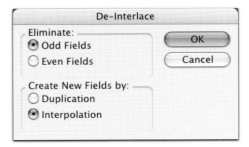

Figure 14

all the odd-numbered lines (1, 3, 5, 7, 9, and so on) of the frame, while Field 2 (lower or even) has the even-numbered lines (2, 4, 6, 8, 10, and so on). So when you capture a single frame image, you are really looking at only half of the image. Add that to the fact that there are 30 frames in every second of footage, and you realize what a tiny moment in time you're actually dealing with.

The De-Interlace filter is used to remove the interlace lines from images captured from video sources. It's important to note that these interlace lines do not appear every time, but if they do appear, this filter can really be a lifesaver.

You usually apply the filter when you want to use a video image in print or as a static graphic in another multimedia application. When you bring a video image into Photoshop, a series of horizontal artifacts, or interlace lines, may be visible in the image. The De-Interlace filter removes pixels from every other row of pixels and then replaces those pixels by doing its own interpolation, which usually produces sharper images. The following tutorial shows how to de-interlace an image that has been digitized using a video capture board.

Step 1
Open your image in Photoshop. The image in *Figure 12* came from a VHS tape that was used with a low-end recreational camcorder.

Step 2
Change the image magnification to 200% so that you can get a clear view of the interlaced lines (horizontal banding) that appear in the image (*Figure 13*).

Step 3
Choose Filter>Video>De-Interlace. When the dialog opens, you will have the option of eliminating the odd or even fields by using either the Duplication or Interpolation methods. Choosing to eliminate the odd fields with the interpolation method works most of the time, so I recommend this method for your default (*Figure 14*).

Figure 15

Step 4

Notice how the interlaced lines disappear after the filter is applied (*Figure 15*).

This image started as a low-resolution, 72-dpi camcorder shot that was one of 30 frames shot in a single second. Using Photoshop's De-Interlace filter allows us to repair the existing data, as well as add some data back into the image. However, if you were to use this image for print, you would still need to adjust levels, run an unsharp mask, and do all the other things necessary to make a picture look great on paper.

Hopefully, this chapter has given you the explanations, tools, and solutions you need to prepare your graphics for use on television, in video, and on film. I look forward to seeing your work soon!

START MOVIE

CHAPTER INDEX

BEHIND THE SCENES

DVD VIDEO

Go to
www.peachpit.com/
dreamteam.html
to download files for
this chapter.

CHAPTER ELEVEN
MAKING DVD MENUS

Richard Harrington

Richard Harrington is a certified Project Management Professional, Apple Certified Trainer in Final Cut Pro, and Adobe Certified Expert in Photoshop and After Effects. Additionally, he has completed Avid's Master Editor Workshop and the Avid Certified Instructor Program.

His visual communications consultancy, RHED Pixel, specializes in creating effective vehicles to carry client messages. RHED Pixel designs motion graphics and produces video and multimedia projects at its integrated production facility. Richard is a faculty member at the Art Institute of Washington, a popular speaker at conferences, and an instructor for Future Media Concepts.

RHED Pixel:

http://www.rhedpixel.com

info@rhedpixel.com

BOOKS AND TRAINING DVDS

Photoshop CS for Nonlinear Editors, 2nd edition (CMP Books, 2004). This comprehensive guide to the video tools in Photoshop is filled with techniques for combining still and moving images to create compelling graphics for use in television, video, the Internet, and DVD.

Final Cut Pro 4 On the Spot: Tips and Shortcuts from the Pros (CMP Books, 2003). This book presents immediate solutions in an accessible format. You can zero in

HOW TO GET AHEAD IN VIDEO OR FRY TRYING

I am both amazed and pleased at how many people are taking an interest in video production these days. At every PhotoshopWorld there are more and more people at the motion graphics/video sessions (although that might just be because people find out that I bring candy…).

What surprises me is how optimistic these folks are that video will cure their creative and financial woes. Don't get me wrong; video and motion graphics are a blast. There is nothing cooler than seeing your design in motion or crafting an engaging story. But if you are thinking of switching to video, let me offer a little bit of career advice.

There is nothing more difficult for an average desktop computer to do than video and animation. It is slow and RAM-consuming, and it just takes time. However long you think it will take, triple it. After four years you can just double it.

Bill for your render-and-digitize time. Half of the equation is the computer, electricity, and software; if you are tying up those items, then you need to charge for it. Charge more for an actual designer or editor, but do charge for the machine, too.

The software does not make the man/woman. Despite what the marketing departments want you to believe, buying an animation/music creation/digital photography/ Web compression/DVD suite in one box will not make you good at those things. Start with the basic tools and move up. Learn how to use Apple's iLife suite (or the Windows equivalent) to put your pieces together. Then take the leap to the next step. Dropping $50,000 on gear and software won't make you a better professional. Grow into your tools.

Work on the triad approach. I recommend that video

continued on next page

quickly on just the solution you need, the moment you need it. Co-written with noted Apple trainer Abba Shapiro.

After Effects On the Spot: Time-Saving Tips and Shortcuts from the Pros (CMP Books, 2004). Packed with more than 400 techniques, this book gets readers up to speed efficiently by teaching them what they need to know, when they need to know it. Co-written with Rachel Max and Marcus Geduld.

Photoshop CS: Essentials for Digital Video (www.vasst.com). This training DVD teaches video pros the essential skills needed to create graphics for use in video. Award-winning editor Richard Harrington clearly demonstrates techniques he uses.

SEMINAR

Photoshop for Nonlinear Editors (www.fmctraining.com/photoshop). This full-day seminar enables experienced video professionals to move to a higher level of confidence using Photoshop. Complex techniques come to life as Richard Harrington shares timesaving production tips for use with video projects.

pros tackle things in threes. First go after editing–motion graphics–still graphics. This could mean learning a nonlinear editing package with Adobe After Effects and Photoshop thrown in. After a while, go up a notch and learn color correcting (making the image look its best), audio mixing (getting the right sound), and compression (DVD and Internet distribution). I do believe that a few people can "do it all" but that it takes a lot of time to get good.

If the computer is misbehaving (which it will do at least five times a day, regardless of platform), shut it down, count to 20, and reboot. Not only will you feel better, but you'll also be amazed how many things work again.

Remember, 90 percent of problems are cable problems: loose cables, bad cables, or even unplugged cables. Before you panic, check all your connections. I am serious here— this is a mantra at our shop.

Pick jobs based on opportunity. If you are trying to get into the industry, pick your projects based on the quality of work. You need to quickly build up your motion graphics and video portfolio. That may mean giving away some services to charities or community events to get yourself established.

Backup your project files every night, because video has the meanest gremlins. Also, backing up to the internal or media drive doesn't count—use a USB thumb drive or a CD.

You can never save too much. No matter what you hear, computers and applications do crash. Video folks often have software and hardware from 20-plus manufacturers running at one time… What do you think is going to happen?

The best job I ever had that prepped me for the video industry was bartending. I got to be a good listener; I learned how to make jokes; and if the stress level got too high, I learned solutions to mellow everyone out. Seriously, though, clients will be tough, and videos are often high-profile. Be supportive and understand that your clients need to annoy you at times.

If you can sleep on it, do so. Fresh eyes are better for making artistic decisions.

And don't forget about your family. The field is tough and time-consuming. Try hard to remember that you have loved ones, and make time for them. You work so that you can live—remember that.

Push pixels! See you at the next PhotoshopWorld …

CREATING A DVD MENU

Do you DVD? Chances are you do, or soon will. The digital versatile disc, or DVD, format has helped jump-start several industries. It is also the hottest way for designers to distribute their content. If you want to capture viewers' attention, creating great menus will invite them to explore the contents of a disc.

For many, the world of video production can be a confusing place. It is common to come across conflicting information (even the software companies disagree; sometimes they even contradict themselves). Let's try to dispel a few myths, teach a few tricks, and get some immediate results.

In this chapter, I'll help you:

- Learn the proper size for DVD menus *(Figure 1)* and how to work with non-square pixels.

- Discover how to set text and create buttons with the title safe area in mind.

- Choose colors that work well on a television.

- Learn how to extract frames from a video to use in Photoshop.

- Build exciting backgrounds by harnessing the power of blending modes.

- Discover advanced collaboration using Photoshop and After Effects side by side to put your menus into motion.

- Create highlight layers and rollover effects.

Figure 1

Figure 2

Why Does It Have to Be So Hard?

Hey, if DVD were easy, everybody would do it, so it'd be just as cluttered and unrewarding as your email inbox. With that in mind, accept that there are some new "rules" you must follow and that you are going to have to learn how to thrive under severe limitations. The DVD format is one of many compromises, and for all its coolness it's remarkably low-tech. You're going to need to think of creative ways to stay inside of the box (and get your audience to come in and join you).

The Rules: Design Specifications and Constraints

When designing a DVD, you must keep a few key specs in mind:

Square-pixel versus non-square-pixel aspect ratio. DVDs use non-square pixels *(Figure 2)*. If you are building in Photoshop CS, this is no problem. If you are using an earlier version of Photoshop, you will have to resize your graphics.

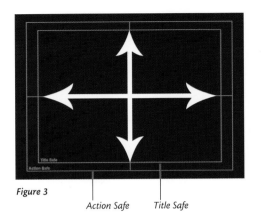

Figure 3

Action Safe   Title Safe

The screen is smaller than you think. A certain portion of the menu design will be lost by consumer TV sets. To counterbalance this, we reserve a bleed area. All words must fall within the Title Safe area, which is 80 percent of the screen. All logos or elements meant to be seen in their entirety must fall inside the action safe area, which is 90 percent of the screen (*Figure 3*). Video graphics, however, are designed edge-to-edge, and must fill the entire canvas.

Final file ends up 720x480 pixels. Whether it's wide-screen or standard, you still only have an area that's 720 pixels across and 480 pixels tall to design for. Extra ppi (often called dpi) are as useless as an elephant at a backyard barbeque.

Buttons use grid slices. You need adequate separation around buttons. Links are assigned to a rectangular target, and you must be able to draw a clean rectangle with no overlapping between button areas.

Swapping layer or a motion menu. Many designers like to build "Photoshop-style" menus where different layers are substituted during the click or highlight stages (think GIF rollover). Other designers build elaborate menus with video and motion using After Effects and other content apps. Never shall the two meet—you can have layers that sub in and out, or a motion menu with a colored highlight layer.

Get Your Stuff Together

The first step to designing a DVD requires that you have a plan. You can't build a menu without knowing the layout of the DVD. The form is often shaped by the contents, so you need to create a disc map. If you've ever built a Web site, the process of making a site map is very similar. Be sure to get client sign-off on the outline, though, or else your redesigns may become painful as you struggle to squeeze extra buttons into your design.

Once you've got a blueprint, you need to get your bricks. Gather your still images, video clips, and logos. I find the more source material I have the better, as it opens up more options and new ideas. But chances are that source material will need some special preparation in order to be ready for the television screen.

Prepare Movie Assets

Most DVD menus use footage as their primary ingredient. If you have access to video software, follow these instructions (if someone else is prepping the files,

Figure 4

Figure 5

you can still share this advice). Depending on your software package, language may vary slightly. It is important to export your movies at the highest quality possible. To harness the full power of the original sequence, choose to export with the native compression rate.

1. Mark In and Out points in your sequence or on an individual clip.

2. Ensure that all media is rendered between the In and Out points.

3. Choose File>Export>QuickTime Movie (*Figure 4*).

4. Set a destination for your target file. Be sure to select a destination that has adequate space.

5. Make sure the movie is self-contained in order to future-proof your project (it's a checkbox in the Export dialog).

6. Be sure to manually add the proper .mov extension to ensure maximum compatibility.

Using Still Frames from Video in Your Menu Design

Get video clips from your client or access them from your NLE (nonlinear editing) system. Most NLE systems allow you to place the playhead indicator on a frame and export a still (see your NLE documentation).

You are going to need the video as a QuickTime or AVI file in order to author a DVD menu with it. You cannot work with MPEG-2 streams, as they are too compressed and do not read into most authoring and design tools.

Step 1
If you need a Frame Grab still, open the clip in QuickTime Pro. You can open both QuickTime and AVI files using QuickTime Player. Place the playhead on the frame you want, and press Command-C (PC: Control-C).

Step 2
Switch to Photoshop and create a new document. It will be automatically sized for your clipboard. Paste the frame by pressing Command-V (PC: Control-V).

Step 3
Choose Filter>Video>De-Interlace to remove interlaced lines. This will create a smoother image for static frames (*Figure 5*).

Figure 6
Color and contrast
are enhanced
(bottom) by using
a duplicate layer,
blurring it, and
setting the layer
blend mode
to Overlay or
Soft Light.

COURTESY AMERICAN DIABETES ASSOCIATION

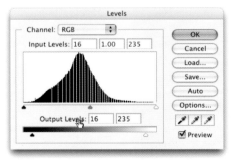

Figure 7

Step 4

To bring the video frame back to RGB levels that are appropriate for video, you need to run a levels adjustment by pressing Command-L (PC: Control-L). In the Levels dialog set the white Input point to 235 and the black Input point to 16 . This restores the proper contrast to the image.

Step 5

To get the color back, duplicate the frame by pressing Command-J (PC: Control-J). Blur this new layer with a Gaussian Blur filter (set to a pixel radius between 15 and 50, according to your preference). Change the blending mode of the blurred copy; Overlay or Soft Light often works well, but you will need to experiment here (*Figure 6*).

Flatten the image. If you are in Photoshop CS, be sure to adjust the Pixel Aspect Ratio settings to match the tape format from which you acquired the video (usually D1/DV NTSC [0.9]).

Using Photos in Your Menu Design

Scan your images to be larger than the size needed for the final menu layout. This will give you extra resolution for restoring the picture. Make any adjustments to the image quality as needed. If you intend to use the image full-screen or want to size the image to the correct video aspect, you need to perform a power crop.

Step 1

Select the Crop tool by pressing "c." In the Options Bar enter a Width of 720 px (for pixels) and a Height of 534 px. The resolution does not matter, as video works with the total pixel dimensions.

Crop the image to taste; remember, video is a medium that works better with tighter shots. If you intend to use an image full-screen, however, keep the action safe area in mind, and leave some headroom.

Step 2

Add a levels adjustment to make the image broadcast safe. You need to clamp the output levels to keep the image in the proper luminance range for television usage. Set the Output Levels to 16 for black and 235 for white (*Figure 7*). Copy and paste or drag and drop the image into your DVD menu.

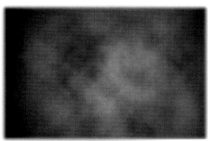

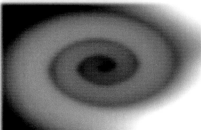

Figure 8
Playing with gradients and filters can lead to some interesting source material for the creation of DVD menu backgrounds. From top to bottom are gradients combined with the Clouds filter, the Twirl filter, and the Wave filter.

When you add the images to a non-square document, Photoshop will automatically scale the images to size.

Making Backgrounds from Stills

When designing a DVD, you are going to need a backdrop to hold your menu. There are several sources for these, but let's go ahead and make our own from scratch. By harnessing gradient layers and blending modes, we can quickly create rich backgrounds with depth and color.

Create random gradient layers using the Gradient tool ("g") and filters (the Distort and Render categories are good places to start). Be sure the gradients are at least 800x600 pixels to enable design flexibility. Limit yourself to working in the Grayscale mode or working with blends between black and white. You can also try creating a gradient and then adding a filter effect to it (*Figure 8*). The important thing is that we are going to combine these layers and only want to affect the results based on luminance. If you need some examples of gradients, try visiting the following Web sites for free samples: the Plugin Site (www.thepluginsite.com), Auto FX Software (www.autofx.com), and Pixelan Software (www.pixelan.com).

We are now going to create a new document to mix our ingredients together.

Step 1

Choose File>New or press Command-N (PC: Control-N). In Photoshop CS choose New 720 X 480 DV NTSC preset; in Photoshop 7 choose New 720 X 534 DV/DVD NTSC preset.

Step 2

Add three to four gradients into your composition by dragging them in. Turn off the visibility of all but the two bottom layers.

Select the layer that is second from the bottom. We are now going to blend…but let's use a shortcut. Press Shift-= or Shift-– (hyphen) to cycle through the blending modes. If you have a tool selected with modes, it changes those; if you have a tool without modes, the layer's mode will change. Pick the Move tool, and press Shift-= to change the layer's mode. Stop when a resulting effect satisfies you.

Turn on the next layer and blend. Repeat as needed.

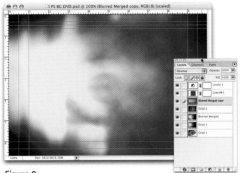

Figure 9

Step 3

When satisfied, we will make a flattened copy of these layers. Make a new layer at the top of the layer stack, and then choose Merge Visible while holding down Option (PC: Alt) (be sure to keep Option [PC: Alt] pressed down until you see the new layer thumbnail appear in the new layer). Apply a slight blur using Gaussian Blur or Median filter.

To bloom it out, duplicate the flattened layer and blur it heavily. Try blending again to get a softer pattern.

Step 4

We are now going to add color. You can do this by placing a solid-color fill layer or a color gradient above the composite. Then adjust the layer's blending mode to taste. You can also try using a Gradient Map adjustment layer. This, too, can be further refined with blending modes (*Figure 9*).

Step 5

Tweak the layer stacking order and modes to refine the background. Add a levels adjustment layer. Clamp the Output Levels by adjusting white to 235 and black to 16.

Make Your Own Title Safe Guides

If you are working in Photoshop 7 (or earlier), you will need to create your own title safe guides. I still choose to add my own, as I do not like using Photoshop's guides as much as an actual layer to mark out my design areas.

Step 1

Create a new layer, name it Title Safe, and highlight it. Choose Select>All or press Command-A (PC: Control-A).Choose Select>Transform Selection.

Step 2

In the Options Bar for the selection, link the width and height by clicking the chain link icon between the width and height fields, and scale the selection to 90% (*Figure 10*). Click Commit (the checkmark button on the right side of the Options Bar) or press Enter to complete the transformation.

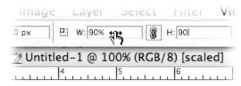

Figure 10

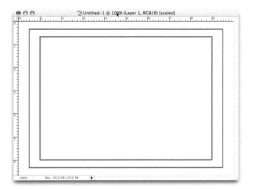

Figure 11

Step 3

Choose a high-contrast color such as red. Choose Edit>Stroke and apply a 4-pixel centered stroke.

Step 4

Once again, choose Select>All or press Command-A (Control-A). Then choose Select>Transform Selection. In the Options Bar for the selection, click the chain icon to link the width and height, and scale the selection to 80%. Click Commit.

Step 5

Choose Edit>Stroke and apply a 4-pixel centered stroke (*Figure 11*). Now you have your title safe guides on a separate layer so that you can always refer to them. Design your menu.

The Split in the Road

At this point you can choose to stop your journey. Stay in Photoshop and finesse your design—the comfortable path. When you finish your design, resize it to 720x480 and save it as a PICT or Targa file. Even basic DVD applications like Apple's iDVD allow you to import your own backgrounds. (Unlike other video apps, though, iDVD wants a 640 x 480 square pixel image.)

But if you are up to the challenge, you can take the leap into Adobe After Effects. This great application makes it easy to take the plunge into a full-motion menu. After Effects is often called "Photoshop with a timeline," and for good reason. Your .psd file will come in easily, including type layers and blending modes. If you're ready for more, keep reading. If you don't own After Effects, be sure to visit Adobe's Web site for a fully functional 30-day trial.

Keep It Moving

You can now import into After Effects the still menu you designed in Photoshop and bring motion to your design.

1. You can replace the static background with an animated one.

2. Try replacing stills with moving clips for background layers or buttons.

3. Feel free to add gentle blurs, fades, and moves. Be sure your first and last keyframes are identical if you want to maintain a loop.

USING TYPE

Remember when you were a kid watching Saturday morning cartoons? Did your mom or dad yell at you for sitting too close to the TV? "You'll go blind!" Well, that's good advice to remember. Type for the television screen is very different than for print or the Web. Here are some things to keep in mind:

- Use a larger point size. Stand up and walk 20 feet away from the computer screen. Can you still read it?

- For video production, white is 235 on an RGB scale and black is 16. When picking colors for screen usage, do not exceed this color range for any of the RGB values.

- Be sure to anti-alias your type for smoother edges at low resolutions (*Figure 12*).

Figure 12

- Layer styles help readability. Don't over-bevel; however, a light bevel can help make the text more readable. Also add a contrasting edge with either a glow or a drop shadow. If you add layer styles, you must flatten the styled layer so that it will import correctly into After Effects or your NLE software. Do this by linking the affected type layer to an empty layer. Then choose Merge Linked from the Layers palette menu.

- Sans serif fonts are often easier to read on television sets. If using a bold version of a serif font, be sure to use a true bold version, not a faux bold effect.

4. When finished, you'll need to render the file out for encoding. End in Non-square pixel size (*Figure 13*).

5. Render to a high-quality codec such as Animation.

6. Loop and add audio in a video editing program or in AE.

7. Loop video multiple times but carry music throughout.

8. Encode to MPEG-2 or bring into DVD authoring as QT (QuickTime).

In After Effects: Let There Be Motion

We must now animate our layered PSD file to create movement. We will employ transfer modes, scaling, pre-compositions, overlapping, and color mapping. This method of creating looping backgrounds requires very little effort. You must be comfortable with blending modes, however, to achieve results.

Create a new project

Step 1

Import the PSD document you created for the back-ground by choosing File> Import and specifying as a Composition.

Select the composition from the project window and modify its settings by pressing Command-K (PC: Control-K). From the preset menu, choose NTSC DV, 720 x 480 and rename the comp. Also, set the duration to 20:00 (*Figure 14*).

Step 2

All of your Photoshop layers and blending modes should have been imported into After Effects (*Figure 15*). If you used a gradient map adjustment layer in Photoshop, you can re-create or improve the effect using AE's Colorama filter (Photoshop gradient maps cannot be imported by other programs properly).

```
Custom

Small, 160 x 120
Medium, 320 x 240

NTSC, 640 x 480
NTSC, 648 x 486
✓ NTSC DV, 720 x 480
NTSC DV Widescreen, 720 x 480
NTSC D1, 720 x 486
NTSC D1 Square Pix, 720 x 540
PAL D1/DV, 720 x 576
PAL D1/DV Square Pix, 768 x 576
PAL D1/DV Widescreen, 720 x 576

HDTV, 1280 x 720
D4, 1440 x 1024
Cineon Half, 1828 x 1332
HDTV, 1920 x 1080
Film (2K), 2048 x 1536
D16, 2880 x 2048
Cineon Full, 3656 x 2664
```

Figure 13

The Composition Settings preset list in After Effects.

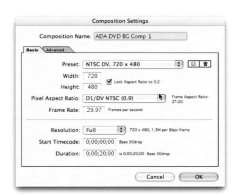

Figure 14

Figure 15

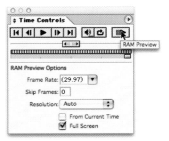

Figure 16

Step 3

Turn off visibility for all layers except the bottom. Select the bottom layer and press "s" for Scale. Then hold down the Shift key and press "r" for Rotation and "a" for Anchor Point. By using Anchor Point instead of Position, we get better results (especially when rotation is involved).

Step 4

Turn on the stopwatch icons for all three properties. Choose random values for the start and end keyframes. All you are trying to accomplish is movement (just be sure that the image always fills the entire screen). Activate RAM Preview to see your results (*Figure 16*).

Step 5

Activate the next layer and repeat the animation technique. Try to achieve a different motion path (thus creating "interference.")

 Adjust the blending mode and/or opacity to achieve a soft look. Repeat for all the remaining grayscale layers (*Figure 17*).

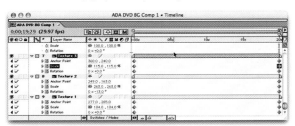

Figure 17

Step 6

To create the soft bloom, add an adjustment layer. Apply the Gaussian Blur effect, and adjust the layer's blending mode and Opacity settings.

Make the Loop

Now it's time to create the loop.

Step 1

Highlight all of your grayscale layers, and create a pre-composition by choosing Layer>Pre-compose or pressing Command-Shift-C (PC: Control-Shift-C). Name it BG.

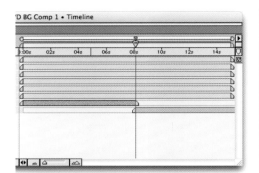

Figure 18

Figure 19

Step 2

Access your composition settings by pressing Command-Shift-K (PC: Control-Shift-K), and shorten the comp to 15:00.

Go to the 8:00 mark by pressing Command-G (PC: Control-G) and entering 8:00.

Step 3

We are now going to split the layer in half, thus creating our loop point. Select the layer and press Command-Shift-D (PC: Control-Shift-D) (*Figure 18*).

Step 4

We now must overlap the layers. With Layer #1 active, jump to the end of the composition by pressing End. Press the right bracket key (]) to move the layer's Out point. Select Layer #2 and then press Home. Press the left bracket key ([) to move the layer's In point.

Step 5

Activate Layer #1 and press "i" to jump to the layer's In point. Press "t" for Opacity and activate the stopwatch. Set a keyframe for 0% Opacity.

Jump forward 4.5 seconds by pressing Command-G (PC: Control-G) and then typing +415 in the Go To Time dialog (*Figure 19*).

Step 6

Set a keyframe for 100% Opacity. Flip the quality switches to Best Quality. Add an adjustment layer at the top of your stack.

Step 7

Apply a colorization effect such as Colorama (Effect>Image Control>Colorama), Tint (Effect>Image Control>Tint), or Hue/Saturation with the Colorize option selected (Effect>Adjust>Hue/Saturation). You might also experiment with other effects on the adjustment layer, such as Glows, Blurs, or Trapcode's Shine.

You may now choose to add video clips of moving footage, as well as additional logos or type.

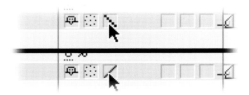

Figure 20

Figure 21

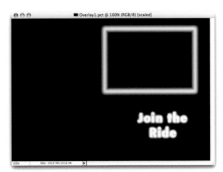

Figure 22

Step 8

Flip all your quality switches to Best Quality, and render at Lossless settings (*Figure 20*).

Export highlight layer

Your DVD authoring app is going to need a map image to determine what lights up. This grayscale image identifies where the glows appear. It is an overlay for the moving video file.

Step 1

Complete your DVD menu and render out the final version. Save your After Effects file to capture any changes.

Set your Comp Window to 100% and Full Quality. Go to an appropriate frame and choose Composition>Save Frame As>Photoshop Layers.

Step 2

Open the file in Photoshop. Turn off the visibility icons for all layers that are not part of the overlay.

Select one of the visible layers, and choose Merge Visible from the Layers palette menu.

Step 3

Lock the transparency for this new merged layer by clicking the Lock Transparent Pixels icon (*Figure 21*).

Choose Edit>Fill, and fill with black (or white, depending on your DVD application).

Step 4

Create a new empty layer, and place it in the stack below the layer you just finished editing. Choose Select>All, and fill this layer with white (or black, again depending on your DVD application).

Delete any unused layers (*Figure 22*).

Step 5

Choose File>Save As, and save a flattened PICT or Targa file to create an overlay layer. Again, you don't need to save layers or alpha channels.

Save the layered .psd file in case you have changes.

Step 6

Duplicate the flattened file, open it, and choose Select>All. Press Command-I (PC: Control-I) to invert the image. This way, you'll have both for your DVD authoring application, if needed.

The End?

Well, not quite—how you put the DVD together will depend on your authoring application. Fortunately, those usually come with decent tutorials and documentation. Where the breakdown usually occurs is in the Photoshop and After Effects integration. I hope this tutorial encourages you to take your designs to a higher level. If you get stuck or need more help with Photoshop and video integration, catch me at the next PhotoshopWorld or at Creative Cow (www.creativecow.net).

Go to
www.peachpit.com/
dreamteam.html
to download files for
this chapter.

CHAPTER TWELVE

FAKING STUDIO SHOTS WITH PHOTOSHOP

Scott Kelby

Scott is Editor-in-Chief and cofounder of *Photoshop User* magazine, Editor-in-Chief of Nikon's *Capture User* magazine, and Editor-in-Chief of *Mac Design Magazine*. He is President of the National Association of Photoshop Professionals (NAPP), the trade association for Photoshop users, and President of KW Media Group, Inc., a Florida-based software education and publishing firm.

Scott is author of the best-selling books *Adobe Photoshop CS Down & Dirty Tricks* (New Riders, 2003) and *The Adobe Photoshop CS Book for Digital Photographers* (New Riders, 2003), and coauthor of *Photoshop CS Killer Tips*. He is also the creator and series editor for the Killer Tips series of books from New Riders.

Outside of Photoshop, Scott has written several books on the Macintosh operating system, including *Mac OS X Killer Tips* (New Riders, 2004), *The Mac OS X Conversion Kit* (Peachpit Press, 2003), and *Macintosh…The Naked Truth* (New Riders, 2002), and he coauthored *The iTunes for Windows Book* (Peachpit Press, 2004).

Scott is Training Director for the Adobe Photoshop Seminar Tour, Conference Technical Chair for the PhotoshopWorld Conference & Expo, and a speaker at graphics trade shows and events around the world. He is also featured in a series of Photoshop training DVDs and has been training Photoshop users since 1993.

For more background info on Scott, visit www.scottkelby.com.

OPENING THOUGHTS

I've always felt that one of the reasons that Photoshop has reached the level that is has, the reason for its amazing success, is the program's sheer depth. You never feel like you've "hit the wall" and can't go any further. In fact, in all the years I've been teaching Photoshop, I've yet to meet anyone who's said "I've done all I can do in Photoshop." That's because the program doesn't limit you. It doesn't put up walls or boundaries—it lets you take it where you want to go, and the better you get at Photoshop, the more you discover there is to learn. You never really feel like "Oh, I know this program inside and out." You always feel like "Wow, I can't believe what people are doing with Photoshop."

Bert Monroy is a perfect example. He's a genius, and every time I see his work, I'm simply amazed. I've been using Photoshop for years, and yet I look at Bert's work and I wouldn't even know where to start. He uses Photoshop in a way that just astounds me and even though I can't begin to do what he does, just knowing that Photoshop can take you there is very inspiring.

Few software programs have ever been written that have the power to do that. To change. To empower. To move and inspire. Photoshop does all of that, it is all of that, and so much more. That's why Photoshop has earned its place in history, in our vocabulary, in our art and culture and in our lives. And the fact that we get to use it, to play with it, to create with it, and to have fun with it—to me that's just incredibly cool.

CREATING YOUR OWN STUDIO SHOTS

One of the techniques I've been showing at recent PhotoshopWorlds (in my "Down & Dirty Tricks" session) is how to create your own digital studio shots. The idea is to make it look as if you spent lots of time setting up a complicated studio lighting rig, but actually the entire illusion is created right within Photoshop.

This "faking studio" concept is ideal for product and portrait shots, and I've gotten so much great feedback on the technique I wanted to share some of these tricks here.

Figure 1

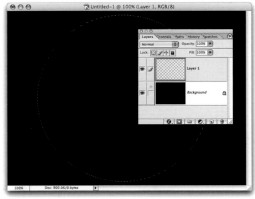

Figure 2

Dramatic Studio Backgrounds

In this first example, we're going to fake a dramatic studio shot (we want to make it look like we went in the studio and set up an elaborate lighting layout, when all we did was shoot the product on a plain white background). The background you'll create here is ideal for products that you want to look elegant (such as expensive electronics, jewelry, and other high-end products).

Step 1

Open a new document at 640x480 pixels, RGB mode, at a resolution of 72 ppi. Set your foreground color to black by pressing "d", and then fill your background layer with black by pressing Option-Delete (PC: Alt-Backspace) (*Figure 1*).

Step 2

Create a new layer by clicking the New Layer icon at the bottom of the Layers palette. Then get the Elliptical Marquee tool, and, holding down Shift (to constrain your selection to a perfect circle), drag out a large circular selection in the center of your new layer (*Figure 2*).

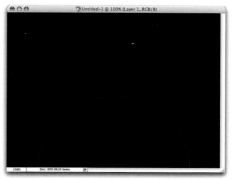

Figure 3

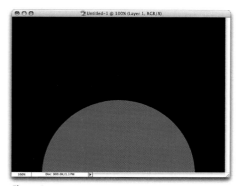

Figure 4

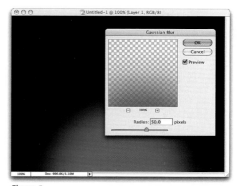

Figure 5

Step 3

While you still have the Elliptical Marquee tool, click within the circular selection and drag straight down until only half of the selection is visible (*Figure 3*).

Step 4

Choose an orangey brown color as your foreground color; then fill this half circle with that color by pressing Option-Delete (PC: Alt-Backspace), and deselect your selection by pressing Command-D (PC: Control-D) (*Figure 4*). (Note: Although we're filling this with a color now, it's just kind of a placeholder color because you'll have the option of changing the circle's color later in this tutorial. That way you can make the circle's color fit better with your product's coloring, so don't sweat getting the exact right orangey brown color at this point.)

Step 5

Now that you've filled the half circle with color, choose Filter>Blur>Gaussian Blur. When the Gaussian Blur dialog appears enter 50 in the Radius field and click OK (*Figure 5*). (Note: Fifty pixels works here because we're working on a low-resolution 72-ppi image. If you're working on a high-res 300-ppi image, use 170 pixels instead.) Applying this blur to the half circle starts to make it look more like a soft light being cast on the black background, but we'll tweak it some more to make it look realistic.

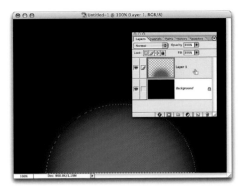

Figure 6

Figure 7

Figure 8

Step 6

Go to the Layers palette, hold down the Command key (PC: Control) and click the circle layer, which puts a selection around the circle (*Figure 6*). Don't let the selection outline fool you—it will look like only the hard-edged non-blurred circle is selected, but in reality even the soft-edged areas are selected.

Step 7

Choose Select>Modify>Contract. In the Contract Selection dialog, enter 40 in the Contract By field, and then click OK to shrink your selection inward by 40 pixels (*Figure 7*).

Step 8

Switch your foreground color to white, then fill this smaller selection with white by pressing Option-Delete (PC: Alt-Backspace). Because the selection was already soft before you contracted it, the white area will have soft edges just like the larger half circle. Now you can deselect by pressing Command-D (PC: Control-D) (*Figure 8*).

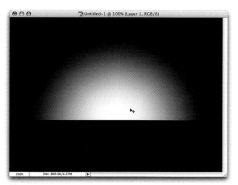

Figure 9

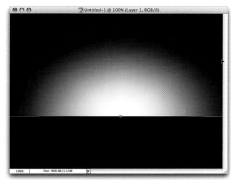

Figure 10

Figure 11

Step 9

Switch to the Move tool, click the circle and drag it straight up (*Figure 9*). This creates the table that the product will sit upon (at least, that's what it will look like).

Step 10

Before we add the product to the background, we need to stretch out our soft light so that the beam is more oval-shaped. Press Command-T (PC: Control-T) to bring up Free Transform. Grab the right-side center point, and drag outward to the right to stretch the soft circle until the edge of the circle almost touches the right edge. Do the same thing to the left center point—drag to the left until the soft edge of the circle almost touches the right edge (*Figure 10*). Then press Return (PC: Enter) to lock in this stretching of the circle.

Step 11

Open your product shot (in this case, it's a product shot taken on a plain white background), and then put a selection around your product (*Figure 11*). (Because the product is mostly made up of straight lines, I used the Polygonal Lasso tool to put a selection around the DVD/VHS player.)

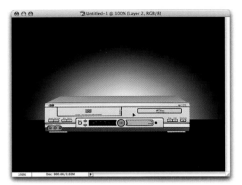

Figure 12

Figure 13

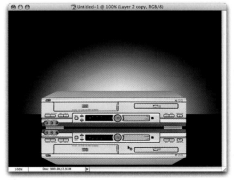

Figure 14

Step 12

Using the Move tool, drag your selected product onto your black background, and position it so that two-thirds of it appears over the spotlight and one-third is over the black background (*Figure 12*).

Step 13

Duplicate your product layer by pressing Command-J (PC: Control-J). Then press Command-T (PC: Control-T) to bring up the Free Transform control. Control-click (PC: right-click) to bring up a pop-up list of transformations and from this list choose Flip Vertical to flip this copied product layer upside down (*Figure 13*). Then press Return (PC: Enter) to lock in this transformation.

Step 14

Using the Move tool, hold down Shift and drag this flipped product straight down until the feet on the bottom of the flipped version touch the feet on the bottom of the top version, creating a mirror image (*Figure 14*).

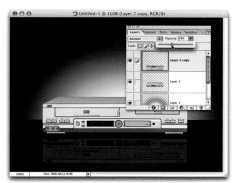

Figure 15

Figure 16

Step 15

Go to the Layers palette and lower the Opacity of this flipped layer to around 35% or 40% to create the illusion of a reflection (*Figure 15*).

Step 16

To take the focus off the reflection, you'll apply a slight bit of Motion Blur to the flipped version: Choose Filter>Blur>Motion Blur. When the dialog appears, set the Angle to 90°, then set the amount to 12 (just enough to apply a slight blurring) and then click OK (*Figure 16*).

Step 17

Now, if you want to change the color of the soft spotlight, go to the Layers palette and click the soft circle layer; then choose Image>Adjustments>Hue/Saturation. Now just drag the Hue slider to the left or right to adjust the overall color of the soft spotlight (*Figure 17*).

Step 18

Finally, add your text (in white) to complete your faked studio shot (*Figure 18*). The text shown here is set in the font Helvetica.

Figure 17

Figure 18

Figure 19

Figure 20

Figure 21

Figure 22

Studio Shot #2

Now we're going to use some of the techniques we learned in the previous tutorial and apply them to an entirely different style of layout—this one is ideal for health and beauty product shots.

Step 1

Open a new document at 5.889 inches by 8.333 inches, RGB mode, at a resolution of 72 ppi. Set your foreground color to a light violet, and then fill your background layer with light violet by pressing Option-Delete (PC: Alt-Backspace) (*Figure 19*).

Step 2

Open the photo of the product you want to use in your fake studio shot. In the example shown here, we're going to use a bottle of fictitious cologne for men called "exuberance" from a made-up company named "Maidup Fragrences" (both words misspelled intentionally) (*Figure 20*). Put a selection around the bottle (in this case I drew a path around the bottle using the Pen tool, and then converted the path to a selection by pressing Command-Return [PC: Control-Enter]).

Step 3

Once your cologne bottle is selected, drag it over onto your light violet background and position it on the left side of the image area (*Figure 21*).

Step 4

In the Layers palette, hold down Command (PC: Control) and click the New Layer icon. This creates a new blank layer directly below your current layer (the cologne bottle layer) (*Figure 22*).

Figure 23

Figure 24

Figure 25

Figure 26

Step 5

Get the Lasso tool and draw a very, very loose selection outside the cologne bottle, leaving plenty of space between the bottle and the selection. Think of it as a wide, rough outline of sorts, and continue your selection so that it extends right off the right side of the image area. Once it's in place, set white as your foreground color and then fill this large selection with white by pressing Option-Delete (PC: Alt-Backspace) (*Figure 23*). Deselect by pressing Command-D (PC: Control-D).

Step 6

Now to soften the white areas and make them look like we're lighting a background, we'll use the same technique we did in the last tutorial: Choose Filter>Blur>Gaussian Blur. In the Gaussian Blur dialog, enter 50 in the Radius field (*Figure 24*). (Note: Again, 50 pixels works here because we're working on a low-resolution 72-ppi image. If you're working on a high-res 300-ppi image, use 170 pixels.)

Step 7

When you click OK in the Gaussian Blur dialog, it softens the white areas and creates the background for your product—but we're not done yet (*Figure 25*).

Step 8

In the Layers palette, click on the cologne bottle layer (Layer 1) and duplicate this layer by pressing Command-J (PC: Control-J). Then press Command-T (PC: Control-T) to bring up the Free Transform control. Control-click (PC: right-click) to bring up a pop-up list of transformations, and from this list choose Flip Vertical (*Figure 26*) to flip this copied product layer upside down. Press Return (PC: Enter) to lock in this transformation.

Figure 27

Figure 28

Figure 29

Figure 30

Step 9

Get the Move tool, and hold down Shift as you drag this flipped cologne bottle straight down until the bottom of the flipped version touches the bottom of the top original bottle, creating a mirror image (*Figure 27*).

Step 10

In the Layers palette, lower the Opacity of this flipped layer to around 35% to create the illusion of a reflection (*Figure 28*).

Step 11

In the Layers palette, click and drag your original cologne bottle layer above the flipped reflection layer. Then hold Command (PC: Control) and click the New Layer icon at the bottom of the palette to create a new blank layer directly below your cologne bottle layer. Press "d" to set your foreground color to black, and then get the Brush tool. Choose a medium-size brush (I chose a 35-pixel brush) and paint a small shadow under the bottom by tracing along the bottom edge (*Figure 29*).

Step 12

Lower the Opacity of this shadow layer to around 50% to make it look more natural (*Figure 30*).

Figure 31

Figure 32

Figure 33

Figure 34

Step 13

In this step, we'll add a paint stroke to make it look as if the cologne bottle is sitting on some sort of surface and not just floating. Get the Eyedropper tool and click up in the left corner of your image area to sample that light violet color and make it your foreground color. Get the Brush tool, and increase the size of your soft-edged brush to 60 pixels. Holding down Shift, paint a straight line along the area where the bottle is sitting (*Figure 31*). Make sure your stroke extends off both sides of the image area.

Step 14

In the Layers palette, lower the Opacity of this shadow layer to around 35% so that it doesn't get too much attention (*Figure 32*).

Step 15

To make this stroke blend in even better, in the Layers palette change the blend mode of this layer from Normal to Multiply (*Figure 33*).

Step 16

The final step is simply to add some type to complete the ad (*Figure 34*).

Go to www.peachpit.com/dreamteam.html to download files for this chapter.

CHAPTER THIRTEEN
BUILDING AN ADDITION TO YOUR PHOTOSHOP

Julieanne Kost

Joining Adobe Systems in 1992, Julieanne Kost has learned her craft through hands-on experience and now serves as Adobe's Senior Digital Imaging Evangelist. Spanning digital imaging and illustration, her role includes customer education, product development, and market research. She is a frequent contributor to several publications, a speaker at numerous design conferences and trade shows, and a teacher at distinguished photography workshops and fine art schools around the world. She is also a contributor to www.adobeevangelists.com.

A passionate photographer, Julieanne brings her psychology background to her artwork, which has been seen in several showings and published in a number of magazines. She is also the author behind the Adobe Photoshop CS Fundamentals and Adobe Photoshop CS Advanced Techniques training CDs, published by Software Cinema (www.software-cinema.com).

THE CREATIVE CHALLENGE

The possible combinations for mixing of media are infinite—print the image to canvas, and then paint on the canvas; take an image to eight colors using indexed color, apply the Mosaic Tiles filter, and use ceramic tiles to reproduce the original image; you can use the Posterize effect for embroidery templates or for creating the film for silkscreens; and on and on.

For inspiration, I tend to turn to things that are highly personal to me. Creativity is like a muscle—it needs to be exercised, even challenged.

Give yourself a "dream assignment"—design the cover of your autobiography (even if you don't plan to write one). Design a CD cover or create an ad campaign about your favorite product. All these arise out of your experiences. Above all, play, play, play!

Second only, perhaps, to love, art can be the most intimate thing you share. Hence, there is no right or wrong. You don't need to explain it, justify it, or even help people make sense out of it. Simply do it.

THE BASIC PREMISE:
BITS AND BYTES AREN'T THE FINAL PROJECT

Just past its 10th birthday, Photoshop has become an indispensable tool to many photographers, illustrators, and graphic designers, as well as to people working in a myriad of other disciplines. It has evolved, adding features as innovation and computing hardware allowed. Perhaps its greatest feature has been the gift of "what if." With the luxury to "undo" almost any action, we're free to take risks knowing that we can undo it. You can essentially go backward in time and see where a different path might lead. This has allowed a fundamental shift in the process: experimentation without penalty.

But I suggest to you, dear reader, that there is a price to be paid for all this flexibility. Going back to the physical world without the Undo command can seem rather daunting. Why would you want to give up this incredible gift of flexibility?

Personally, I find myself longing for the feel of good paper, for seeing the ridges in a paint stroke—in short, for something more tangible than pixels. I believe Photoshop should be just one of many tools at the disposal of any creative individual. It is an indispensable tool, but it is not the only tool. While my job is to evangelize Photoshop and its many uses, I believe tools should serve creativity, not the other way around.

For many traditional artists, like painters, sculptors, and darkroom photographers, the finished product is a unique piece of work—tangible, physical, and tactile. It's A painting, A sculpture, or A print. The As are emphasized because those results are one of a kind. The Mona Lisa, surprisingly small for her fame, is singular in all the world. If a disaster struck that painting, we would be left with only reproductions of those meticulous and legendary paint strokes. We couldn't simply generate another one. The physical "being" of that piece would be lost.

In the digital realm, I have found there to be a barrier between artist and medium. The common ground is a mouse or a Wacom tablet. The artist is never in contact with the actual piece. While this prevents you from smearing the pixels or leaving a big fingerprint on the finished piece, it also means that far fewer of your senses are involved—your eyes are as busy as ever, but your fingers don't sense the texture of the paint, you don't hear the palette knife scraping, nor do you smell (for better or worse) the chemicals involved in almost any media.

In the past, the image itself has essentially been the product for the digital fine artist. Once the image is created, it's as easy as hitting the Print command to create another copy. You can print the image in color or in black and white, large or small, on canvas or on high-gloss paper. (Of course, getting calibrated color from an inkjet printer walks a fine line between art and witchcraft.) The ability to make exact duplicates has given us immediate access to artwork that might otherwise have taken days, weeks, or even months to generate any other way.

So what is the role of Photoshop in the creative process? Has it changed creativity into a bunch of sliders, layers, and blending modes? Are people less creative because Photoshop is available? I think the reverse is true. Photoshop allows people to experiment with the creative process without being hindered by the physical limitations of a particular medium.

This new technology brings its own challenges. Sure, the learning curve can be steep. But how long before you learn the "feel" of a brush painting with oil on canvas? Or understand how to read the tonal values of a scene that you want to photograph? It's a lifelong process, constantly evolving as you change brushes, paints, film, or—today—digital capture devices. I would encourage anyone using Photoshop to try to master the technology so well that it truly becomes an asset that allows you to focus on the creativity and ideas behind the content.

It took me a long time to decide how to combine these two worlds, which I thought were so different but turn out to have much in common. They are both essential parts of the new creative process, and I want access to as many tools as possible to express myself and what I see. I urge you to consider making Photoshop a part of the process, rather than the entire process. Use its flexibility to develop the image you're after, and then use it in conjunction with another medium.

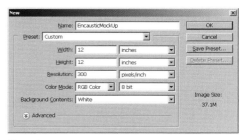

Figure 1

The Project

OK, enough preaching. In this example I'll retrace the steps I took to create this painting with a technique called *encaustic*, which involves painting with wax. From initial inspiration to collecting raw images and physical materials, to manipulating and blending these pieces together to explore what would later become a physical piece, I'm quite certain that you'll see how indispensable Photoshop was to the process.

A book inspired the eventual image, and I knew early on that I wanted the final piece to be a three-dimensional collage—more specifically, an encaustic painting. The process sounds simple: Heat up the wax, mix it with pigments and resin (which hardens the resulting mixture), and then apply the heated wax to any one of several materials. The process is similar to painting, but with unique textures and variations based on the temperature of the wax at various points.

Like oil paint, wax has some amount of flexibility in terms of what you can "undo"—you can always strip off the wax by simply melting it and begin again. (These mistakes, in fact, melt down to produce my dark brown wax. I have a lot of dark brown wax.)

But here is a place where using Photoshop is ideal. Instead of starting the project with wax, I started with a digital camera. Taking pictures of my existing wax images allowed me to experiment with different colors and textures. The choices I would be making in Photoshop would eventually determine what I would do in wax. This is a case where an existing texture—a "known quantity"—can be used in the Photoshop piece for prototyping purposes.

Step 1

To begin mocking up the collage, I created a new document 12 inches square. (This is the typical size of my wax "canvases," known as clayboards.) I set the resolution to 300 pixels/inch so that I had the option to use actual elements from Photoshop in the end piece (*Figure 1*). More about that later.

I often use this image size, so, while still in the New dialog, I clicked the Save

Figure 2

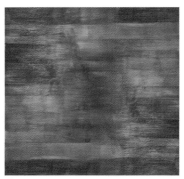

Figure 3

Figure 4

Preset button and saved the dimensions and resolution as a preset called "12 in x 12 in encaustic." For my next project, I'll simply choose my preset from the preset list.

Step 2

I opened various photographs of encaustic paintings and cropped them down to the areas I wanted to keep (*Figures 2, 3, and 4*).

Step 3

Next, I needed to get all of the elements into a single document. After cropping, I dragged them from their individual documents into the new master document. Layers in Photoshop would allow me to experiment with the three different backgrounds as I worked, trying different combinations of textured wax with various images (*Figure 5*).

Figure 5

Now I was ready to start adding other elements to work with. While you can certainly use a camera to gather images, don't limit yourself to that approach. You can also place objects directly on a flatbed scanner (this creates unusual lighting effects, a very shallow depth of field, and no lens distortion). Even though I knew that I would use the actual objects in the final piece, scanning would allow me to play with the quantity and positions of these elements ahead of time.

Step 4

Removing the cover of my Epson scanner, I placed multiple beads and charms directly on the glass. I covered them with a white piece of paper (to make removing the background easier later on) and scanned them at 100% size using the same resolution as my master document (300ppi). This ensured that the sizes of the scanned items would be the same sizes as the actual items that would be used in the final artwork.

Figure 6

Figure 7

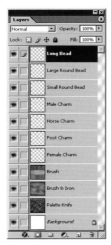

Figure 8

Figure 9

Step 5

Using the File Browser to organize the scans, I flagged the images I thought I would be most likely to use (*Figure 6*). I could then view and open only the flagged images. I dragged each of them into the master image.

I didn't hesitate to add elements even if I thought I would later discard them (*Figure 7*). I'd rather have the images on layers in my Photoshop file while I'm compositing than later have to stop and look for an image—in other words, it's easier to subtract than to add.

Step 6

At this point, I took a minute to rename and organize the layers by double-clicking their names in the Layers palette (*Figure 8*). This is a very good habit to get into. There's nothing more frustrating than working with a document containing 20 layers with names like "layer 01," "layer 02," "copy of layer 02," and so on.

Step 7

This is a great tip for organizing layers into layer sets: Target (click on) the first layer in the Layers palette that you'd like to place in a set, and link it to the other layers. Then, from the Layers palette menu select New Set From Linked, and name the set. (It's almost more important to name sets than to name individual layers because layer sets don't have thumbnails.) Using this method, I placed all the bead layers into their own layer set. Next, I linked all the charms together, but this time I dragged one of the linked layers to the New Set icon at the bottom of the Layers palette. This shortcut automatically creates a layer set containing the linked layers. As with a regular layer, double-clicking the layer set's name allows it to be changed (*Figure 9*).

Step 8

After I created the layer sets, I unlinked the layers from one another so that I could later reposition each of them independently (*Figure 10*). (After placing layers in a set this way, I often forget to unlink them, which prevents them from moving independently. Layers in a set are effectively linked, anyway.)

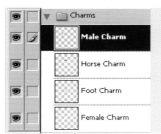

Figure 10

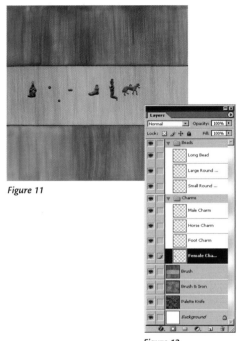

Figure 11

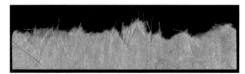

Figure 12

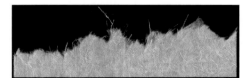

Figure 13

Scaling the set, for example, will scale all images within that set.)

Step 9

To remove the unwanted areas from around the beads and charms, I chose the Magic Wand tool and clicked in the white area to select it, and then hit the Delete key to remove the extra information. Checking the Contiguous option in the Options Bar prevents the selection of any similar areas of color not touching the background. Because these scanned objects were only for reference, I wasn't too concerned with the edges. To quickly select each layer, with the Move tool selected I held down Command (PC: Control) and clicked the layer to auto-select it. I repeated this technique for the beads as well and moved them into the middle of the image (*Figures 11 and 12*).

Step 10

I also wanted to incorporate some torn paper in the collage, so I tore a piece of textured cream-colored paper in half (frankly, sometimes tearing a piece of paper and scanning it is much faster and far more convincing than any Photoshop technique). I added tears to make the pieces different from one another, and placed each half on the flatbed scanner, covering the pieces with a piece of black paper this time (since the paper was light, scanning it against a black background would make it easier to separate in Photoshop) (*Figure 13 and 14*).

I added the paper scans to the composite file (again, by dragging and dropping each on its own layer, and placing the layers into their own set), saving the original torn papers so that they could be used in the final artwork if desired. In order to quickly remove the black background, I used a different approach.

Step 11

Many times, you can create a selection of an object from the image itself. The lighter something is, the more it will be selected; the darker it is, the less it will be selected. In this case, I wanted the paper but not the background. I could load the document as a selection based on brightness. I hid all of the layers except for Bottom Paper, and then used the keyboard shortcut Command-Option-~ (tilde) (PC: Control-Alt-~) to load the layers' luminosity values as a selection. Clicking the Add Layer/Vector Mask icon at the bottom of the

Figure 14

Figure 15

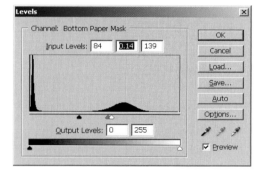

Figure 17

Figure 18

Layers palette added a layer mask to the layer based on the selection (*Figure 15 and 16*).

Step 12

The mask was allowing too much of the image through, so I adjusted the mask by targeting it (I clicked the Add Layer/Vector Mask icon to make it active) and selecting Image>Adjustments> Levels. I dragged the black and white input triangles to shift the values of the mask so that I could fine-tune the transitional areas between opaque and transparent. I used the gray triangle to shift the semitransparent areas of the mask until the mask was the way I wanted it (*Figure 17*). I repeated this process for the other layer.

Figure 16

Step 13

The side of the paper that wasn't torn was too straight, so to soften it I simply painted on the layer mask using a soft-edged brush. Making sure that I was targeting the layer mask, I began painting with black to hide the sharp edge. Holding down Shift while painting constrained the strokes to a straight line (*Figures 18 and 19*).

Step 14

It was time to add some photographs, and I decided on an image of a female model and an old diesel locomotive. The model image was heavily retouched, but the locomotive had hardly been manipulated at all.

To remove the model from the background, I used the Pen tool to draw a path around her arm, neck, and head. I stayed close to her chin and face, removing her hair from the image because I found it distracting (*Figure 20*). From the Paths palette menu I selected Make Selection to turn the path into a selection.

Figure 19

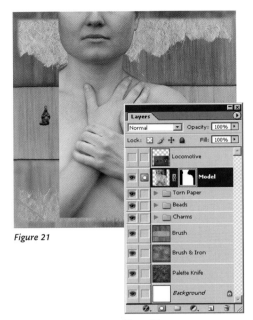

Figure 21

Figure 22

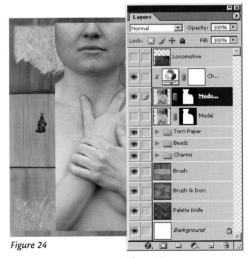

Figure 24

Figure 25

While a selection is active, clicking the Add Layer/Vector Mask icon on the Layers palette converts the selection to a mask. Doing this hid (but didn't delete) the background and hair, while revealing the model (*Figures 21 and 22*).

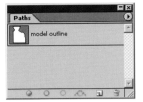

Figure 20

Step 15

In order to remove color saturation as well as add the high-contrast effect I wanted for the model, I added a Channel Mixer adjustment layer (Layer>New Adjustment Layer>Channel Mixer). In the New Layer dialog, I checked the box next to Use Previous Layer to Create Clipping Mask. This would isolate the effect of the Channel Mixer adjustment layer to the model. In the Channel Mixer dialog,

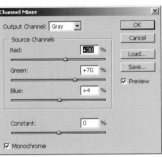

Figure 23

I checked the Monochrome box and then used the RGB sliders to mix the amount of each channel used to create the monochrome image (*Figures 23 and 24*).

Since I was going to explore some filter effects next, I duplicated the Model layer (just in case I didn't like the effects of the filter and wanted to return to the original version of the layer). For the time being, I hid the extra layer by clicking the Eye icon next to it (*Figure 25*).

Step 16

Before experimenting with filters, I set my foreground and background colors to their defaults by pressing "d," since some filters use these color swatches to apply the filter. Then I selected Filter>Filter Gallery. After trying out filters in different combinations, I decided to apply a single filter, Diffuse Glow (*Figure 26*).

Step 17

I added a Curves adjustment layer (Layer>New Adjustment Layer>Curves) and once again checked the option to Use Previous Layer to Create a Clipping

Figure 26

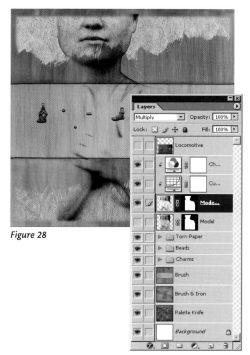

Figure 28

Figure 29

Mask. I added contrast by lowering the shadows and raising the highlight areas in the Curves dialog (*Figure 27*).

Figure 27

Step 18
Knowing that I was going to print the image on vellum (which is semi-transparent) to be used in the collage, I changed the blending mode for the Model layer to Multiply. This produced an effect similar to that of printing on vellum but removed too much of the lighter values. It became clear that just one blending mode on one layer wouldn't achieve what I was after (*Figures 28 and 29*).

Step 19
To bring back some of the detail in the model and more accurately imitate the look of vellum, I duplicated the Model layer and changed the blending mode of the duplicate back to Normal, decreasing the Opacity to 40% (*Figures 30 and 31*).

To keep my Layers palette organized, I put all the layers associated with the model into a set and then repositioned the Model set below the paper in the Layers palette. This made the paper look as if it were sitting on top of the model (*Figures 32 and 33*).

Step 20
I added the image of the locomotive, repeating the technique I used on the model for imitating the look of vellum. I knew that I was going to tear the edges of the locomotive image, so I scanned in another piece of torn vellum for use as a

Figure 30

Figure 31

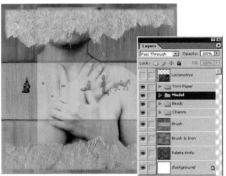

Figure 32

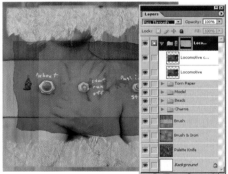

Figure 34

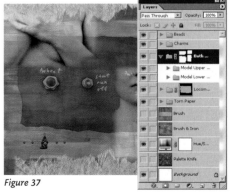

Figure 37

Figure 33

Figure 35

Figure 38

mask. To add this torn edge as a mask to both locomotive layers at once, I added a new layer set and placed the two layers inside. I made a mask out of the torn vellum, by Option-clicking (PC: Alt-clicking) the layer set's mask to make it visible, and pasted in the edges (*Figures 34 and 35*).

Step 21

At this point, I simply began to play. I used the Move tool to move images around, varying the placement and opacity of various elements. I added an adjustment layer to change the colors of the backgrounds and repositioned layers in the layer stack to see the effects. Each time that I felt I had a good candidate, I saved the layers as a layer comp. Using layer comps is a bit like saving multiple versions of the image but takes up a whole lot less room (*Figure 36*). Layer comps are not available in versions of Photoshop prior to CS.

Figure 36

Step 22

I used the Move tool to reposition the model so that her lips were over the text with the "push when starting" button. But I felt that this cut off too much of the bottom of the model. I decided to "tear apart" the model's image in Photoshop to see how it would look. I duplicated the entire Model layer set and repositioned the duplicate in the upper-left corner. To hide the areas in both layer sets at once, I nested them in a new layer set and then added a layer mask to the set. This enabled me to mask all the layers within the layer set using a single mask (*Figures 37 and 38*).

Step 23

In order to simulate adhering the photographs and the paper to the wax in the final piece, I made a duplicate of my chosen texture layer and repositioned

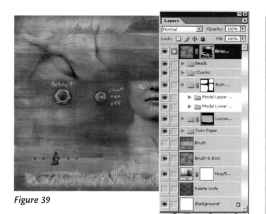

Figure 39

Figure 40

Figure 41

Figure 42

Figure 43

it at the top of the layer stack. Adding a layer mask filled with black hid the layer. Then I edited the layer mask to allow some of the texture to show through over the underlying images (*Figures 39 and 40*).

I moved the charms around and added multiple beads by duplicating the original scan. Then came the hardest part—realizing when I was done.

Step 24

Once I was satisfied with the finished work, I made a straight print of the collage for reference. I began the collage by painting the background with wax using a brush and the colors in the reference image. From Photoshop, I printed the photographic elements in the collage by simply soloing their individual layers (*Figure 41*) and printing the document (*Figures 42 and 43*).

After printing the images, I tore the photographs and adhered them to the wax piece. Here, Photoshop was more than just a prototyping tool—the prototype actually became part of the final piece. The paper, beads, and the icon were added based on the reference print (*Figure 44*).

Figure 44
The finished artwork.

CHAPTER FOURTEEN
PHOTOREALISM TECHNIQUES

Bert Monroy

Bert Monroy was born and raised in New York City, where he spent 20 years in the advertising industry as an art director and creative director for various agencies, including his own.

Upon discovering computers, with the introduction of the Macintosh 128 in 1984, he embarked on a new, digital, career. He embraced the computer as an artistic medium and today is considered one of the pioneers of digital art. Bert's work has been seen in virtually every major magazine and has also been featured in scores of books.

Bert co-authored *The Official Adobe Photoshop Handbook*, which was the first book on Photoshop—the only one for almost two years. He's also co-authored a number of other books, including *Photoshop Channel CHOPS*. His first solo effort, *Bert Monroy: Photorealistic Techniques with Photoshop & Illustrator*, was released in 2000 by New Riders Press. Upon the release of Photoshop 7, Bert created *Photoshop Studio with Bert Monroy*. These titles concentrate on the techniques he has established over the years in the creation of his fine art works. In his most recent book, *Commercial Photoshop with Bert Monroy*, Bert concentrates on the techniques and work habits that have made him a sought-after commercial illustrator.

He has appeared on many television shows both in the U.S. and Japan; since May of 2001, he has appeared monthly on TechTV's *The Screen Savers*.

Bert is an accomplished teacher and lecturer who has served on the faculty

PAINTING WITH PHOTOSHOP

I have heard the question a million times: "Why don't you just take a photograph?" Well, for one thing, I'm not a photographer. To me, it is not the end result that is important, it is the journey. When I start a painting, I am filled with excitement. It is an excitement that grows with each new development; an excitement that comes to an end when the piece is completed. At that point, my urge is to start the next piece.

continued on next page

BERT MONROY, *continued*

of The School of Visual Arts (NYC, NY), Center for Creative Imaging (ME), Dynamic Graphics Educational Foundation (IL), and California College of Arts and Crafts (CA). He lectures at many other institutions and conferences around the world. He currently teaches at San Francisco State University, and lives in Berkeley, California.

He continues to serve his installed base of clients that include Apple Computer, Adobe Systems, Pioneer Electronics, Fujitsu, Sony, AT&T, Chevron, and American Express. Bert has also done a considerable amount of film work for Industrial Light & Magic, Pacific Data Images, and R/Greenberg Assoc.

Products:

Bert Monroy: Photorealistic Techniques with Photoshop & Illustrator
   (New Riders, 2000)

Photoshop Studio with Bert Monroy
   (New Riders, 2002)

Commercial Photoshop with Bert Monroy
   (New Riders, 2003)

Photorealism with Bert Monroy: Using Adobe Photoshop and Illustrator
   (CD-ROM) available through Lynda.com (2003)

CREATING A SIGN WITH METAL LETTERS AND NEON TUBES

I am the guy they call to create the photograph when a photograph cannot be taken. I create realistic-looking images entirely from scratch using the tools available within Photoshop. To cover all the techniques I use in the creation of one of my pieces would require an entire book. That is why I have written many books on the subject. In this book, however, I am limited to a single chapter, so I will concentrate on one detail.

Figure 1
The painting "HAMBURGERS" was created entirely in Photoshop.

Figure 2
A detail of the metal letters that house the neon tubes.

Neon signs—I find myself doing a lot of those. I am drawn to them and seem to pick up a lot of clients that want me to illustrate neon signs. The painting in *Figure 1* is one of my personal paintings. The location is Orlando, Florida. Adobe Systems sent me there to attend the PMA show, where it was announcing Photoshop 7. I was one of the "Magnificent Seven," a collection of artists and photographers from all over who would be used to promote the new upgrade.

I took a series of reference photos with my Nikon Coolpix 995. It would have been nice to paint on location, but the sun would never stay in one place, and the shadows were perfect at that precise moment when I saw the scene (in my mind's eye, I was already seeing it as a painting). Reference shots are just that— reference. I never incorporate scans or photos in any of my fine-art pieces. Commercial work—that's another story.

The section I discuss in this chapter is the word *HAMBURGERS* that runs along the bottom edge of the sign. Zooming in on the image, as seen in *Figure 2*, we see the detail that I created to make the image seem real.

Looking at the image in Figure 1, we see that the sign is made up of metal boxes that are in the shapes of the letters. Each letter is hollow, containing a neon tube. The first thing to do was to create the metal

Figure 3
*The word
HAMBURGERS
was typed using a
standard font.*

Figure 4
*The word
"HAMBURGERS"
was skewed to
match the angle
needed for the sign.*

Figure 5
*The layer with the word
HAMBURGERS was
duplicated; the letters
were filled with gray and
moved to form the depth
of the metal letters.*

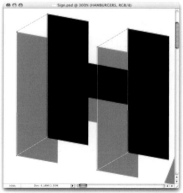

Figure 6
*Using the Pen tool, a path
was made connecting the
edges to form the sides of
the letters.*

boxes that make up the sign. Using the Text tool, I typed the word *HAMBURGERS* using a font that closely resembled the one used for the actual sign (*Figure 3*).

The text was skewed to match the angle of the sign (Edit>Transform>Skew), as seen in *Figure 4*. I did a slight distortion to make the letters get smaller as they went back in space (Edit>Transform>Distort).

The layer of the text was duplicated. The text in back was filled with a gray color and moved with the Move tool to a position that would serve as the back portion or depth of the thick metal boxes (*Figure 5*).

Using the Pen tool, shapes were made that connected the corners of the letters (*Figure 6*). A path was made for all the sections of the letters that made up what would eventually be the sides of the metal boxes. In a new layer, the paths were filled with a green color that appeared on the real sign (*Figure 7*).

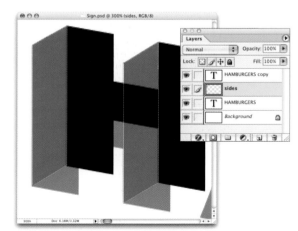

Figure 7
*The paths for the sides of the letters were filled
with a green color.*

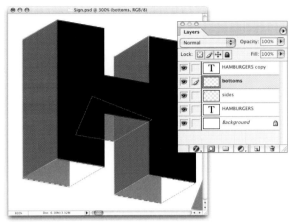

Figure 8
Paths for the bottoms of the letters were created.

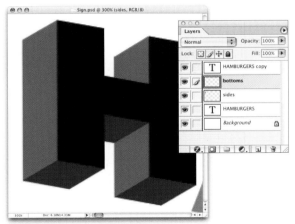

Figure 9
The paths for the bottoms of the letters were filled with a darker green color.

Paths were created for all the sections that made up the bottom of the metal boxes. In *Figure 8* we see the paths. In *Figure 9* we see them filled with a darker version of the green in a separate layer that I created to contain all the sides of the letters.

Creating a hollow effect for the letters is a matter of applying the exact same technique as that used to create the outside of the letters. The positions of the shapes create the illusion of interior space.

The layers that contained the outside portions of the letters were turned off so that they would not obstruct my view of the basic letter shapes (gray and black letters).

The black letters in front were reduced in opacity to allow the gray letters beneath to be visible (*Figure 10*).

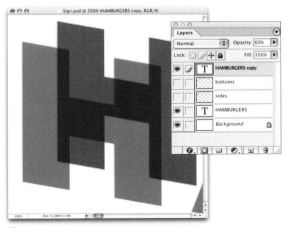

Figure 10
The opacity of the black letters was lowered so that the letters beneath would be visible.

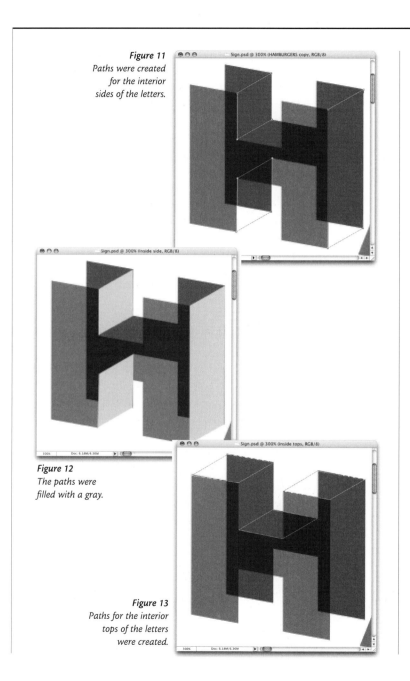

Figure 11
*Paths were created
for the interior
sides of the letters.*

Figure 12
*The paths were
filled with a gray.*

Figure 13
*Paths for the interior
tops of the letters
were created.*

As with the outside shapes, paths were drawn to connect the shapes of the letters. *Figure 11* shows the paths that make up the sides of the insides of the letters. In *Figure 12* those paths have been filled with a gray tone. In *Figure 13* the paths for the top inside portions of the letters are visible. *Figure 14* shows the paths filled, in their own layer, with a gray that is slightly different from the gray on the side walls of the interior.

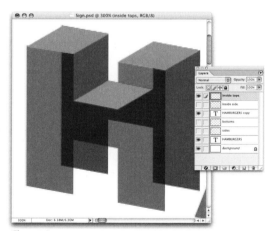

Figure 14
*The paths were filled with
a darker gray.*

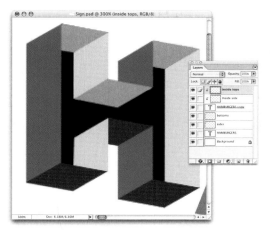

Figure 15
The layers for the interiors of the letter shapes were clipped by the layer containing the basic letters of the sign.

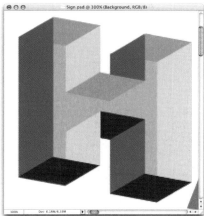

Figure 16
The color of the black letters was changed to a gray to simulate the back of the letters.

The two layers for the interior dimensions of the metal letters were then clipped by the layer that contained the text (*Figure 15*). This made them visible only inside the letter shapes, creating the illusion of the letters' being hollow and deep. To create a layer clipping mask, highlight the layer in the Layers palette that is immediately above the layer you want to clip it to, and choose Create Clipping Mask from the main Layer menu. Personally, I'm lazy—I prefer to just click between the layers in the palette while pressing the Option (PC: Alt) key. The shape of the bottom layer in a clipping group establishes what is visible on the layers above that use it as a clipping mask.

Figure 16 shows how the color of the black text has been changed to a gray tone to simulate the inside back of the metal letter-shaped boxes.

A little grime was now needed to make the sign look right. It was, after all, outside. Without any grime it would look flat and unreal. I chose one of the Spatter brushes that come with the Photoshop CS (*Figure 17*). In the Brushes palette I made a few alterations to add randomization to the brushstroke as it is applied to the art (*Figure 18*). In a layer that

Figure 17
Selecting a Spatter brush in the Brushes palette.

Figure 18
Making alterations to the Spatter brush in the Brushes palette.

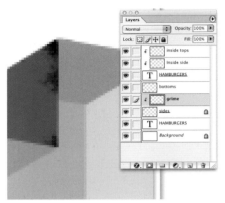

Figure 19
Applying the grime with the modified brush in a layer that was clipped by the layer containing the sides of the letters.

Figure 20
The finished letter shape in position.

was clipped by the layer of the sides of the letters, I added a few splotches of grime here and there (*Figure 19*). Grime was added to all the other sections of the letters, as well as some shadows and highlights with the Dodge and Burn tools.

The shapes of the metal letters were roughened up a bit. Using the Eraser tool, I traveled along the edges of the text, adding small dents and softening those sharp corners. Then I put the final letters in position over the art (*Figure 20*).

Now it was time to create the neon tubes that sit inside the metal letters. With the Pen tool, paths were created to form the shapes of the tubes (*Figure 21*).

Since the tubes overlap each other in some cases, it was necessary to separate the paths into separate elements for the positions of the tubes. In *Figure 22* we see the completed path for the letter *H. Figure 23* shows the path as it was split, so we see only the portion of the path that would be used to create the part of the neon closest to the outside of the sign.

Figure 21
The paths that make up the neon tubes.

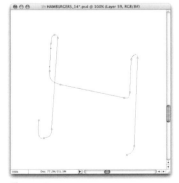

Figure 22
The completed path for the tube of the letter H.

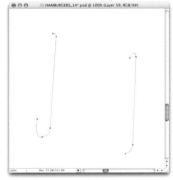

Figure 23
The portion of the path for the tube that would fall in the front of the sign.

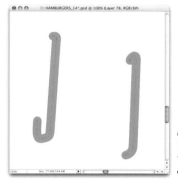

Figure 24
*The path was stroked
with the Paintbrush to
create the neon tube.*

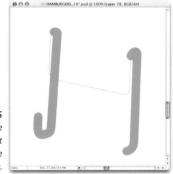

Figure 25
*The path for the
portion of the tube that
was bent to form the
back of the tube.*

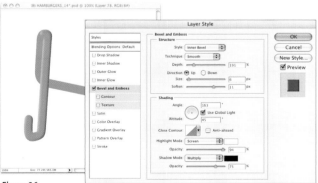

Figure 26
A Layer Style of Bevel and Emboss gives the tubes dimensionality.

The stroking of the paths to complete the tube shapes was executed in individual layers for each. To stroke the paths, I used the Paintbrush tool with a hard-edged brush tip. In order to get the effect I needed, it was necessary to make a slight alteration to the brush from its default state. First I changed the size to one that was perfect for the girth of the neon tubes. (Keep in mind that the brush sizes are dependent on the resolution of the image you are working on.) I then changed the Spacing to 1% to ensure that a solid stroke would result.

With the Paintbrush tool selected and a green shade for my Foreground color, I clicked the Stroke Path icon at the bottom of the Paths palette. The result was the thick tube shapes visible in *Figure 24*.

In *Figure 25*, we see the path for the part of the neon tube that falls in back about to be stroked in a separate layer.

To add a little dimension to the tubes, I gave the layer a Layer Style of Bevel and Emboss (*Figure 26*).

In *Figure 27*, the opacity for the two layers has been reduced to make them look like transparent glass.

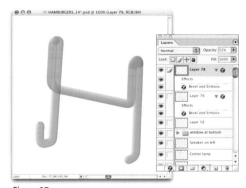

Figure 27
*The opacity of the two layers that make up the tubes
was lowered to make them look transparent.*

Figure 28
Create Layer separated the Layer
Style effects into layers of their own.

Figure 29
The area where the two layers of tubes
overlapped.

Figure 30
With the Eraser tool, the overlap is
eliminated.

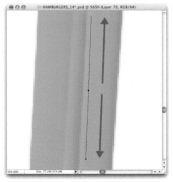

Figure 31
Two paths are created traveling in
different directions.

It was necessary to make the tubes look like one continuous tube. The fact that the front and back parts of the tubes were in separate layers with Layer Styles applied meant that it was not so easy to simply erase the portions where the two layers overlapped. The Layer Style effects would have clashed, thus preventing the look of continuity in the tubes. To make this alteration possible, I separated the Layer Styles into their own layers. The Create Layer command (Layer>Layer Style>Create Layer) allowed me to make that separation (*Figure 28*).

Figure 29 shows the overlap of the layers of the tubes. In *Figure 30* we see that overlap being eliminated by using the Eraser tool on the layers of the tubes and the layers for the effects that were a result of the previous step.

A little sheen here and there was needed to create the sense of light being reflected onto the surface of the neon tubes. When a path is used to guide the Paintbrush tool, the stroke is applied in the direction that the path was created in. Since I wanted the light reflections to appear as shimmers that faded out from the center, I created two separate paths that started from the center and traveled outward in opposite directions as seen in *Figure 31*.

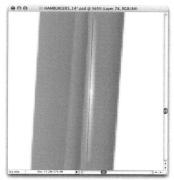

Figure 32
*The paths were stroked with the
Paintbrush tool set to Fade Out.*

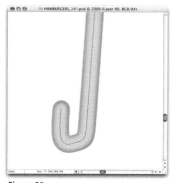

Figure 33
*The path for the tube was stroked with
a soft-edged brush to simulate the light
beam inside the neon tube.*

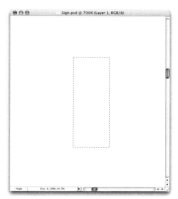

Figure 34
*A shape was selected with the
Rectangular Marquee tool to form the
rods that would attach the neon tubes
to the metal letters.*

Figure 35
*With the Elliptical Marquee tool, a
rounded edge was added to the bottom
of the rectangular selection.*

Using a Paintbrush that had been set to Fade Out
(in the Other Dynamics section of the Brushes palette),
the paths were stroked with white (*Figure 32*).

The light inside the tubes was created in yet another
layer. The same paths that were stroked to form the
tubes were then stroked with a soft-edged brush shape
using a very light shade of the green (*Figure 33*).

Finally, the neon tubes needed to be connected
to the metal letter shapes that housed them. Little
connector rods had to be created to hold the wires
that held the neon tubes in place.

In a new layer, a small rectangle was selected with
the Rectangular Marquee tool (*Figure 34*). Since these
were to be cylindrical rods, it was necessary to make
them look rounded. To achieve this effect I added
a rounded bottom edge to the selection with the
Elliptical Marquee tool (*Figure 35*).

Figure 36
The selection was filled with a gradient.

Figure 37
With the Elliptical Marquee tool, a rounded shape was added to form the top of the rod.

Figure 38
The top was filled with a gray color.

Figure 39
A small black ellipse was added to form the hole from which the wires would protrude.

In *Figure 36* we see the selection filled with a gray-colored gradient. The top of the rods was selected with the Elliptical Marquee tool (*Figure 37*) and was filled with a light gray (*Figure 38*). A small opening, where the wires will protrude, was selected and filled with black as seen in *Figure 39*.

The rod shape was rotated to the angle of the sign and duplicated into various positions within the hollow portions of the metal letters (*Figure 40*).

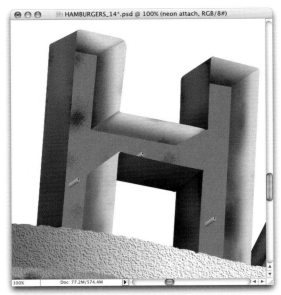

Figure 40
The rods were placed throughout the sign.

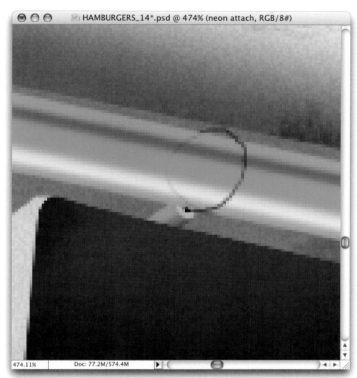

Figure 41
With a small-sized paintbrush, the wires were painted over the neon tubes.

For the final touch, using a tiny paintbrush, the wires were painted over the neon tubes. Using a lighter gray, the wires visible through the tubes were also added. *Figure 41* shows the wire wrapped around the neon tube running into the rod.

In the End...

This has been a small sampling of what went into the final piece. It is that attention and devotion to detail that makes my images seem like photographs. However, what I want to leave you with is not the step-by-step on how to make a neon sign, but the introduction to a series of techniques. When you study them individually, you might find the answer to another imaging problem you are faced with.

Photoshop is filled with effects waiting to be found—happy accidents that pave the way to masterpieces. It is just a matter of sitting there and playing. No—not moving down virtual hallways looking for aliens to blow up, but playing with the Paintbrush in all its many shapes and modes. Then applying a layer style to the brushstroke. Then trying a couple of filters. Then…

i

Go to
www.peachpit.com/
dreamteam.html
to download files for
this chapter.

CHAPTER FIFTEEN

PHOTOSHOP POWER FOR DIGITAL PORTRAIT PHOTOGRAPHERS

Todd Morrison

Todd Morrison, founder of Zero2Digital.com and owner of Morrison Photography, in Nashville, Tennessee, has acquired more than 14 years of experience in the professional photographic industry. Todd's experience includes commercial, editorial, stock, and portrait photography, as well as managing all aspects of a professional photo lab.

Todd brings real-world experience and advanced Photoshop techniques to digital photographers. Clients include Epson America and Adobe Systems. Todd also serves as a contributing writer for *Photoshop User, Professional Photographer, Focus on Imaging, Create*, and *Digital Capture* magazines.

Todd is the author of *Photoshop for Portrait Photographers* and *Creating Art from Your Digital Images*. Both are interactive video training sets from Software Cinema (www.software-cinema.com).

Specializing in streamlining and simplifying the digital workflow, Todd teaches techniques to replace the work in digital production with excitement and creativity. Todd's unique training methods are ideally suited for any photographer or studio making the transition from traditional film-based imaging to a digital capture environment. Todd's consulting services include the following: group training, one-on-one training, calibration of input and output devices, virtual training, digital production system design and configuration, workflow and creativity enhancement, and marketing and business plan development.

www.Zero2Digital.com

Email: todd@zero2digital.com

A DECADE IN THE LIFE OF A PIXEL-CRAZED BABY PHOTOGRAPHER

As you may guess by the images in this chapter, my beautiful wife, Kathy, and I operate a portrait studio specializing in images of infants and children. My background as a nature and wildlife photographer offered me a glimpse into the pulse-quickening anxiety that can only be experienced while capturing images of a 2-year-old.

This magical journey into the wilds of child photography began with creating simple outdoor portraits of my beautiful daughter Ashley. Little did I know that taking a secondhand Mamiya 645 to the park would be the death of my arsenal of Nikkor lenses and cases of Fuji Velvia. Soon boxes marked Hasselbad began arriving at my door, and my 35mm canisters grew into 220 rolls of medium-format negative film. My Lowepro backpack collected dust, while Photoflex soft boxes were raised on their light stands like mighty sails carrying me to unknown shores.

I can still remember the first time I used Photoshop's Rubber Stamp tool, back in the days of version 2.5. If memory serves me correctly, I utilized its power to create a third eye on the forehead of a dear friend. Hours upon hours were spent mixing and blending and painting and searching for the right tool, the best technique, the most effective use of Sharpen More....

continued on next page

A DECADE IN THE LIFE OF A PIXEL-
CRAZED BABY PHOTOGRAPHER, *continued*

Digital capture was a distant dream for photographers at that time, and the most cost-effective method for getting my negatives into that beige monster known as a PC was a scanning service called Pro Photo CD, offered by the local pro lab. I would carefully select the images for scanning and wait patiently for the magical transformation to be complete. Then at last I could place the golden CD into the motorized tray, which would propel me into the infinite world of pixels.

Then, at last, digital capture was born, in Kodak cameras with no preview screens, internal hard drives, and dismal battery life. Not long after I dove into digital capture, my attention was drawn to a sleek machine dressed in a Bondi Blue and ice shell. The original iMac tugged at my hot-rod heart, forcing comparisons to '57 Corvettes and '56 F-100s. This silicon machine disguised as retro art pulled me into the secret society known as the Mac faithful.

Today I type on my Titanium G4 PowerBook, having been completely immersed in the ways of the softly glowing apple. Tomorrow I will most certainly find new adventure. Maybe a new computer will catch my eye, a hot rod of a different flavor sporting dual Pentium chips and flying an XP flag. Maybe I will dust off the Lowepro backpack and buy a new 300 f:2.8 lens for my digital SLR. One thing is for sure: the latest version of Photoshop will be installed on my fire-breathing machine of choice.

I feel very fortunate to live in this tiny slice of time. The wonderment of photography colliding with the technology of digital imaging at this very moment creates the ultimate pinnacle in creativity for photographers. This revolution also offers the freedom of expression to once and for all solidify photography as an art form.

We all are now working at the pixel level of expression, digital artists connected by this society known as Photoshop.

BRINGING BACK THE LOOK OF FILM

Part 1—Don't Be Afraid of the Curves

Many newcomers are a bit overwhelmed by the Curves tool. This technique provides a more predictable method for using the Curves tool to build contrast in specific values contained in your image.

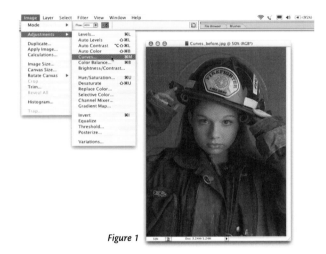

Figure 1

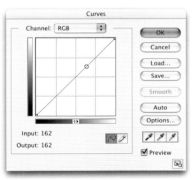

Figure 2

Step 1

With your image open, start by choosing the Curves tool from the Image menu: Image>Adjustments>Curves or press Command-M (PC: Control-M) (*Figure 1*).

Step 2

With the Curves dialog now open, move your cursor onto your image. Your cursor becomes the Eyedropper tool. You can click any point in your image and the current value (on a 0–255 scale) of that point will be displayed at the bottom of the Curves dialog. You will also notice that a temporary circular marker appears on the Curves control line to indicate the control point of that value (*Figure 2*).

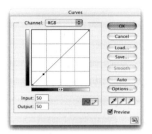

Figure 3

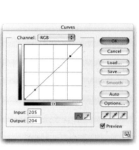

Figure 4

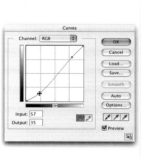

Figure 5

Step 3

In order to build some contrast in this image (which is a bit flat), we want to first locate a spot that contains shadow information including detail. The value of this point usually falls between 25 and 50. When you Command-click (PC: Control-click) this point in your image, a permanent control point is added to your Curves control line (*Figure 3*).

Step 4

We want to repeat this process for the highlight information in your image. Locate a spot that contains highlight information and also some detail. The value of this point will usually fall between 190 and 225. Command-click (PC: Control-click) this point to place a permanent control point on your Curves line that corresponds with this value (*Figure 4*).

Step 5

Click the control point at the lower left of the control line (shadows), and drag this point down and to the right diagonally. You want to be careful here, since a small adjustment goes a long way in Curves. Stop dragging this control point when you have reached a shadow density you are happy with (*Figure 5*). Don't worry what the highlights may be doing at this point; we'll fix them in the next step.

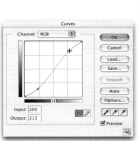

Figure 6

Step 6

Click the control point at the upper right of the control line (highlights), and drag this point up and to the left diagonally. Stop dragging this point when you have sufficiently brightened the highlights (be careful to avoid blowing out highlight detail; move your cursor over that area of the image and keep an eye on values in the Info palette). When you are satisfied with your adjustment, click OK (*Figure 6*). If you have a problem with your adjustment and you would like to start over, simply press Option (PC: Alt) to change the Cancel button to Reset.

Part 2—Adjustment Layer Vignette

I'd tried many different burn (darkening) techniques in Photoshop and couldn't find a technique that faithfully emulated the look that I obtained with film images. After many frustrating attempts, I finally created a technique that provided the result I wanted. Now in Photoshop CS we can perform this technique in 16-bit mode. Most of the higher-end digital cameras offer the ability to output image files in a format with a bit depth greater than 8 bits. Depending on the camera, this larger bit-depth mode may provide 12-, 14- or 16-bit images, but Photoshop will switch to 16-bit mode when opening any image with a bit depth greater than 8 bits.

The 16-bit RGB color images have twice the color information of 8-bit color RGB images, which offers greater latitude when making color and contrast adjustments to these images. Larger Curves and Levels adjustments on 8-bit color RGB images will cause the quality of the images to suffer; 16-bit images have more color pixel information available and will be less affected by larger adjustments to color balance and contrast.

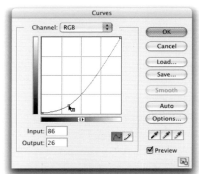

Figure 7

Figure 8

Step 1

Create a new Curves adjustment layer by clicking the Adjustment Layer icon at the bottom of the Layers palette and selecting Curves. Now click the Curves adjustment line at the first grid intersection from the bottom. Drag the line down and to the right at a 45° angle (*Figure 7*). Disregard the density of your subject matter in the center of the image, and watch the edges of your image (or wherever you want the burn effect). As you pull the Curves adjustment line down and to the right, the shadow information in your image will darken dramatically. Stop when the overall density level of your image reaches the required level for the burn. Click OK to make this adjustment.

Step 2

Select the Brush tool ("b"). Select black as your foreground color on the Toolbox, and make sure that you still have your new Curves adjustment layer activated in the Layers palette.

Step 3

Choose a soft, round brush (a large brush works best), and set the Opacity of the brush to 40% in the Options Bar. You may also want to use the Airbrush mode for this step. Set your brush's Opacity to 100%, and click the Airbrush icon at the right end of the Options Bar. Set the Flow to the left of the Airbrush icon to 20% (*Figure 8*).

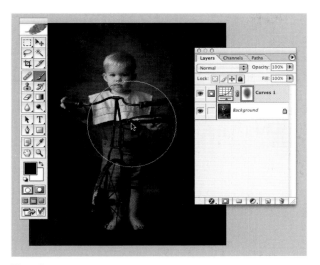

Figure 9

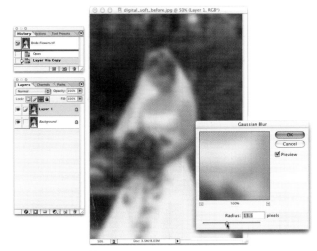

Figure 10

Step 4

Choose an area you'd like to lighten (typically the subject of your portrait in the center of the image) and paint away the darkness with the Brush. If you're using the Airbrush feature, simply pause over areas you want to appear lighter in the image and they'll gradually lighten. If you're using the traditional Brush, you can increase the lightening effect by using multiple paint strokes over areas you want lighter (*Figure 9*). The areas you paint will be restored to the original density settings. You'll be left with a very nice burn around your subject with a smooth transition from light to dark.

Danger: Sharp Objects Ahead (Digital Soft Focus)

Many photographers (especially portrait photographers) find that digitally captured images lack the warmth of film and may appear a bit harsh in comparison. I find that with many of my portrait images, I prefer a soft glow around my subject (similar to what you get with a traditional Softar filter) while retaining detail in critical subject areas. The following technique will give you the tools to selectively enhance your images by softening specific areas.

Step 1

Create a duplicate layer of your background image by selecting Layer>New>Layer via Copy or pressing Command-J (PC: Control-J).

Step 2

With the duplicate layer selected apply a Gaussian Blur to this layer by selecting Filter>Blur>Gaussian Blur. Adjust the Radius to a point that excessively blurs the image. Do not worry about retaining detail at this point; you want to create a soft glow on the entire image (*Figure 10*).

Figure 11

Step 3

Adjust the Opacity of the blurred duplicate layer by clicking the triangle button next to the Opacity setting in the Layers palette. Adjust the slider to the left to lower the opacity and provide a bit more detail while retaining a soft glow (*Figure 11*).

Step 4

Click the Add Layer Mask icon at the bottom of the Layers palette to add a layer mask to the blurred duplicate layer (*Figure 12*).

Step 5

Select the Brush tool ("b"), and select black as your foreground color. With a soft brush and the layer mask targeted, begin painting with black the areas of the image where you want to restore detail (*Figure 13*). If you go too far, you can select white as your foreground color ("x") and paint away your mistake by painting with white on the layer mask.

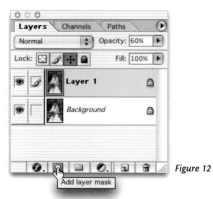

Figure 12

Figure 13

Figure 14

Figure 15

Hip to Be Square: Square Crop from a Vertical Image Trick

Many photographers diving into digital are converting from medium-format film cameras. One of the more popular formats for medium format is the 6 x 6 cm square. Many of my customers were accustomed to (and expected) square images. Providing square images from vertical rectangular images can be a challenge. This quick and easy technique will make you square in record time.

Step 1

With your image set to full-screen mode ("f"), configure your Crop tool for a format (5 x 5) and drag your initial crop selection.

Step 2

Grab the corner handles and enlarge your crop selection to create the square crop as though you have extra image area available to you. It's OK if the crop box extends out onto the gray area surrounding the image (*Figure 14*). Double-click inside the selected area to complete the crop.

Step 3

You now have an image with solid bars on the left and right, created by cropping outside of the image area, resulting in additional canvas. Select the Rectangular Marquee tool ("m"), and drag a selection starting at the edge of the image and extending into the image, just avoiding the primary subject (*Figure 15*).

Figure 16

Step 4

Choose Edit>Free Transform or press Command-T (PC: Control-T), and drag the outside handle of the selection toward the outside edge to stretch the image (*Figure 16*). When the image has been stretched to fill the extra canvas, press Return (PC: Enter) to accept the transformation. Repeat this process for the other side of the image (*Figure 17*). Although you will experience a bit of distortion in the stretched area, in most cases the transformation will not be readily apparent.

Figure 17

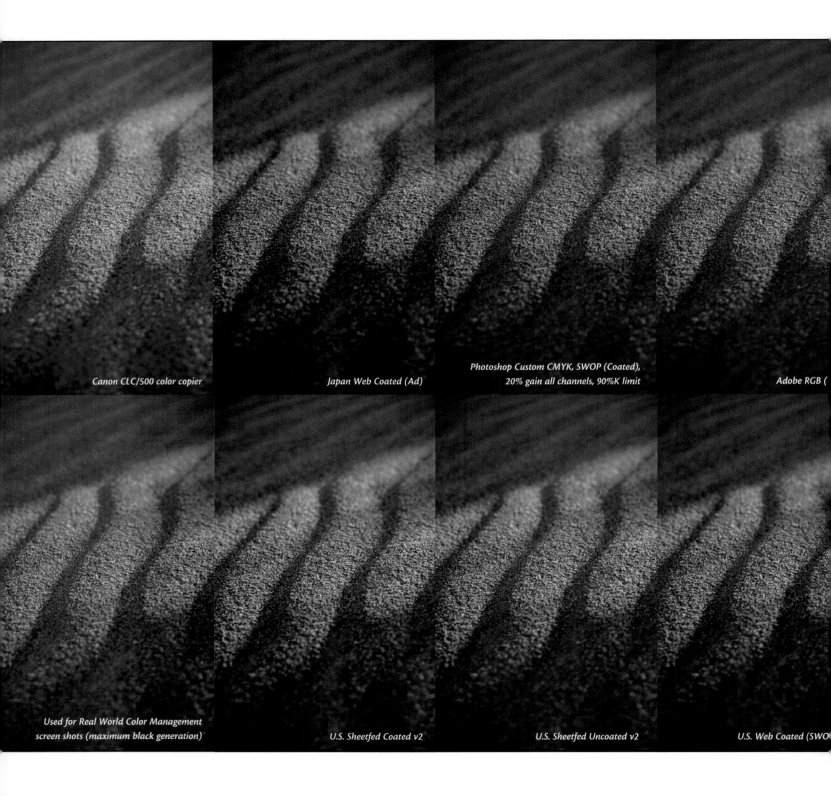

Canon CLC/500 color copier

Japan Web Coated (Ad)

*Photoshop Custom CMYK, SWOP (Coated),
20% gain all channels, 90%K limit*

Adobe RGB (

*Used for Real World Color Management
screen shots (maximum black generation)*

U.S. Sheetfed Coated v2

U.S. Sheetfed Uncoated v2

U.S. Web Coated (SWO

CHAPTER SIXTEEN
COLOR MANAGEMENT INCANTATION

Chris Murphy

Chris Murphy, of Boulder, Colorado, is president of Color Remedies (www.colorremedies.com), specializing in worldwide training and consulting in emerging color technologies. He has extensive experience in implementing color management workflows, and he is a respected speaker at conferences and seminars, including Seybold Seminars. He is also a coauthor of *Real World Color Management* (Peachpit Press, 2003). Chris has been involved in computers and technology for 20 years, the past seven years of them as a professional trainer. Some people believe he has extra-sensory vision, but he assures us that he does not.

OPPOSITE PAGE:
What's this spread showing you? The one that should look correct is "U.S. Web Coated (SWOP) v2." That's what the printer asked for. Therefore all the other images, which were separated differently, will look less than ideal. The key point is to show how subtle, but important, getting the right separation settings are. Printing presses print differently throughout the world, and even in the same country there are different inks, dot gain, and papers being used. The more accurate the profile used for converting to CMYK, the better the result.

HOW ABOUT A CAR OR MINI-VAN?

I wish our choices in color management weren't limited to either the tricycle or the space shuttle. It'd be great if the options were powerful enough for professionals, but didn't require a 90-page manual to describe just how to push the ignition button. In any event, I recommend that you start slowly, and work your way up as you find the need. When used properly, color management is not only helpful, saving time and money as well as reducing frustration, but in many situations it is the only sane path.

Here are a few thoughts on embedding profiles. Always embed profiles in RGB images, and have the profile embedded in them when you share them with others. If other users ignore the embedded profile, that's their mistake; at least you sent along the information necessary for them to properly render your file on-screen as well as in print. When using Save For Web and ImageReady, by default the profile will not be embedded, which is just fine because on the Internet, embedded profiles usually don't get used anyway. Photoshop's Save For Web dialog or the ImageReady Optimize palette includes a checkbox for this if you do decide to include the profile.

For grayscale and CMYK images it's a different story. I highly recommend embedding profiles for images you need to archive and for images you're going to share with fellow color management–savvy individuals. But don't hand off such images to people until you've first discussed embedded profiles with them. Save a copy, and uncheck the Embed Color Profile box found in the Save As dialog. Good luck!

COLOR MANAGEMENT INCANTATION

Thinking about color management is like mowing the lawn. You don't really have to do it, but if you don't, eventually you'll have a problem. It will be all that much more work later, and in the end you'll have a mulched lawn. OK, it's not a perfect analogy. How about it's like milk that you've forgotten in the refrigerator? Well, you get the idea. People ignore color management all the time and the world keeps turning. But a few simple steps can result in an amazing difference, substantially reducing the amount of color correction needed later, and also saving you time and money.

We seem to have only two color management options in our applications: tricycle mode, and space shuttle mode. And there is nothing in between. Photoshop's color management implementation is vast, and while it can be configured poorly there is a rarely talked about secret regarding Photoshop: Despite all the valid opinions on what editing space to use, such as Adobe RGB (1998), ColorMatch RGB, ECI RGB, and so on (and on, and on…), you can get reliable prints no matter what your settings are.

Even with bad settings, you can start doing a few things correctly without having to dive into Photoshop's somewhat forbidding Color Settings dialog, and reap substantial benefit. Yes, fellow color geeks reading this are probably gasping for air at this point.

The incantations I have selected for your immediate use are, in order: Proof Setup and Proof Colors to get better on-screen simulations of what you'll get in print; Print with Preview and printer driver settings to get better printed output from Photoshop; and the final incantation will be about preparing images for the Internet.

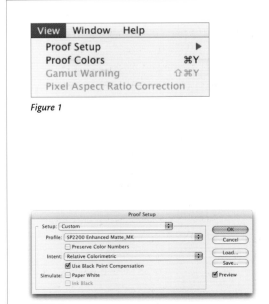

Figure 1

Figure 2

Proof Colors

Proof Colors, found in the View menu (*Figure 1*), causes Photoshop to show you what your document will look like when printed. If you're working on an RGB image, selecting Proof Colors can show you how your image will actually turn out when printed in CMYK or on an inkjet printer. Those vibrant RGB colors that you see on your display are not always printable and the tonal range for printing is also much narrower than what is available on screen. This option allows you to see the limitations of your printer and paper combination in advance.

By default, Proof Colors will simulate whatever profile you have selected as the CMYK Working Space in Color Settings. But you can use Proof Setup to change the profile to anything you want, even that of your desktop inkjet printer or the Web.

Step 1

Choose View>Proof Setup>Custom. Select the profile for your intended output device in the Profile pop-up menu. For example, I have an Epson Stylus

Figure 3

Figure 4
Relative Colorimetric
rendering intent.

Figure 5
Perceptual rendering intent.

Figure 6
Saturation rendering intent.

Photo 2200 inkjet printer with matte black ink, and Epson Enhanced Matte paper installed. That means I need to select the "SP2200 Enhanced Matte_MK" profile, which is one of the profiles installed by Epson's print driver installer (*Figure 2*).

If you're going to print to a printing press, select the printer's supplied profile here, or make the best educated guess you can. U.S. Sheetfed Coated v2 works well for higher line screen (175lpi or higher), computer-to-plate or direct-to-plate printing. If your image will appear in a magazine article or ad, use U.S. Web Coated (SWOP) v2 (*Figure 3*).

Preserve Color Numbers means, "Show me what it will look like if I don't use color management to convert this document when printing, and just print the numbers in the file as they are." This option is only available when the document's color mode and the color model of the profile match, for example an RGB document and an RGB printer

profile or a CMYK document and a CMYK printer profile. You might use this feature with images you've painstakingly worked on for a particular printer/ media combination, and that you'd rather not have to convert to a new media if you can get away with it. Turning this option on will show you how the numbers in the file will print without further conversion.

Step 2

Intent is the rendering intent setting, which is color management's compromise for how to render, or translate, your wonderful, brilliantly saturated RGB image to something for print. For most images, I recommend choosing Relative Colorimetric, although you may prefer the result of Perceptual or Saturation for images that contain fine saturated detail. It might not seem very scientific to give such "loosey-goosey" advice, but what really matters is what you like and how you want the image to look. Some experimentation is often required. *Figures 4 through 6* show the effects of different rendering intents. It's usually pretty subtle, but the result will be more or less pronounced depending on the printer and media used, the profile for that combination of printer and media, and the image. Fancy, huh?

Figure 7
Black Point Compensation On

Figure 8

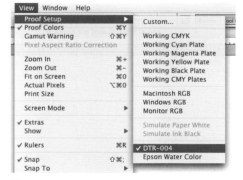

Figure 9

In the Proof Setup>Custom dialog, you're looking to preview the effect of the rendering intent on-screen before making the actual print. That way when it's time to print, you know what rendering intent you prefer for a given document.

Step 3

The Use Black Point Compensation option scales the tonal range of the source color space to that of the destination space. Translated into non-geek, it means that your images will be rendered from screen to print with the best possible contrast and shadow detail preservation. You will almost always want this option selected in Proof Setup since you will also use it when you print the image (*Figure 7*). This can be a rather subtle effect, so you may have to look closely to see any changes. Black point compensation is increasingly important when you print to output devices with a narrower tone reproduction, like printing presses, and use lower quality paper stock.

Step 4

"Simulate Paper White and Ink Black" options do exactly that. They cause Photoshop to simulate on-screen the actual paper white and ink black, which are considerably darker and lighter, respectively, than the white and black produced by your monitor. I often prefer using just the Ink Black option.

Step 5

If you plan on using these particular settings regularly, you can click the Save button and give the settings a name. This name will appear in the Proof Setup>Setup pop-up menu, and in the Proof Setup drop-down menu for handy use (*Figures 8 and 9*).

Once you click OK in this dialog, Proof Colors is automatically enabled.

Web designers can use the View>Proof Setup>Monitor RGB preset to make Photoshop show the same thing as ImageReady and your Web browser. On a Macintosh you can select Windows RGB to see how Windows Web users will see your image, and if you're on Windows you can select Macintosh RGB to see how Macintosh Web users will see your image.

On the Macintosh, Apple made the decision to alter the effective display gamma to be 1.8 because it approximated the behavior of the original Apple Laserwriter. Effectively, it's a form of hardware grayscale management. When calibrating and profiling your display, you can choose whatever gamma you want because the profile will tell Photoshop what the gamma is, and Photoshop will compensate for it regardless. I personally prefer using gamma 2.2 because it alters the display less, but you're welcome to flip a coin if you prefer.

Step 6

Now, color-correct and enhance your image as you usually would, but you can better trust the color and tone reproduction on your display. Of course, the accuracy of any kind of proofing is very dependent on the printer profile's describing actual printer behavior. Printer behavior does drift over time, however, and profiles don't drift with it. This is why creating custom profiles for your printer and media (or having them created for you) is often inevitable for those who want greater accuracy than that provided by the canned profiles supplied by the manufacturer. It also helps to have a calibrated and profiled display so Photoshop knows the behavior of your particular display.

Printing

Naturally, everyone wants to get the best possible print the first time around. Ink and media are expensive, and it's time-consuming to have to manually fix images that look great on screen, but are temperamental when being printed.

The canned profiles that manufacturers supply with their products have improved considerably in recent years, especially if you're using the manufacturer's paper and ink, so it's worth a shot to see if they'll work well enough for your purposes. But chances are, at some point you'll want to make custom profiles.

Regardless of whether you use a manufacturer-supplied profile, or a custom one, the steps are the same. There are two rules to remember:

1. You must reproduce the exact settings in the printer driver that were used to build the profile.

2. You want Photoshop to do the conversion, not the printer driver.

Here are the steps to follow to ensure that you're following these two rules.

Step 1

Get your image looking the way you want it to on screen. Ideally you will also have followed the steps for soft proofing in the previous section. That way you won't be surprised when your print pops out.

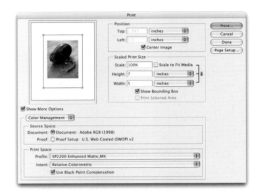

Figure 10

Step 2

With RGB images, you have two choices for printing the image. You can print it as best as your inkjet or laser printer will allow you to print, which is typically much more vibrant than what can be printed on something like a printing press. Or you can ask Photoshop to restrict the color of your image to that of a printing press, and then print the image—that's a proof.

If you want to produce a proof, first follow the steps earlier for configuring Proof Setup, selecting a suitable profile for the output condition you intend to print to.

With CMYK images, the colors in the image are already restricted so you will be producing a proof regardless.

Step 3

From the File menu, select Print with Preview. Check the "Show More Options" checkbox, and from the resulting pop-up menu, choose Color Management (*Figure 10*).

Step 4

In Source Space, select Document if you want your image to look as good as possible, or select Proof if you want to produce a proof.

Step 5

Print Space>Profile pop-up should be set to your local printer profile. If you're printing to an inkjet printer, as I am, select the profile for that printer and the media you will use. I'm using Enhanced Matte paper, with matte black (_MK) ink so that's the profile I have selected. If I were using a custom profile, I'd select that instead.

Step 6

In the Print Space>Intent pop-up, select the rendering intent you chose when playing with this setting in Proof Setup. If you haven't done this yet, either go and play first, or just set it to Relative Colorimetric. Black Point Compensation should be turned on.

If you're printing proofs (as opposed to a final print) then you have two options. In either case you want Black Point Compensation turned off so that

Figure 11

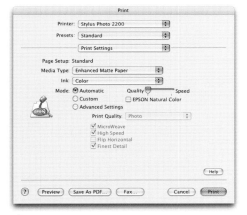

Figure 12

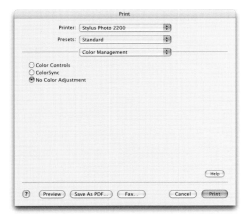

Figure 13

black will be properly proofed. Most other printers and presses will print a lighter black than your personal printer, and turning this off will ensure an accurate simulation.

I generally prefer using Relative Colorimetric when proofing. But you're welcome to try Absolute Colorimetric, which is technically more accurate, since it also simulates the source paper white. For example, magazine paper white is gray and slightly yellow, so Absolute Colorimetric rendering will cause your inkjet or laser printer to tint the whole image grayish-yellow to simulate the effect of printing on stock of that color. If you do decide to use Absolute Colorimetric, be prepared to trim the printed piece to the imaged area or your proofs won't look right. It's a chromatic adaptation thing…long story.

Step 7

Click the Print button.

You will now see your printer's Print dialog box (*Figure 11*).

Step 8

In this example with my Epson 2200, I need to reproduce the same settings that were used when building the profile for this printer/media combination. These are found in two sections of the Print dialog, depending on your operating system.

Mac OS X

a. In the main pop-up menu, which defaults to "Copies & Pages", choose Print Settings (*Figure 12*).

b. Set the Media Type for the paper you are using.

c. In the main pop-up menu, choose Color Management (*Figure 13*).

d. Select the "No Color Adjustment" option.

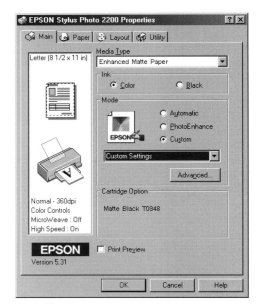

Figure 14

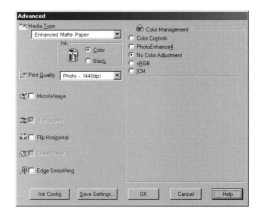

Figure 15

Windows

a. Open the Properties for your printer (*Figure 14*).

b. Under Mode, choose Custom, which will then activate the Advanced button. Click the Advanced button.

c. In the Advanced dialog select "No Color Adjustment" (*Figure 15*).

Note: The settings you should use are the same for all of Epson's printers, and similar to those of other brands as well, in that you need to turn off anything related to color management in the printer driver itself. In some cases, you may need to contact the manufacturer to find out specifically what settings to use when with its supplied profile.

Step 9

Print your document.

Prepare for the Web

I'll discuss four ways to tackle this beast:

- Make your corrections so that the image looks good on your display, which means choosing View>Proof Setup>Monitor RGB. This is easy, but it doesn't target your content for the average viewer of your images.

- Test the image on a bunch of different monitors and color correct until you get something you can live with on all of those monitors.

- Target your Photoshop content to sRGB from the word Go and never use anything else.

- Use whatever RGB working space you want to—ColorMatch RGB, Adobe RGB, even a CMYK image—and then convert to sRGB before using Save For Web or ImageReady.

The first two are as practical as you think they are. The second two are more useful and each has its benefits.

Figure 16

TIP

Epson's manufacturer-supplied profiles are designed specifically for Epson media. If you are not using Epson media, see if your supplier has profiles for the printer model/media combination you are using. InkjetMall (www.inkjetmall.com) is one such supplier. The difference in media is one of the biggest reasons for color shifting when printing, so it is important to use the right profile for the printer/media combination you are using. This is one reason that buying whatever paper is on sale is not really a good idea if you're concerned about predictable results. Even two high-quality brands of glossy paper can have completely different behavior. If you can't find a profile, you may need a custom profile built. Check out Imaging Revue (www.imagingrevue.com) and CHROMiX (www.chromix.com) for such services.

Start, Work, and End in sRGB

This option is easy and safe but not particularly flexible. It is the one to use if you have any Web-safe colors in your document that need to remain Web-safe (such as those in text, shapes, or illustrations). It's really simple:

Step 1

Go to Color Settings (*Figure 16*).

Step 2

Choose the "Web Graphics Defaults" color setting.

Step 3

Click OK. Voilà! That's it. Now, be aware that every single image you create or open will be viewed as though it were an sRGB image. If all you do is Web work that's OK.

But if you want your images for other things as well, I recommend setting the RGB Color Management Policy to Preserve Embedded Profiles. Anything you save directly from Photoshop will have a profile embedded, and anything you open that has a profile embedded will have its intended color appearance preserved, which is what you want. See the next section.

Use Whatever Editing Space You Like, Convert to sRGB Later

Step 1

Open your image, and get it to where you want it. There is no need to soft proof using Proof Colors.

Step 2

Choose Image>Mode>Convert to Profile.

Figure 17

TIP

You can make an action of this sequence that will perform the necessary conversion and drop the image into either Save For Web or send it to ImageReady.

Step 3

If the Source Space is already sRGB, no need to convert. You can skip all remaining steps and proceed to Save For Web or ImageReady. Otherwise, Set Destination Space to "sRGB." On any given machine there is often more than one than one choice for sRGB, and usually the differences are subtle. I use the setting at the top of the list, which is the one supplied by Adobe called "sRGB IEC61966-2.1". Dang—and all you thought you were doing was stickin' an image up on the Web (*Figure 17*)!

Step 4

Set Conversion Options:
Engine = Adobe (ACE)
Intent = Relative Colorimetric
Black Point Compensation = active

Step 5

Click OK.

Step 6

The image data has now been converted to preserve the color appearance of the original image in sRGB, which represents average display behavior. You may proceed with using Save For Web or ImageReady.

Go to
www.peachpit.com/
dreamteam.html
to download files for
this chapter.

CHAPTER SEVENTEEN
PHOTO REALISTIC ILLUSTRATION TECHNIQUES

Felix Nelson

Felix Nelson is the Creative Director for a number of tutorial-based publications, such as *Mac Design Magazine* (KW Media Group); *Capture User* magazine (Nikon USA); and *Photoshop User,* the Adobe Photoshop how-to magazine (National Association of Photoshop Professionals [NAPP]). He is also the Creative Director for the NAPP.

His design and illustrative work has been featured on NHL-, NFL-, NBA-, and MLB-imprinted licensed sportswear including high-profile sporting events such as the Super Bowl, the World Series, NCAA Championships, NASCAR, and Penske Racing. He has also created cover art for some of the industry's best-selling Photoshop books, including *The Photoshop Elements Book for Digital Photographers* (New Riders, 2003), *The Adobe Photoshop CS Book for Digital Photographers* (New Riders, 2003), and the *Photoshop Down and Dirty Tricks* book series (New Riders).

Felix is a contributing writer for *Photoshop User* magazine (NAPP), and was also a contributing writer for *Photoshop 6 Effects Magic* (New Riders, 2001). He is co-author of the bestselling *Photoshop Killer Tips* series (New Riders), and an instructor with the Adobe Photoshop Seminar Tour.

IS IT REAL, OR IS IT PHOTOSHOP?

In this era of instant gratification, when you can capture an image with a digital camera and have it instantly appear on a laptop via wireless connections, I'm often asked, "Why would you draw a photorealistic image? Can't you just shoot what you want and save yourself some time?" Well, maybe.

But when you think about it, in the time it takes you to set up the shot you want, set up the right lighting conditions, decide on the correct exposure, ISO, and eventually bring the image into Photoshop to make the final tweaks, color adjustments, and other modifications, you could probably draw the image just as quickly. In the time it takes to search the Web or all the hundreds of stock photo companies for the image I want, I can just draw the correct angle, color, or position I'm looking for.

Plus, there's the fun factor. It's just plain fun to draw with Photoshop. We spend enough time making layer adjustments and color corrections, sharpening images, removing red-eye, and doing other day-to-day Photoshop tasks. The time I spend actually using Photoshop as a painting tool is the time I enjoy most. Being able to create a fantastic scene or image that looks so real that it makes someone wonder if it's real or if it's Photoshop is what it's all about.

PHOTOREALISM IN PHOTOSHOP

What's photorealistic illustration all about? It's about making your digital illustrations come to life. It's about making the viewer wonder whether the image is photographed or illustrated. In this tutorial I'll show you some tips and techniques you can use to make your illustrations more lifelike. You'll learn which Photoshop tools to use and which ones make it easy to create realistic effects.

In the first part of this tutorial you'll learn how to create visual depth, conveying shape and form with a single highlight, from one common light source. You'll learn that it isn't always necessary to draw every detail into your illustrations—you can let the eyes fill in where the illustration leaves off.

Then I'll show you how to take flat-looking vector-based images and make them look more dimensional with the Dodge and Burn tools. You'll be able to add depth to any image with two easy-to-use but powerful tools.

Finally, you'll learn how to combine the techniques in the first two sections, along with some other time-saving illustration techniques, to create a digital illustration completely from scratch, using only Photoshop.

Note: You can download the files used in this chapter from the companion Web site, www.need-to-know-the-url.com

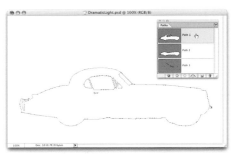

Figure 1

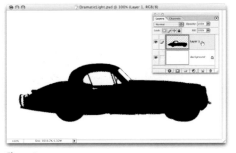

Figure 2

Using Highlights to Add Depth and Reveal Shapes

Step 1

Download the file DramaticLight.psd from the companion Web site, and open it in Photoshop. Command-click (PC: Control-click) Path 1 in the Paths palette to make it an active selection (*Figure 1*).

Step 2

Create a new layer (Layer 1) by clicking the New Layer icon at the bottom of the Layers palette. Press "d" to set the foreground color to black, and then press Option-Delete (PC: Alt-Backspace) to fill the selection with black (*Figure 2*).

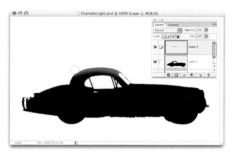

Figure 3

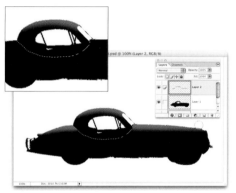

Figure 4 (top) and 5 (bottom)

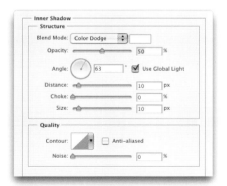

Figure 6

Step 3

Create a new layer (Layer 2). Click the foreground color swatch, choose a dark brown color, and click OK. Press "b" to choose the Paintbrush tool, then click the Airbrush button in the Options Bar. Use a large soft-edged brush (about 50 pixels), and draw a highlight on the roof of the car (*Figure 3*).

Step 4

Press "l" to choose the Lasso tool. We'll be subtracting the top of the selection (the passenger compartment), by holding down Option (PC: Control) and drawing around the top of the selection (*Figure 4*). Now use the Airbrush tool once again to draw highlights on the trunk and the hood. Press Command-D (PC: Control-D) to deselect (*Figure 5*).

Step 5

Click the Add Layer Style icon at the bottom of the Layers palette, and choose Inner Shadow from the pop-up menu. Change the Blend Mode to Color Dodge. Click the Color Swatch, choose white, and click OK. In the dialog, change the Opacity to 50%, Distance to 10, and Size to 10, and click OK (*Figures 6 and 7*).

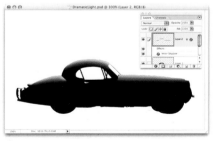

Figure 7

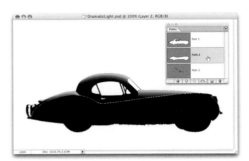

Figure 8

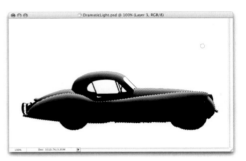

Figure 10

Figure 11

Step 6

Command-click (PC: Control-click) Path 2 to load it as a selection, and fill the selection with black (*Figure 8*). Create a new layer (Layer 3). With the foreground color set to brown again, use the Airbrush tool to add highlights to the front and rear fenders as shown. Press Command-D (PC: Control-D) to deselect. Now, click on the word Effects under Layer 2, and drag it under Layer 3 to add the effect to Layer 3 (*Figures 9 and 10*).

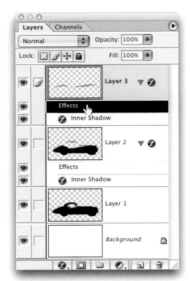

Figure 9

Step 7

Create another new layer (Layer 4). Choose the Elliptical Marquee tool from the Toolbox. Hold down Shift while drawing a perfect circle to constrain the selection just inside the rear tire. The same brown color we have been using should still be in your foreground color swatch. From the Edit menu choose Stroke. In the Stroke dialog, enter 3 for Width, choose Center for Location, and click OK (*Figure 11*).

Figure 12

Figure 13

Figure 14

Figure 15

Step 8

From the Select menu choose Transform Selection. In the Options Bar enter 30% for both Width and Height (*Figure 12*). Press Return or Enter twice to apply the transformation. From the Edit menu choose Stroke. In the Stroke dialog, enter 3 for Width, choose Center for Location, and click OK (*Figure 13*).

Step 9

"d" and then "x" to set the foreground color to white. Now choose the Brush tool with a large soft-edged brush. Lower the Brush Opacity to 50% in the Options Bar, and paint in some highlight areas on the lower right of each selection. Press "x" again to set the foreground to black, and paint in some shadow areas on the upper left of the selections. Press Command-D (PC: Control-D) to deselect (*Figure 14*).

Step 10

Choose Filter>Blur>Gaussian Blur. Enter 2 pixels and click OK. Create a new layer (Layer 5). Choose dark brown as the foreground color. Choose the Pencil tool from the Toolbox. With a small hard-edged brush (about 3 pixels), draw a line from the center of the wheel down toward the edge of the wheel rim (*Figure 15*). Holding down Shift as you draw constrains the stroke to a straight line.

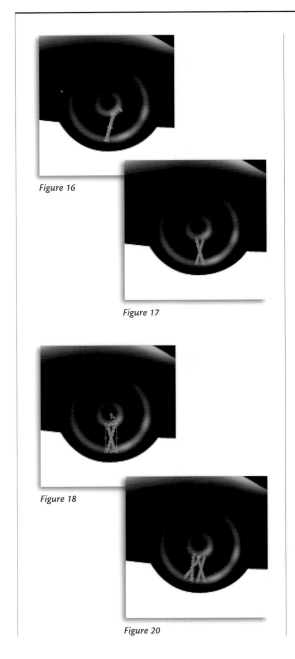

Figure 16

Figure 17

Figure 18

Figure 20

Step 11

Press Command-T (PC: Control-T) to bring up the Free Transform bounding box. While holding down Shift, move the pointer outside of the bounding box. When the pointer turns into a double-sided arched arrow, click and drag in the direction in which you want the selection to rotate. Press Enter or Return to apply the transformation (*Figure 16*). Command-click (PC: Control-click) Layer 5 to make it an active selection.

Press Command-Option-T (PC: Control-Alt-T) to bring up Free Transform (holding down the Option [PC: Alt] key automatically duplicates the selection on the same layer when the transformation is applied). Now Control-click (PC: right-click) in the center of the Free Transform bounding box, and choose Flip Horizontally. Press Enter or Return to apply the transformation (*Figure 17*).

Step 12

Command-click (PC: Control-click) Layer 5 to make it an active selection. Press Command-Option-T (PC: Control-Alt-T) again. Move the rotation point from the center of the Free Transform bounding box to the center of the wheel

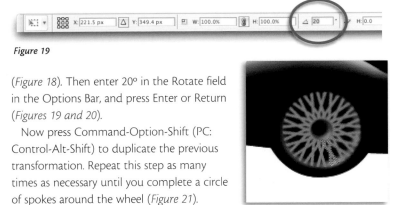

Figure 19

(*Figure 18*). Then enter 20° in the Rotate field in the Options Bar, and press Enter or Return (*Figures 19 and 20*).

Now press Command-Option-Shift (PC: Control-Alt-Shift) to duplicate the previous transformation. Repeat this step as many times as necessary until you complete a circle of spokes around the wheel (*Figure 21*).

Figure 21

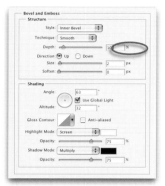

Figure 22

Figure 23

Figure 26

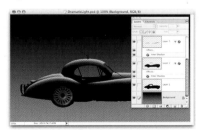

Figure 27

Step 13

Click the Add Layer Style icon at the bottom of the Layers palette, and choose Bevel and Emboss. In the Layer Style dialog, enter 2 in the Size field (*Figure 22*). Choose Gradient Overlay from the Styles list. Choose Multiply from the Blend Mode pop-up menu, enter -41 for Angle, and click OK (*Figure 23*). Press Command-D (PC: Control-D) to deselect. Then move Layer 5 below Layer 4 in the Layers palette. Now use the Move tool to center it with the wheel's inner and outer rings (*Figure 24*). Link Layers 4 and 5 together by clicking the box to the left of Layer 4 in the Layers palette. Now click the right-facing arrow in the top right of the Layers palette, and choose Merge Linked Layers. Lower the Layer Opacity to 75%.

Duplicate Layer 5 by dragging it to the New Layer icon at the bottom of the Layers palette. Then use the Move tool to center it with the front wheel (*Figure 25*).

Figure 24

Figure 25

Step 14

Create another new layer (Layer 6), and press "d" to set black as the foreground color. Command-click (PC: Control-click) Path 3 in the Paths palette. Press Option-Delete (PC: Alt-Backspace) to fill with black (*Figure 26*). Click on the Background layer in the Layers Palette to make it active. Choose brown as the foreground color and black as the background color. Choose the Gradient tool from the Tool bar and draw a gradient from the bottom towards the top of the document (*Figure 27*).

Figure 28

Figure 29

Step 15

Create a new layer (Layer 7). Choose the Elliptical Marquee tool and make a large oval selection across the bottom of the illustration. Press Command-Option-D (PC: Control-Alt-D) to bring up the Feather dialog. Enter 25 for the Feather Radius and click OK. Choose white as the foreground color and press Option-Delete (PC: Alt-Backspace) to fill with white. Change the layer blend mode to Overlay (*Figure 28*).

Step 16

Create a new layer (Layer 8). Set the foreground color to black. Create a thin oval selection under the car (*Figure 29*). Press Option-Delete (PC: Alt-Backspace). Press Command-D (PC: Control-D) to deselect. Choose Filter>Blur >Gaussian Blur. Enter 3 pixels and click OK to complete the illustration (*Figure 30*).

Figure 30

Figure 31

Figure 32

Figure 33

Figure 34

Nothing Is Perfect

One thing to remember is that most objects hardly ever look perfect. The problem with some computer-generated illustrations is that they look too good, too perfect. Giving your illustrations some imperfections is one way to make them appear more natural. Using basic shapes does simplify the illustration process, but don't forget to look for the little imperfections and add them to your work.

Step 1

Open the ThinBarArt.psd file. You'll notice that the illustration looks stiff and unnatural (*Figure 31*). So the first thing we want to do is soften some of the hard edges and bend some of the straight lines. Click Layer 1 in the Layers palette. In the Filter menu choose Liquify. In the Liquify dialog, choose varying brush sizes to bend some of the edges (*Figure 32*).

Step 2

Choose the Dodge tool from the Toolbox. What you want to do is draw some highlight imperfections; the more varied and arbitrary the highlights, the better. The thing to remember is that white and light-colored areas appear closer to the foreground (*Figure 33*).

Step 3

Now you'll want to use the Dodge tool to add some dark, or shadow imperfections (*Figure 34*). The rule here is that dark areas recede, or appear further away from the foreground. So anything you want to appear sunken or pushed in should be darker. Remember, the more random, the better.

Figure 35

Figure 37

Step 4

Duplicate Layer 1 by dragging it to the New Layer icon at the bottom of the Layers palette. Now press Command-Shift-U (PC: Control-Shift-U) to Desaturate. Choose Filter>Sharpen>Unsharp Mask. Enter 500 for Amount and click OK. Choose Filter>Artistic>Plastic Wrap. Enter the settings shown in *Figure 35*—Highlight Strength: 14; Detail: 9; Smoothness: 13—and click OK.

Step 5

Change the layer blending mode to Soft Light. You might want to slightly lower the layer Opacity (to between 50% and 75%) if the effect is too strong (*Figure 36*). Add a Drop Shadow, and flatten the image to complete the effect (*Figure 37*).

Figure 36

By comparing the final result with the original EPS artwork, you can see that simply adding some highlight and shadow imperfections has made the image come to life right before your eyes (*Figure 38*).

Figure 38

Double Your Pleasure

We're always looking for ways to save time—to speed up the process or find ways to do things faster. Sometimes we just overlook the obvious. In this section we'll explore some more-advanced techniques, but more important, we'll look at how duplicating and copying some or all of your illustration can cut your production time in half.

Step 1

Open FararriPaths.psd. Press "d" to set the foreground color to black, and press Option-Delete (PC: Alt-Backspace) to fill with black. Choose the Elliptical Marquee tool, and make a selection of the lower center portion of the document (see example). Press "d" and then "x" to set the foreground color to white. Click the New Layer icon at the bottom of the Layers palette (Layer 1). Press Command-Option-D (PC: Control-Alt-D) to bring up the Feather dialog. Enter 40 pixels and click OK. Now press Option-Delete (PC: Alt-Backspace) to fill with white. Change the layer blend mode to Hard Light and lower the layer Opacity to 75% (*Figure 39*). Press Command-D (PC: Control-D) to deselect.

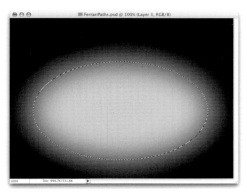

Figure 39

Step 2

Create a new layer (Layer 2). Click Path 1 in the Paths palette. Use the Direct Selection tool (the hollow arrow) to select the tire portion of Path 1. Click the Load Path as Selection icon at the bottom of the Paths palette to make it an active selection (*Figure 40*). Set the foreground color to black and the background color to gray. Choose the Gradient tool from the Toolbox and make a gradient from the left to the right of the selection (make sure that Foreground to Background is selected as the gradient type in the Options Bar). Choose the Pencil tool from the Toolbox. Use different-size brushes to draw in the tire treads as shown (*Figure 41*). Press Command-D (PC: Control-D) to deselect.

Figure 41

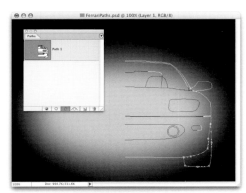

Figure 40

Figure 43

Figure 44

Step 3

Go back to Path 1, and with the Direct Selection tool, choose the rear window and lower bumper portions. Make them active selections. Press Option-Delete (PC: Alt-Backspace) to fill the selection with black. Press Command-D (PC: Control-D) to deselect. Choose the Lasso tool to make a selection of the lower part of the rear window (*Figure 42*). Choose Filter>Blur>Gaussian Blur. Enter 4 pixels and click OK (*Figure 43*).

Figure 42

Step 4

Choose the seat portion of Path 1 with the Direct Selection tool, make it an active selection, and fill with black. Set the foreground color to gray. Choose the Brush tool from the Toolbox, and, using a soft-edged brush, draw a highlight on the upper right of the selection, as shown in *Figure 44*. Press Command-D (PC: Control-D) to deselect.

Choose the rear window and roofline portion of Path 1, and make it an active selection. Use the Lasso tool, and hold down Option (PC: Alt) to subtract the area just on the lower left (*Figure 45*). Set the foreground color to white and the background color to dark gold. Choose the Gradient tool to make a gradient from the top toward the bottom right of the selection (*Figure 46*). Press Command-D (PC: Control-D) to deselect.

Figure 45

Figure 46

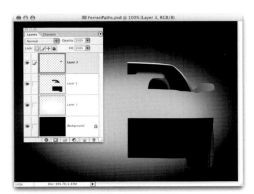

Figure 47

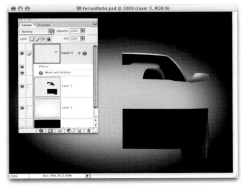

Figure 49

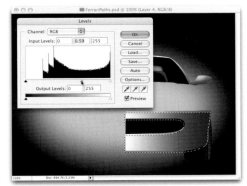

Figure 50

Step 5

Create a new layer (Layer 3). Choose the side mirror portion of Path 1 and make it an active selection. Change the foreground color to light gold and make another gradient from the right toward the left of the selection (*Figure 47*). Click the Add Layer Style icon at the bottom of the Layers palette, and choose Bevel and Emboss. Enter 300 for Depth and 50 for Size, and lower the Shadow Mode Opacity to 50 (*Figure 48*). Press Command-D (PC: Control-D) to deselect (*Figure 49*).

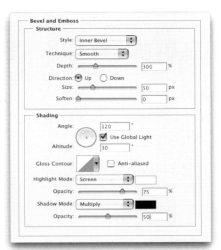

Figure 48

Step 6

Create a new layer (Layer 4). Choose the lower bumper portion of Path 1, and make it an active selection. Change the foreground color to white, and make a gradient from the left toward the right of the selection. With the Marquee tool selected, use the arrow keys to move the selection down and toward the left. Press Command-L (PC: Control-L) to bring up the Levels dialog. Move the Midtone adjustment point (the one in the middle) toward the right, and click OK (*Figure 50*). Use the Burn tool to add some detail to the shadow areas. Now press Command-Shift-I (PC: Control-Shift-I) to inverse the selection, and use the Dodge tool to add some highlight details (*Figure 51*).

Figure 51

Figure 54

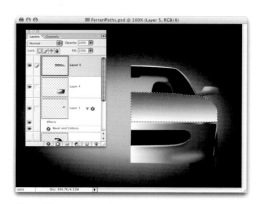

Figure 55

Step 7

Command-click (PC: Control-click) Layer 4. Use the Lasso while holding down Option (PC: Alt) to subtract two-thirds of the top of the selection (*Figure 52*). Press Delete (PC: Backspace). Choose the Elliptical Marquee tool and make an oval selection around the lower part of the bumper. From the Select menu choose Transform Selection. Move your cursor outside of the Transform bounding box until you see a double-arrow arch, and then rotate the selection into the desired position; press Enter or Return (*Figure 53*). Press Command-Option-D (PC: Control-Alt-D) to bring up the Feather dialog. Enter 5 pixels and click OK. Press Command-L (PC: Control-L) to bring up the Levels dialog. Move the Midtone adjustment point (the one in the middle) toward the left and click OK (*Figure 54*).

Figure 52

Figure 53

Step 8

Create a new layer (Layer 5). Choose the hood portion of Path 1, and make it an active selection. Change the foreground color to dark gold and the background color to white. Use the Gradient tool to make a gradient from the top toward the bottom of the selection (*Figure 55*). With the Marquee tool selected, move the selection down just a bit. Press Command-L (PC: Control-L) to bring up the Levels dialog. Move the Midtone adjustment point (the one in the middle) toward the left, and click OK. Move the selection down just a bit more. Set the foreground color to white. Use the Brush tool with a large soft-edged brush to draw in some highlights (*Figure 56*).

Figure 56

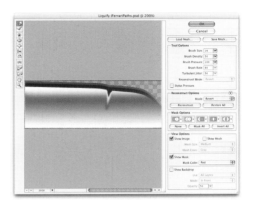

Figure 57

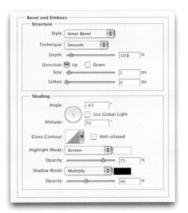

Figure 59

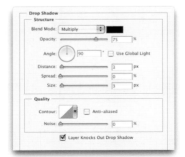

Figure 61

Step 9

Command-click (PC: Control-click) Layer 5. In the Filter menu choose Liquify. In the Liquify dialog, use the Warp tool to push down the highlight reflection (use a small brush), and click OK (*Figure 57*). Once again use the Dodge and Burn tools to add some details (*Figure 58*).

Figure 58

Step 10

Choose the headlight portion of Path 1, and make it an active selection. Press Command-J (PC: Control-J) to place the selection on its own layer (Layer 6). Press Command-L (PC: Control-L) to bring up the Levels dialog. Move the Midtone adjustment point (the one in the middle) towards the right, and click OK. Click the Add Layer Style icon, and choose Bevel and Emboss. Uncheck the Use Global Light box; enter -65 for Angle, 70 for Altitude, and 40% for Shadow Mode Opacity, and click OK (*Figures 59 and 60*).

Figure 60

Step 11

Create a new layer (Layer 7). Choose the grill portion of Path 1, and make it an active selection. Change the foreground color to gray. In the Edit menu choose Stroke. Enter 2 pixels for Width, choose Center for Location, and click OK. Choose the Pencil tool, and with a point of about 3 pixels create three horizontal lines in the selection from left to right. Click the Add Layer Style icon in the Layers palette, and choose Drop Shadow. Uncheck the Use Global Light box, and enter 90 for Angle, 3 for Distance, and 3 for Size (*Figure 61*). Choose Bevel and Emboss from the Styles list. Enter 1000 for Depth, 15 for Size, 120 for Angle, and 65 for Altitude, and change the Highlight Mode Opacity to 100. Click OK (*Figure 62*).

Figure 62

Figure 64

Figure 66

Create a new layer (Layer 8). Use the Pencil tool to create three vertical lines. Click the word Effects under Layer 7, and drag it under Layer 8 to apply the same layer style. Choose the inner and outer fog lamp portions of Path 1, and make it an active selection. Press Option-Delete (PC: Alt-Backspace) to fill the selection with gray (*Figure 63*).

Figure 63

Step 12

Create a new layer (Layer 9). Choose the inner fog lamp, the turn signal portion of Path1, and make it an active selection. Set the foreground color to white, and fill the selection. Now choose the Rectangular Marquee tool. While holding down Option (PC: Alt), subtract from the selection until you have only the right side of the turn signal selected. Change the foreground color to yellow and fill the selection (*Figure 64*). Click the Add Layer Style icon, and choose Inner Glow from the pop-up menu. Enter the settings shown in *Figure 65*.

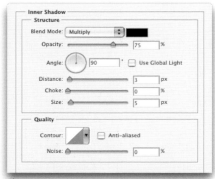

Figure 65

Step 13

Choose Bevel and Emboss from the Styles list, and enter the settings shown (*Figure 66*). Choose Satin from the Styles list. The default settings in the Satin dialog will work fine, but make sure to choose Rounded Steps as the Contour (*Figure 67*). Now choose Pattern Overlay from the Styles list and enter the

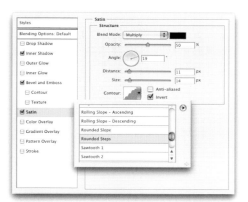

Figure 67

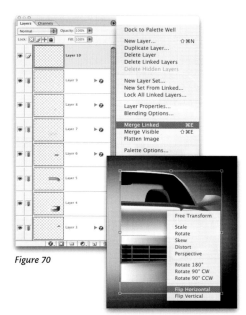

Figure 70

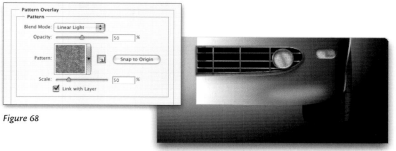

Figure 68

Figure 69

settings in the Pattern Overlay dialog shown in *Figure 68* (choose Oil Pastel on Canvas from Artistic Surfaces as the pattern). Click OK (*Figure 69*).

Step 14

Create a new layer (Layer 10). Link all the layers together (except for the background layer and Layer 1) by clicking the box directly next to the layer name. Hold down Option (PC: Alt), click the right-facing arrow at the top of the Layers palette, and choose Merge Linked from the menu (*Figure 70*). Duplicate Layer 10 (call it Layer 10 Copy) by dragging it to the New Layer icon in the Layers palette. Press Command-T (PC: Control-T) to bring up Free Transform, Control-click (PC: right-click) in the center of the bounding box, and choose Flip Horizontal. Press Enter or Return to apply the transformation (*Figure 71*). Use the Move tool to reposition the other half of the car. Press Command-E (PC: Control-E) to merge down (*Figure 72*).

Figure 71

Figure 72

Figure 73

Step 15

Duplicate Layer 10 again (Layer 10 Copy again). Press Command-Shift-U (PC: Control-Shift-U) to Desaturate. Choose Filter>Artistic>Plastic Wrap. Enter these settings—Highlight Strength: 14, Detail: 10, Smoothness: 6 (*Figure 73*)—and click OK. Change the layer blend mode to Overlay, and lower the Opacity to 85%. Use the Eraser tool to remove any areas you do not want to appear shiny or metallic (the tires, for example). Finally, add the hood ornaments and logos to complete the illustration (*Figure 74*).

Figure 74

ALASKA LIGHT

CHAPTER EIGHTEEN

PHOTOSHOP AND ACROBAT WORKFLOW: CAPTURING, CORRECTING, PROTECTING, AND DISTRIBUTING YOUR IMAGES

Taz Tally

Go to
www.peachpit.com/
dreamteam.html
to download files for
this chapter.

Dr. Taz Tally is president of Taz Tally Seminars, a computer-publishing consulting and training company. Taz is the author of numerous books, among them his most recent book, *Acrobat 6 and PDF Solutions* (Sybex, 2004), as well as *Electronic Publishing: Avoiding the Output Blues* (Prentice Hall PTR, 2001), a textbook on electronic publishing fundamentals and PostScript file preparation; and *Avoiding the Scanning Blues: A Desktop Scanning Primer* (Prentice Hall PTR, 2000), a comprehensive guide to desktop scanning that was a featured selection of the Doubleday Book Club. In addition, Taz has published the *UMAX MagicScan® Manual* and *SilverFast: The Official Guide*, which are distributed worldwide. He has produced numerous instructional videos and CDs on scanning, prepress, Photoshop, Microsoft Publisher, font management, and keyboard shortcuts, and was the codeveloper and instructor for the video training series *DeskTop to Print*. Taz has invented and produces a ten-step scanner and digital camera calibration target and kit. He is a frequent presenter at seminars and trade shows throughout the United States, including GraphExpo, and is a member of the Photoshop Dream Team at the biannual PhotoshopWorld conventions. Taz also is a frequent contributor to *Photoshop User* magazine, for which he

Opposite: *Fall in the Kenai Peninsula, looking through the crystal-clear autumn atmosphere across Kachemak Bay toward the snow-and-glacier-draped southern Kenai Mountains near our home in Homer, Alaska. I took this photograph in the fall of 2003 during one of my many daily bike rides. I always take my camera on outings, as there is always a spectacular view to enjoy and capture.*

MY PASSION OUTSIDE OF THE DIGITAL REALM

When I'm not hogging the bandwidth and digitizing everything in sight, I am an outdoor nut. My wife, Jaz, and I love to kayak, mountain bike, canoe, hike, and engage in nature photography—we are basically digital gypsies. This is one of the reasons why we live in Alaska most of the year. We spend much of our time outdoors there. Most of Alaska is still a frontier and looks like what you see on the opposite page. Alaska is still a land with plenty of pristine landscape, sky, and wildlife.

Not only do we enjoy Alaska ourselves, but we also set up custom adventures for those who want to get an inside look at Alaska. Jaz's and my passion for enjoying the great Alaskan outdoors includes working to protect this unique environment, one of last unspoiled ones on Earth. We think the future of Alaska is not in exploitation and overextraction of its oil, gas, mineral, forest, and marine resources, but in the sustainable preservation and enjoyment of Alaska's unique landscapes and ecosystems through a wide variety of recreational uses. This is one of the key reasons why we started our Alaska Light Adventures. We present Alaska seminars all over North America and operate a free "Alaska Image of the Month Club" service, through which we send out an Alaskan image each month with some info about the scene. If you are interested in receiving our free images, just email me

continued on next page

TAZ TALLY, *continued*

writes a regular prepress column. He is perhaps best known for his entertaining, content-rich seminars and his ability to present complex materials in a simple, easy-to-understand fashion. He is currently working on developing online training courses with Lynda.com (www.lynda.com) and StaffingTools (www.staffingtools.com).

When Taz is not touring the country by plane or motor home presenting his seminars, he splits his time between houses in Homer, Alaska, and Fort Myers, Florida, with his fabulous partner, Jaz, and their Cardigan Welsh corgi, Zip. In their "spare time" Taz and Jaz generally head off to the outdoors. They can be found hiking or mountain biking in Alaska, skiing the powder snow in Utah, or diving with the whales in the waters off Hawaii.

Taz is available for custom training and consulting.
Contact Taz at:
ttallyphd@aol.com or taztally@alaska.net
www.tazseminars.com
Florida Address: 16175 John Morris Rd. #10, Ft. Myers, FL 33908
Alaska Address: 41195 Turkington Circle, Homer, AK 99603

MY PASSION OUTSIDE
OF THE DIGITAL REALM, *continued*

at taztally@alaska.net and ask to be added to our club. And if you or your travel club or organization is interested in having us make a presentation on Alaska, just let us know by contacting us at the same email address. As the great caravan travelers during the Middle Ages used to say when greeting and parting, Yol Bolson!—Let there be road!

THE MEAT

Unlike other chapters in this book, which are authored by enormously creative and talented folks (I hate them!), this one is written by a production bum. I typically have three goals when I sit down to work: (1) do it right, (2) do it right the first time, and (3) do it fast. The *it* in this case is the production stuff, such as calibration, scaling, adjusting resolution, and image and color correction, (a more complete list will follow)—all the production stuff that needs to be done properly to capture, prepare, present, and distribute your images. If you do all the production stuff properly and fast, you will have more time to devote to the more fun and creative aspects of your image manipulations, *and* your images will be of consistently higher quality, with more consistent results.

In a word, we're talkin' 'bout *workflow.* Workflow is not just about what you do, but it's also about the tools you use and when (the order in which) you use them. In this chapter I am focusing on two tools, Photoshop and Adobe Acrobat, because they are both such powerful and flexible tools, and they are becoming progressively more integrated. One of the keys to a good (fast, flexible, and effective) workflow is knowing your tools inside and out—what they are capable of and how to best use those capabilities. There are dozens, maybe hundreds, of image editing and distribution tools out there in the vast digital world, and in fact you could spend much of your time sampling, trying, and testing these tools—and never get anything done. I am a big fan of sticking to a couple of tools that you know really well. For me it is Photoshop and Acrobat. Photoshop provides all the image-editing muscle I need, while Acrobat provides an extremely flexible presentation and distribution tool.

There are as many different creative workflows as there are people who work in them. The key is to construct a workflow that meshes with your image capture, editing, and distribution needs. As an example, I will be using one of my digital photographic workflows. Your specifics will vary from mine, but perhaps the case study of my workflow will give you some ideas about how to best construct or improve your own. I routinely follow one of two digital photographic workflows: one for my landscape and nature photography, and another for the real estate image presentations that I create for my wife, Jaz. The two workflows have much in common and vary mostly in the details. I will use the workflow for the real estate images here.

Set a Specific Goal

It is good to have a clear understanding of your goal to begin with, because the goal of your workflow will likely affect the workflow production steps and tool choices. For instance, in the real estate workflow, my goal is to create a presentation of multiple images of multiple properties primarily for out-of-town real estate clients to view on a monitor, from a CD, or over the Web. I typically shoot 10 to 15 images of each property and usually include five to ten properties in each presentation. My goal is to create and send, usually on a CD, a client-customized, address-labeled, self-playing presentation of multiple properties that can be readily viewed on just about any computer. The PDF format fits my needs to a T. High-quality printing, such as commercial printing, is not an issue, but the images need to be high enough quality to be attractive onscreen, so proper highlight and shadow assignments, brightness and contrast, and color-correction adjustments are important.

And speed is critical! We want to quickly get these images together in a presentation to send to the client, who is usually located out of town. We know that the client may not even end up purchasing one of these houses we show them, but because they are out of town, sending them presentations of numerous houses and listening to their feedback allows Jaz to customize the selection of properties that she will show them when they do get to town. My choices of tools, steps, and settings reflect these twin requirements of good image quality and speed of completion. As we will see, Photoshop and Acrobat are just the right tools to help us quickly and accurately meet our goal.

Production Chores

Constructing an effective workflow boils down to three key steps:

1. **Make a list of all the production steps.** List every step you need to perform to reach your stated goal.

2. **Determine the best order in which to perform those steps.** Do you resize or resample first? And when should you perform your RGB-to-CMYK conversion?

3. **Figure out ways you can streamline 1 and 2.** Use actions and batch functions galore, and remember that there are often several ways to perform a specific production step— such as the myriad ways to make PDF documents—with one method often being much more appropriate, because it may be faster or of higher quality than other methods.

The Steps

Here are the tasks I perform, sequentially, for my real estate images workflow:

1. Recharge batteries (two sets) in preparation for the shoot.
2. Set a low image resolution/dimension for screen viewing.
3. Make the initial front-of-house shot.
4. Calibrate and color balance for lighting conditions (interior).
5. Shoot the house in proper sequence.
6. Download the images.
7. Rename the images by address.
8. Flag, cull, and sort the images.
9. Rotate the vertical images.
10. Apply initial highlight and shadow adjustments and color correction.
11. Crop each image as needed (conditional)—an opening for creativity here!
12. Make the final image adjustments.
13. Apply sharpening.
14. Create the PDF presentation.
15. Do the final sort in Acrobat.
16. Place copy on images.
17. Add the promo.
18. Copy the presentation to CD.

> **NOTE**
>
> *Some steps, such as cropping and selective area image adjustments, may be conditional and thus not applied to all images. I try to design each step to maximize speed, minimize mistakes, and leave me time to tackle specific problems and infuse a bit of creativity into the presentation…yes, contrary to popular belief, some production folks can have a modicum of creativity!*

Figure 1 *A resolution of 640 x 480 is enough for presentation display. If you expect that you may want to make prints, however, it's best to use a larger resolution.*

Figure 2 *A front shot of the house is always the first image in the shooting sequence.*

Here are the steps expanded, with descriptions of some of the specific tools and tips I use to perform them.

Step 1: Recharge the batteries

I always keep a set of rechargeable batteries in a 12V charger in my vehicle. This pretty much guarantees that I will have power to shoot. I use a thin rapid-charge (1-hour) charger.

Step 2: Set low resolution/dimension and mild compression for screen viewing

I will typically set a capture resolution/image dimension of 640 pixels by 480 pixels. I shoot my images with a 5-megapixel 2560x1920 Minolta DiMAGE 7 but only use the 640 x 480 dimension (the lowest resolution/smallest dimension available on my camera). The 640 x 480 resolution/dimension creates an appropriately sized 8.8 x 6.6-inch image onscreen (*Figure 1*). Lowering the capture resolution does *not* reduce the image quality, only its dimensions, and it eliminates the need for later downsampling and resizing (speeding up the production process and increasing final image quality as well, because you've avoided interpolation). I use mild JPEG compression to speed up image writing during shooting. The mild compression does not noticeably reduce image quality onscreen.

Step 3: Make the initial shot of the front of the house with daylight balance

I set my camera on daylight balance and shoot the front of the house as the initial image for that address. Setting a daylight color balance will provide me with a decent initial exposure for my first outside shot. My first shot is always the front of the house (*Figure 2*).

Step 4: Calibrate and color-balance for interior lighting conditions

I use a ten-step calibration target to create a custom color balance by performing a simple color balance on my grayscale

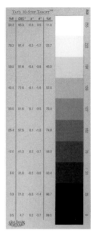

Figure 3 *I photograph my 10-Step Calibration and Color Correction Target to create a custom color balance.*

Figure 4 *The image-capture sequence, starting with the front of the house.*

Figure 5 *The Transfer Storage partition is for initial copying, sorting, and moving, as well as for writing to CDs and DVDs.*

target under the interior light conditions of each house. I set my digital camera to Custom Color Balance mode, focus the camera on just the target, and partially depress the shutter release to record the custom color balance profile (*Figure 3*). I will use this profile to shoot the remainder of the interior shots in that house. If lighting conditions change dramatically from one room to the other, I may perform several custom color balances. Creating and using custom color balances results in higher-quality initial images and reduces the amount of correction necessary later in the production process.

Step 5: **Shoot the house in proper sequence**

After the initial shot of the front of the house, I try to follow a particular order: entryway and hall, living room/great room, kitchen, dining room, lanai, master bedroom, master bath, other bedroom and bath pairs, individual baths, other interior rooms, and the garage, and then finish up with outdoor shots (*Figure 4*).

Step 6: **Download the images**

To begin, I simply drag the images off of my camera's flash card onto my hard drive. I want to copy the images onto a faster read-write media (aka my fast internal hard drive) prior to viewing them. Once on the hard drive, the images will be more rapidly accessible for viewing, sorting, moving, and editing.

I use a special large hard-drive partition, called Transfer Storage, for my initial image copying, moving, and sorting. I routinely defragment this partition to maintain fast read-write times. Using this separate partition prevents all this copying, sorting, and moving from degrading the performance of other partitions. I use this same Transfer Storage partition for writing to CDs and DVDs, as I always keep plenty of extra free space on this partition. The plentiful free space and routine removal of images and defragmentation allow for consistent, uninterrupted image data flow onto a CD or DVD (*Figure 5*).

Figure 6 The Medium Thumbnail preview selection.

Figure 7 Sequential image selection in File Browser.

Figure 8 Configuring the Batch Rename dialog settings.

Figure 9 Flagged, isolated, and sorted images in Photoshop's File Browser.

Step 7: **Rename the images with Photoshop File Browser**

a. I use the ever-cooler Photoshop File Browser to view, sort, and rename my images. I expand the thumbnail window to a large size to accommodate as many preview images as possible. Then I select the Medium Thumbnail preview from the View menu (*Figure 6*).

b. I select all the images for each property (my initial front shot of each house makes it easy to identify the start and end of each property sequence). I make a range selection by Shift-clicking the first and last images of each property-shot sequence (*Figure 7*).

c. From the File Browser's Automate menu I select Batch Rename.

d. In the Batch Rename dialog I configure the rename settings, which include the property address + a single-digit serial number + extension (*Figure 8*).

I repeat the same process for each property I have photographed.

Step 8: **Flag, cull, and sort**

a. Sometimes I will flag and isolate the images for each property as I work on it. To flag the images, simply Shift-click the first and last images of a property-shot sequence, and click the flag icon at the top of the File Browser. To view just the flagged images, select Flagged Files from the Show pop-up menu at the upper right of the Browser window (*Figure 9*). This clears the visual decks and removes the confusion.

b. Once all the images are renamed, I select (with Command-click [PC: Control-click]) and delete (with the Delete key or the trash can icon at the top of the File Browser) any images I do not want.

c. At this point I may reorder the images by simply clicking and dragging to move them to different positions in the Browser window.

Figure 10 Selected and rotated thumbnail images in the File Browser.

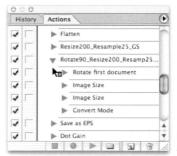

Figure 11 A rotation action, shown in the Actions palette.

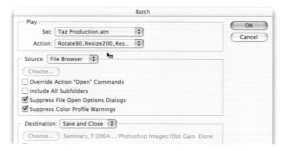

Figure 12 A rotation action applied through a batch function.

Step 9: Rotate vertical-format images

If any images have been shot with a vertical format—typically 30 to 50 percent of my interior images—I rotate them now. This can be accomplished in one of two ways:

a. Select the images in the File Browser and click the Rotate icon (either clockwise or counterclockwise) at the top of the Browser window. A rotational arrow icon appears below thumbnails that have been rotated (*Figure 10*).

> **NOTE**
>
> *The high-resolution image is not actually rotated until the images are opened. Photoshop will inform you of this via a message window.*

b. In Photoshop you can create and use a rotation action, which can be combined with other action-controlled steps as well (*Figure 11*).

To perform a rotation on multiple images, apply the rotation action through the batch function (Automate>Batch in the File Browser) (*Figure 12*).

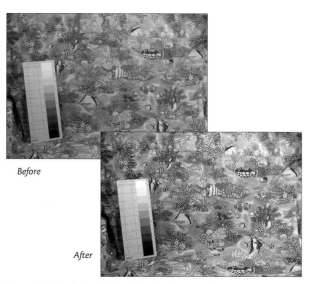

Before

After

Figure 13 *Before and after target-based color correction.*

Figure 14 *Access the auto levels adjustment with preset options through the Levels dialog.*

Step 10: **Apply initial highlight and shadow adjustments and color correction**

Here is where I really save some time. I can apply highlight and shadow adjustment and basic color correction (if neutrality is my goal) in one of the following ways:

a. If I have placed a copy of my calibration target in my image somewhere, I can perform a target-based image adjustment. I open the Levels dialog, select the highlight eyedropper, and click the top white swatch (*Figure 13*).

> **TIP**
>
> *You can preset highlight and midtone eyedropper RGB values by double-clicking the dropper icons before using them. I generally use 242 for the highlights and 127 for the midtones.*

b. If no target is available in the image, you can access auto levels by clicking Options in the Levels dialog (*Figure 14*). You can preset the values for the auto levels tool in the Auto Color Correction Options dialog. Be sure to check the Enhance Per Channel Contrast box if your goal is a neutralized image.

> **TIP**
>
> *I avoid using auto levels on images that have specular (blown-out) highlights. On these images I perform a manual levels adjustment instead. In most cases I perform levels corrections on individual channels (rather than the master channel) to help remove any unwanted color cast in the image.*

Before   *After*

Figure 15 *A creatively cropped image.*

 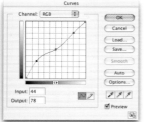

Figure 16 *Using the Curves dialog to selectively lighten a dark portion of an image.*

Step 11: Crop each image as needed—a creative opportunity

Not all images need cropping. This is a manual adjustment that is performed on a per-image basis. Some images can be enhanced significantly through the removal of busy, extraneous, or poorly lighted areas (*Figure 15*).

Because we are going to output these image to PDF, don't be afraid to use some creative crops. Our PDF document will display the graphics at whatever dimensions we choose. And if our images are displayed in presentations (aka full-screen) mode, all the images, regardless of their initial dimensions, will be displayed at full-screen size!

Remember also that an auto levels adjustment can be applied as an action, or as an action through a batch function.

Step 12: Make final image adjustments

Where needed, apply selective area lightening and contrast adjustments. I usually perform this with the Curves tool, often to lighten a dark portion of an image or bump up the contrast of some images. Due to the low power and quality of my flash lighting, many of my interior shots can routinely be enhanced with a bit more contrast, which can be applied through the use of the Auto Contrast command (Image>Adjustments>Auto Contrast). However, I tend to favor the creation and use of my own curves (*Figure 16*). A custom curve or the auto contrast tools can both be applied with an action or as an action through a batch function.

Figure 17 *Sharpening should be applied last and should be appropriate for the image use.*

Figure 18 *Photoshop's PDF Presentation dialog.*

Figure 19 *Photoshop's PDF Options dialog.*

Step 13: Apply sharpening

Since the digitizing process tends to soften images, sharpening can improve most digitally captured images. Sharpening should be the last step of the image-enhancement process. While Photoshop has several sharpen tools, the Unsharp Mask tool provides the most control. For these low-resolution JPEG images, which will only appear onscreen, I typically apply just a moderate amount of Unsharp Mask. Here are some typical value ranges: Amount = 50–75, Radius = 0.5–1.0, Threshold = 3–5 (*Figure 17*).

Step 14: Create a PDF presentation (from the Photoshop File Browser)

For our use (low-resolution, on-screen only), the PDF Presentation tool, available through the File Browser, is the perfect solution for creating our PDF-based presentation—it's easy and fast.

a. In the Photoshop File Browser select all of the final real estate images you want to go into the presentation.

b. In the File Browser, select Automate>PDF Presentation (*Figure 18*).

c. In the PDF Presentation dialog, indicate whether you want to create a multipage PDF or a presentation. If you select Presentation, choose among your Presentation options of transitions, looping, and advancing.

d. Click Save and complete the PDF Options dialog (*Figure 19*).

You can always change your mind about any of this later by adjusting the PDF in Acrobat.

> **NOTE**
>
> *We are using the PDF Automate option here (because it suits our specific purpose), but notice that Photoshop offers an array of other display and presentation options, including Photo Web Gallery, a Picture Package, and a contact sheet, any of which might suit your needs to a T!*

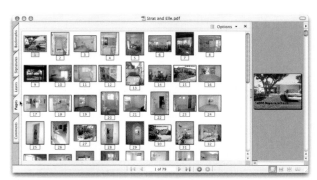

Figure 20 Move PDF pages around in the Acrobat Pages pane.

Figure 21 The Full Screen pane of Acrobat Preferences.

Figure 22 The Initial View pane of Acrobat Document Properties.

Step 15: Do the final sort and presentation control in Acrobat

Once you have created your PDF presentation, you can manage your PDF through Acrobat.

a. You can sort your images in the Acrobat Pages pane (*Figure 20*).

b. You can control the presentation characteristics of your PDF on your computer through the Acrobat Preferences: select Acrobat>Preferences>Full Screen (PC: Edit>Preferences>Full Screen) (*Figure 21*).

c. The display characteristics of your PDF on other computers can be controlled through Document Properties: File>Document Properties>Initial View (*Figure 22*).

Figure 23 *Address and contact copy placed on layers in Photoshop.*

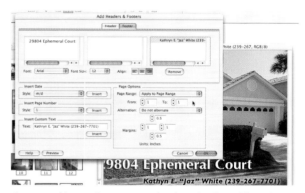

Figure 24 *Address and contact copy placed as a header and footer in Acrobat.*

Figure 25 *Jaz's e-business card added with the Insert Pages command.*

Step 16: **Add info to image(s)**

Because I know it is hard for Jaz's clients to keep track of which property they are viewing, I have gotten in the habit of placing the addresses on the images in the PDF. And just so that they don't forget who has sent them this lovely presentation (and whom they will be buying their house from!), I place Jaz's name and phone number on the PDF as well. Sometimes I will just place the copy on the first image, and sometimes on all of them. I set the type in one of two ways:

- I place the copy as type on layers in Photoshop. I might do this if I am placing the text just on the first image (*Figure 23*).

- I use Acrobat to place the address and contact copy as a header and a footer (Document>Add Headers and Footers) (*Figure 24*).

> **NOTE**
>
> *Placing type in Photoshop is more precise than in Acrobat and offers far greater flexibility and design options. Placing the type as a header or footer in Acrobat is a fast and easy, if somewhat pedestrian, method for adding type. You make the call!*

Step 17: **Add the promo**

Never one to miss an opportunity to promote Jaz, I add a digital e-business card (also a PDF document) to the last page of the presentation. I do this in Acrobat by pressing Command-Shift-I (PC: Control-Shift-I) (*Figure 25*).

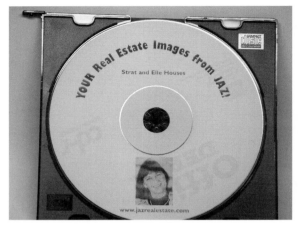

Figure 26 *A customized CD label with logo and photo.*

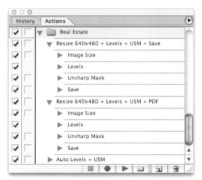

Figure 27 *A multistep Photoshop action.*

Step 18: **Copy the presentation to CD**

We copy the PDF presentation onto a JazRealEstate logo CD (complete with a photo of Jaz on the label), personalized with the client names (*Figure 26*). In addition to the PDF presentation we have both Mac and Windows versions of Adobe Reader included on the CD, so even if clients do not have Reader installed, it is available for them to use to view their personalized real estate presentations.

As we have discussed, many of these 18 steps can be automated, and any of them can be customized at any point. Several steps, such as resizing and resampling, using auto levels, and using the Unsharp Mask filter, can be applied to an image sequentially as one Photoshop action (*Figure 27*).

For my workflow, at each step I have struck a balance between image quality and speed that is suitable for the project's output requirements. Your needs are likely to be different, possibly very different, from those served by this workflow, but perhaps this will give you some ideas on how you can modify your process to speed up and simplify your production chores to better suit your needs.

Go to
www.peachpit.com/
dreamteam.html
to download files for
this chapter.

CHAPTER NINETEEN

REMOVING GLASS GLARE

Eddie Tapp

© AMY CANTRELL

Eddie Tapp is a photographer, lecturer, consultant, and author on digital imaging issues. As an award-winning photographer with more than 20 years of experience in computer technology, Eddie has been actively involved in educating and advising corporations, studios, and agencies in the applications of digital imaging workflow, color management, prepress, and digital photography globally through workshops, seminars, on-site consulting, and training.

Clients include Epson, Eastman Kodak, Foveon, Polaroid, Apple Computer, the Society for Imaging Science and Technology, Dynacolor Graphics, Marathon Press, American Color Lab, Millers Color Lab, H&H Color Lab, CPQ Color Lab, PhotoLogic (Ireland), PGC (Japan); the U.S. Department of Defense, Department of Education, Army, and Navy, and other government agencies; and many photographic studio operations. He has also served as print judge at many professional photographic competitions and is a Nationally Qualified Juror in Electronic Imaging for the Professional Photographers of America (PPA).

Eddie is director of the Institute of Visual Arts in Maui, Hawaii. He served six years as the chairman of the Committee on Digital and Advanced Imaging for the PPA, from which he received Master of Photography, Master of Electronic Imaging, and Photographic Craftsman degrees; API (Approved Photographic Instructor) certification; and the title of Certified Professional Photographer. He has also served as the Commercial Council representative to PPA for the GPPA.

He has created a series of interactive instructional CDs on professional

BECOME ONE WITH THE GRAY OBIS OF DIGITAL

What a blessing to be invited to create a chapter for this book that features so many powerful and talented artists. The Glass Glare project isn't my image creation, but is a lesson designed to show a technique that I feel is worthy for helping to develop the experience to use a brush tool effectively and to understand the concepts that are the foundation for any rebuild project.

The art of creating images becomes an extension of oneself, one's visual interpretation, one's ability to communicate a feeling or moment. Thinking back over my past 30-plus years of image creation, it wasn't until I learned how to use the computer to enhance images that I felt I could create images that were more satisfying for myself. And now when I have a vision, I'll work that into something visual for my own experience. Sometimes that becomes a very creative composition, sometimes less is more, but the bottom line is that the ability to create images using Photoshop presents the potential to follow my heart's visual desires, and for that I am thankful.

Learn to accept the "gray obis of digital"! I know from experience that learning the science of digital imaging and Photoshop has some intimidating arenas (the gray obis of digital), and we sometimes feel we'll never be able to learn enough to comprehend the application or use it as we really want to. I also know

continued on next page

EDDIE TAPP, *continued*

enhancement techniques, color management, and digital workflow, available from Software-Cinema (www.software-cinema.com). Eddie is working on his first book, *Production Techniques in Photoshop and Digital Photography*, to be published later in 2004 by Amherst Media. His articles have appeared in *The Professional Photographer, Photo Electronic Imaging, Infoto* magazine, *Southern Exposure Digital Capture*, and other publications, and he serves on Adobe's Photoshop beta team and is a member of NAPP's PhotoshopWorld Dream Team.

> etapp@aol.com
> www.eddietapp.com
> Eddie Tapp, M.Photog., Cr., MEI, API, CPP

BECOME ONE WITH THE GRAY OBIS OF DIGITAL, *continued*

from experience, however, that if we learn one thing at a time, the pieces begin to fit together and we can suddenly start to approach various projects with more certainty and less gray obis.

Accept the opportunity of truly getting to know the gray obis of digital, and enjoying the adventure of exploring and discovering what lies beyond. Contemplate the final image; use your deepest feelings, expression of life, and aspirations to determine what you want to create; and then educate yourself in the direction that you want to learn.

Light, composition, and exposure are ingredients that create a wonderful image. Concept, style, and technique are ingredients that develop a unique form.

I go through many stages of image-creation learning; it's kind of like eating. Sometimes I'll go on an eating binge and eat peanut butter and jelly sandwiches. Then banana sandwiches. Then I'll go on a turkey-sandwich binge for a while. The photographic analogy is that sometimes I go on a wide-angle binge, then a telephoto binge, then a combo-image binge, and so on. Right now I'm in the middle of a wide-format binge, using Photomerge in Photoshop CS to create panoramas (see Chapter 5 for more on the Photomerge feature), and at the early stages of experimenting with various compositions.

It's been an exciting venture to work in the digital media for the past several decades. I remember when Apple first came out with the happy face Mac (1984, I think). After one evening's session with that I had completely designed a killer studio workflow and setup using MacDraw. At that time, I was really hooked on producing projects in the computer and after my first experience with a digital camera in 1993 I made a quick conversion over to digital from film.

Little do we know what little do we know! That is a famous quote from Jane Conner-ziser, and one that seems to fit perfectly in my experiences with digital imaging. There is always something to learn, and I find myself learning something new every day—from my peers, my students, and my clients, and especially at conferences such as NAPP's PhotoshopWorld.

Remember this one truth: There is no right way or wrong way to do anything in Photoshop, but a variety of ways to do the same thing. Explore the experience, accept the gray obis of digital, and take pleasure in creating your heart's visual desires.

GLASS GLARE PROJECT

Two key words for this project are *rebuild* and *blending*. Once you've become accustomed to the techniques used here, you'll find yourself working at a whole new level: You'll be able to quickly and easily create solutions for image problems that in the past have been almost impossible to solve in a way that looks natural. In this project, you're going to learn how to merge the two primary ingredients that we always work with, chrominance and luminance—better known as color and tone—to blend and restructure shape and texture that doesn't exist in a given area into an acceptable (for lack of a better word) concealment.

The master tool we'll use for this project will be the Brush tool along with the Option (PC: Alt) key. The Clone Stamp tool might make a brief appearance, and we'll finish up using the Patch and Burn tools for final blending. The only palette we'll use will be the Layers palette, and we'll pay close attention to our brush size, edge hardness, and options.

Learn to develop your technique! When I see something like glass glare in an image, the first thing that comes to mind is *rebuild*. This single word to me means *Brush tool and working on blank layer: Rebuilding something that doesn't exist.* And the technique we learn is *blending: Blending tone, color, edges and shapes.*

Yes, I know—the first thing you want to do is reach for the Clone Stamp tool. It's not really a bad idea, and the Clone Stamp tool is certainly a vital and important tool for retouching. But when it comes to a rebuild, only certain pieces or areas will require the Clone Stamp tool (also known as the most dangerous tool in Photoshop, according to Jane Conner-ziser, because of a phenomenon called the "cloning blues"—a noticeable repetitive texture).

The following lesson in removing glass glare will present fundamental information and step-by-step procedures for those who have never used Photoshop CS, along with essential information for the experienced Photoshop user.

DEFINITIONS

rebuild
To build again, as something which has been demolished; to construct anew; as, to rebuild a house, a wall, a wharf, or a city.

Thesaurus: do up, doctor, fix, heal, mend, overhaul, patch, reconstruct, reform, rehabilitate

blending
Combining or mixing [syn: merging, mingling] n 1: the act of blending components together thoroughly [syn: blend] 2: a gradation involving small or imperceptible differences between grades [syn: shading]

Thesaurus: combination, consonant, fusion, harmony, musical

Figure 1
The image at 100% zoom ratio.

Figure 2
The Toolbox, showing the Full Screen Mode with Menu Bar button selected.

Figure 3
Position the image in the upper left to have both eyes near the top.

Step 1: Setting up the palettes for the rebuild

Open Photoshop CS, and if only for this one project, the first thing to do is hide all palettes, keeping only the Toolbox and the Options Bar visible (you can do this quickly with the keyboard shortcut Shift-Tab). Then open your image file and set the image to the 100 percent zoom ratio (View>Actual Pixels) (*Figure 1*). Click the Full Screen Mode with Menu Bar button at the bottom of the Toolbox (*Figure 2*) (or press "f").

Now simply hold down the Spacebar (which turns your pointer into the Hand tool) and click and drag in the image window to position the image in the upper left part of your screen. It's especially important to position the image so that you can see both eyes in the face you're going to work on at the same time (*Figure 3*).

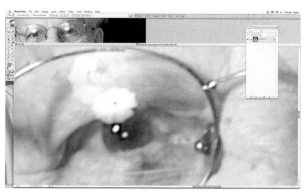

Figure 4
The final rebuild window workspace setup with two views of the same image and the Layers palette. The actual size of the window showing the 100% view will vary depending on your monitor resolution.

Figure 5
Create a new layer and name it "base skin".

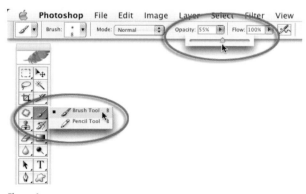

Figure 6
Select the Brush tool and set the options as shown.

NOTE

In Photoshop CS, setting your window in full-screen mode allows you to use the Spacebar to move your image anywhere on the canvas, even off the visible screen. This is an especially wonderful feature for setting up your rebuild workspace. If you're using a version of Photoshop prior to CS, you will be able to zoom in but not move the image around.

Next we're going to open a second window of this same file by choosing Window>Arrange>New Window for *file name*. Position the new window so that you can see the eyes in the full-screen mode behind it, as shown in *Figure 4*, zoom in on the image in the new window to between 400% and 800% to do the rebuild work. Bring out your Layers palette and position it at the right side of the screen.

As we work with this project in the 400% to 800% zoom window, we can quickly and easily see the effects of our work in the 100% zoom full screen view behind our work window. Once you have created your basic workspace, you can save this workspace for future rebuild work (Window>Workspace> Save Workspace). A saved workspace will save the positions of any visible palettes as well as the screen view mode, but it will not record whether you have opened up a second window of your image.

Step 2: First stage to rebuild: base skin color

We'll start by creating a new blank layer and naming it "base skin". Double-click on the name "layer 1" and enter a new name (*Figure 5*).

Select the Brush tool; in the Options Bar choose Normal from the Mode menu and set the Opacity to 50% to start (*Figure 6*). Note that once we start blending, we'll change the opacity often by using the number keys on the keypad (see the sidebar "Review of Shortcuts" later in this chapter for a list of shortcut keys used in this lesson).

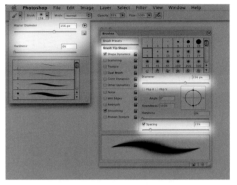

Figure 7
The Brush Picker in the Options Bar (left) and the Brushes palette (right) both contain controls for setting the diameter and hardness of a brush tip (see also "Brush Tool Keyboard Shortcuts").

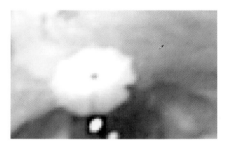

Figure 8
Option (PC: Alt)-click to sample a color from the image to paint with.

Figure 9
First stage of the rebuild: blending new base skin color from either side of the glass glare.

With the Brush tool selected in the Toolbox, bring up the Brushes palette; take a few minutes to become familiar with your Brushes palette and controls (*Figure 7*). We'll be using the left ([) and right (]) bracket keys to quickly change the brush size, and Shift-[and Shift-] to change the brush edge hardness, but it's helpful to see how these shortcuts change the values in the Brushes palette. And we'll also use the Option (PC: Alt) key to access the Eyedropper tool, which will allow us to sample color from the image while using the Brush tool (see the sidebar "Review of Shortcuts").

BRUSH TOOL KEYBOARD SHORTCUTS

Typing the [key increases the brush size, while the] key decreases brush size. Shift-[will create a softer brush edge while Shift-] will create a harder brush edge. While in the Brush tool, holding down the Option (PC: Alt) key will change the cursor to the Eyedropper tool, and then by clicking on a color in the image, it will set that color/tone in the foreground swatch. Holding down the spacebar will bring up the Hand tool, allowing you to click and drag to navigate about the image.

Step 3: First rebuild stage: blending the base skin

Option (PC: Alt)-click to sample the color on one side of the glare (*Figure 8*), then brush into the glare to begin covering it up. Next, Option (PC: Alt)-click on the other side of the glare to pick up color from that area and brush into the glare from the other side. You can almost hear the brush stroke in your head as you do this…*schwoosh!* Do this again and again and again from one side of the glass glare to the other to slowly build up color and tone that will cover up the offending glare. Sample-click, *schwoosh*, sample-click, *schwoosh*. In order to rebuild the glare area on the glasses, you'll sample the color and tone (Option [PC: Alt]-click) from one side of the glare to the other for every brush stroke. By controlling your brush size, edge hardness, and opacity, you gradually blend the color and tone from both sides

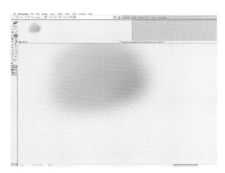

Figure 10
The first stage of blending work is placed on a separate layer (background layer visibility turned off).

Figure 11
Establish the brush edge hardness for the Eraser tool; 50% works great.

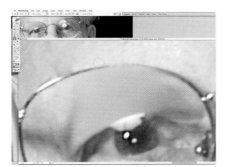

Figure 12
Erasing along the edge of the eyeglasses frame.

until it looks natural (*Figure 9*). Don't worry if it looks a bit too smooth to be natural—we'll fix that in a later step.

At this stage, you should be more concerned with your blending of tone and color than with staying between the lines of the eyeglasses frame and the top edge of the eyelid (*Figure 10*)—after all, we're working on a layer. Next we'll use the Eraser tool to clean up the edges of our retouching "spray." Select the Eraser tool and set its hardness to 50% (*Figure 11*).

Erase around the top edge of the eyeglasses frame and carefully erase along the bottom eyelid edge (*Figure 12*). Here you'll have to decide where the original edge is or should be. Turn off visibility—click the Eye icon to make it disappear—for the background occasionally so that you can see the brushwork you've done so far and judge how well it is blending with the existing image (*Figure 13*). Chances are you'll see some additional overspray that you need to erase. Remember that you're blending an edge, so pay close attention to the brush edge hardness.

Figure 13
First stage: base skin work after erasing edges (background layer visibility turned off).

Figure 14
Create a new layer above base skin and rename it "frame_shadow".

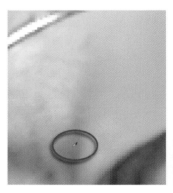

Figure 15
Option (PC: Alt)-click on the glass frame shadow to sample that color.

Figure 16
In the Brushes palette, choose Shape Dynamics and set the Control pop-up menu to Pen Pressure if you're using a Wacom tablet.

Step 4: Second stage to rebuild: frame shadow

Next, we'll create a new layer and name it "frame_shadow" (*Figure 14*).

Option (PC: Alt)-click on the actual shadow of the eyeglasses frame to set that tone and color in the foreground swatch (*Figure 15*). If you're using a Wacom tablet, in the Brushes options window, highlight Shape Dynamics and select the Pen Pressure option from the Control pop-up menu to give you additional control when you create the arch stroke (*Figure 16*).

REVIEW OF SHORTCUTS

- f = standard and full-screen modes

-] = larger brush

- [= smaller brush

- Shift-[= softer brush edge

- Shift-] = harder brush edge

- Spacebar = Hand tool (click and drag to navigate around image)

- Change opacity of a painting tool or layer using the number keys 1–0 (press 1 to get 10% opacity, press 5 for 50%, 0 = 100%, 05 = 5%, and so on). When a Brush tool is active, the brush opacity is changed; when a tool other than a painting tool is selected, the layer opacity is affected.

- Saving your workspace (Window>Workspace>Save Workspace) allows you to create different workspaces for various types of workflows and access them quickly under the same menu.

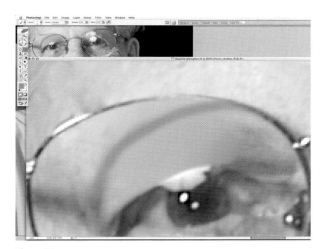

Figure 17
Create a new shadow and check both the 800% and 100% views.

The brush size, brush edge, pressure, and strokes will allow you to create a realistic shadow. Look at the 100% view image to make sure your blending is looking natural and turn off visibility for the shadow layer to check your rebuild work (*Figures 17, 18, and 19*). In selecting your brush size here, be sensitive to the size of the shadow, and choose a soft-edged brush to emulate the size and edge of the shadow you need to re-create. Try starting out with an opacity setting of 60%.

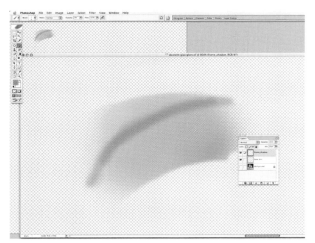

Figure 18
Turn off visibility for the Background to evaluate the rebuild work.

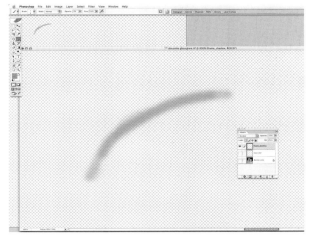

Figure 19
Turn off visibility for the other layers to see only the frame shadow work.

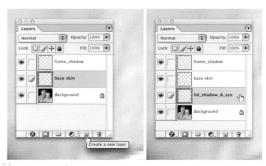

Figure 20
Make the base skin layer active, and then Command (PC: Control)-click to create a new layer below the current layer.

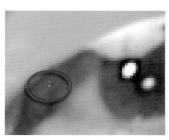

Figure 21
Option (PC: Alt)-click to place lid shadow color and tone in the foreground.

Step 5: **Third stage to rebuild: lid shadow and eye**

To create the lid shadow and eye layer, first click the base skin layer in the Layers palette to make it the active layer. Hold down the Command (PC: Control) key and click New Layer. This creates a blank layer just below the active layer, which is where we want to create the next blending elements. Rename the new layer "lid_shadow_&_eye" (*Figure 20*).

Select the Brush tool (Normal mode at 100% opacity); Option (PC: Alt)-click the shadow under the upper eyelid; and blend in the shadow tone under the eyelid where it is obscured by the studio-umbrella reflection (*Figures 21 and 22*). Then work on the iris, paying close attention to the color and tone values. Work on the pupil and minimize the second catch light (*Figure 23*).

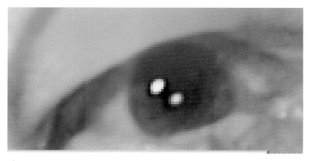

Figure 22
Paint in the eyelid shadow and rebuild the iris and pupil.

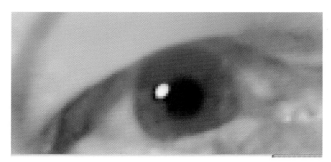

Figure 23
Rebuild the pupil, and paint and minimize the second catch light in the eye.

Figure 24
Create a new layer, and name it "lid_line_edge".

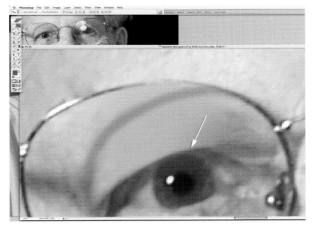

Figure 25
Carefully paint in the lid line edge, checking your work at 100% zoom view.

Figure 26
Link the rebuild layers together and select Merge Linked from the Layers palette menu.

Step 6: Fourth stage to rebuild: lid line edge

Now we're getting close. Create another blank layer above the previous one and name it "lid_line_edge" (*Figure 24*). Option (PC: Alt)-click on the tiny edge-line color/tone to sample it, and paint in a very thin line for the eyelid (*Figure 25*).

Step 7: Fifth stage to rebuild: link and merge layers

In the Layers palette, link all of the rebuild layers together by clicking the Link icon in the column next to the visibility column for each layer, and then selecting Merge Linked in the Layers palette menu. This merges all of the blending work into one single layer (*Figures 26 and 27*).

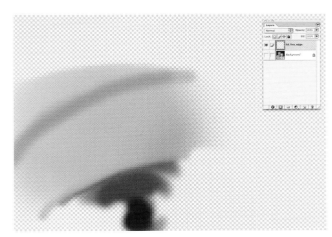

Figure 27
Uncheck the visibility icon on the background layer to view the blended work.

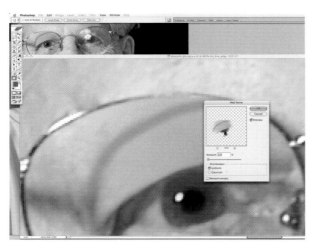

Figure 28
Check both views (100% and 800%) as you set the amount of noise to be added.

Figure 29
After adding Noise, select Edit>Fade Add Noise. Use 55% opacity and the Luminosity blend mode.

Step 8: Sixth stage to rebuild: add resident pixel noise

On the merged layer we want to add noise so that the texture of retouching work matches as closely as possible the actual pixel noise or grain look of the original image. Select the Add Noise filter (Filter>Noise>Add Noise) and add between 0.5% and 1.5%, using the Uniform option to obtain a close match to the resident noise (*Figure 28*). Don't be too concerned about having an exact match at this point because after clicking OK to this, we'll *fade* the Add Noise filter by selecting Edit>Fade Add Noise to refine the blending. Choose Luminosity from the Mode pop-up menu in the Fade dialog; now you can adjust the opacity until you have a close match to the original pixel noise that is resident in the file (*Figure 29*). View the image in the 100% zoom window to check blending.

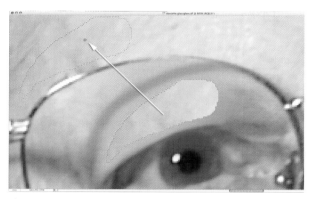

Figure 30
Select an area to patch and while the cursor is inside the marching ants area, click and drag the selection onto the desired skin texture you want to use for the patch.

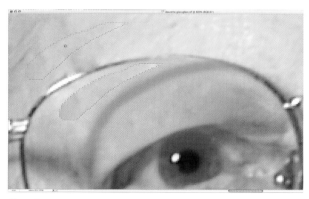

Figure 31
Use the Patch tool to select areas you want to add texture to, keeping the selection away from edges that contain color and contrast that's different from the area you'll be patching.

Step 9: Seventh stage to rebuild: add texture to the rebuild

Before we add texture, flatten the layer to the background by choosing either the Layer>Flatten Image command or Flatten Image from the Layers palette menu. Select the Patch tool and in the Options Bar, click the Source button. With this tool we're going to carefully select several areas in the completed rebuild work and add some resident skin texture to them. When selecting these areas, click and drag the cursor, avoiding the edge or contrast zones—a slight feather of 1 or 2 pixels to the selected area is okay. To do this, you'll have to create your selection with the Patch tool and then from the main menu choose Select>Feather to feather the selection. Once you have created and feathered your selection with the Patch tool, move your cursor inside the marching ants, then click and drag your selection to the desired texture and let go of the mouse. The Patch tool beautifully blends the color, tone, and texture of the two areas together (*Figures 30 and 31*).

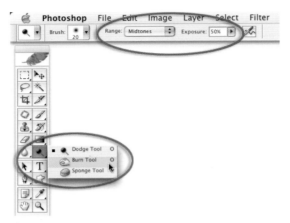

Figure 32
Select the Burn tool, set the Range to Midtones, and set Exposure to somewhere between 10% and 30%.

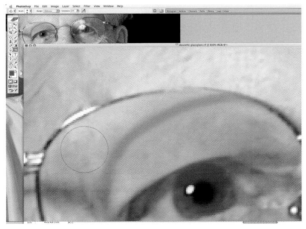

Figure 33
Check the 100% view to finalize blending with the Burn tool.

Step 10: Eighth and final stage to rebuild: final toning

Finally, we'll take the Burn tool, set the Range to Midtones and the Exposure to between 10% and 30% (*Figure 32*). Pay close attention to your brush size, edge hardness, and stroke, and carefully burn in the rebuild area, frequently checking the 100% view image for a natural blended look (*Figure 33*).

Step 11: Repeat steps 2 through 10 on the other eyes

Repeat all the previous stages for the other eyes. Once you become familiar with this technique, it should take approximately 30 minutes to complete a job such as the one in this lesson.

Save, Save, and Save Again!

Save, and save often!!! Famous last words—something that experience will teach us. But if you're just beginning to work in Photoshop, keep in mind that a computer is only a computer, and operating systems do lock up, crash, and occasionally have their little tantrums. I've found that for some reason a computer will lock up during an important work session when we're close to completing a pressing project or have just about finished the most amazing creation in our lives and we haven't saved the image in a while. So learn from the experienced, who have suffered these calamities before, and save…and save often!!!

The rebuild technique is a very powerful method to use when you must restore areas that are completely lacking detail, color, tone, and texture. I find the rebuild technique also works great for replacing walls, clothing, body parts, and much more. This project would serve as a good beginning for a more complex rebuild project, and there are many other techniques to learn as well. I owe a special thank-you to Jane Conner-ziser, who gave me the insights to create and control rebuilds. After repeating this technique several times, you'll become very comfortable with the process of blending and rebuilding.

Figure 34a Before

Figure 34b After

© THE ROMANO SISTERS, PHOTOGRAPHED BY HADI DOUCETTE

Moral of the Story

There are two morals, actually. The first is learning the *techniques* and *mentality* of rebuilding information that doesn't exist and learning where we want to control tone, color, texture, and blending. The second is teaching yourself, your staff, or others how to avoid glass glare, if possible, from the start. The best way to learn the importance of this is to have to create a rebuild on a complicated glass-glare project. This will teach you to watch the effects of your lighting setup and reposition the lights so that the glare is minimized or eliminated *before* you press the shutter button. For tricky situations, you can even use glassless eyeglasses frames, or simply take some shots of your subjects without their glasses that you can use as source material for any rebuild work that has to be done.

Congratulate yourself if you used the Clone Stamp tool only minimally for this particular project. Don't get me wrong—I love the Clone Stamp tool. After all, my first Photoshop retouching experience, nearly 13 years ago, was with this tool, which was then called the Rubber Stamp tool. I use it daily, but I also use the other powerful tools available, such as the Brush, Patch, and Burn tools, as well as the all-important concepts demonstrated in this tutorial, to create successful and convincing rebuilds that will satisfy my clients (*Figures 34a and 34b*).

CHAPTER TWENTY

A CINEMATIC APPROACH TO DIGITAL STILL PHOTOGRAPHY

Vincent Versace

Vincent Versace is a recipient of the 1998 Computerworld Smithsonian Award in Media, Arts & Entertainment and the 2001 Shellenberg Fine Art award. His work is part of the permanent collection of the Smithsonian Institution's Museum of American History.

In addition to being one of the featured artists of Nikon Electronic Imaging, and part of Epson's Stylus Pros team, he is also one of the photographers used by Epson, Lexar, Apple, Dyna-Lite, Photoflex, Luminos, Kodak, LowePro, and Nikon to beta-test their digital cameras, digital backs, flash media, lighting systems, high-resolution printers, ink and inkjet media, and scanners.

WHY TO PHOTOSHOP

When the question is: "How did you shoot that photograph?" it's likely that the answer being sought is not "f5.6, 125sec ISO 200." Instead, what the questioner really wants to ask is: "Why did you shoot that picture that way?"

Understanding the why to do something makes it much easier to find out the how to do something. A problem with many "how to" books is not the quality of the instruction or answers that these tomes provide, it's in knowing the questions to ask. Those answers will always be found in the why. The quest for how comes from our need to find the winning formula, the "secret sauce" or the "just follow these simple steps" that will work every time. It is difficult to put a linearity to a nonlinear thing: Art. In the real world, 2+2=4. We are taught that the whole can never be greater than the sum. In the artistic world, 2+2=FISH or FERRARI or whatever—but it never equals 4.

With the steps I'll demonstrate in this chapter, we'll take care of a couple of ways that the eye sees, by controlling areas of light to dark and areas of focus to blur. I'd love to be able to go further—our next step would be to exploit the aspects of contrast and sharpness. Contrast and sharpness often go hand-in-hand because of the way sharpening uses contrast.

What we will do with this image will get it ready for the next phase of the workflow, which would be the conversion from color to black-and-white while staying within the RGB color space. But that is for another time, another tutorial. The complete workflow for the "Stardust" image will be covered in my book Welcome to OZ: Following the RGB Road.

If you come away with only one thing from reading this chapter, my hope is that it be this: Try to approach the editing of a digital still image from a dynamic and cinematic perspective. By crafting and shaping the light that plays on the image, we can guide the viewer's eye through the scene and create a sense of motion within the confines of a seemingly still image.

ANATOMY OF A PHOTOGRAPH: STARDUST

Using Adobe Photoshop to do classic studio lighting

This chapter is an excerpt from the forthcoming book *Welcome to OZ: Following the RGB Road,* by Vincent Versace, to be published by Peachpit Press. *Welcome to OZ* is a "why to" rather than merely a "how to" book, discussing a cinematic approach to digital still photography. This chapter explores the first of a series of lessons involving the creation of the image "Stardust."

Why to

Whenever one thinks of glamour or Hollywood, it is the images of George Hurrell that come to mind, just as when you think of Yosemite, you think of the images of Ansel Adams. Even if the name doesn't ring a bell, no one is unaware of the images. Hurrell invented the Hollywood glamour photograph. His dramatic use of light and his understanding of the drama of light were second to none. He lit the most famous of his movie star photographs with movie lights, or hot lights, not strobes; and he photographed his subjects with an 8x10 view camera, not an SLR, and did not have the luxury of roll film or CompactFlash cards. He engaged his subjects in a dialogue, and from time to time he'd click the shutter. The images he captured became the result of the experience.

Hurrell most often employed two focusable light sources, diffused them, and then placed the lights above and on either side of the subject. This type of lighting became known as *butterfly lighting* because of the hallmark shadow produced under the subject's nose.

Before we get to the how-to aspect of this chapter, let's explore the reasons for why to. There are some questions surrounding this particular photograph. First, is it actually possible to create the look and feel of this unique stylistic approach using Photoshop? And, if so, is it possible to make the image look not like an exact digitally lit reproduction, but rather like a naturally lit one?

The first consideration is, as it almost always is, light. The image in *Figure 1* was lit naturally rather than with strobes or hot

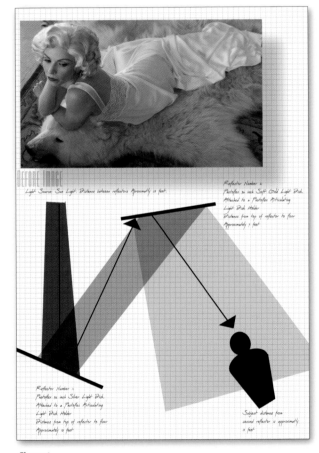

Figure 1
The lighting setup for the "Stardust" image: Two reflectors are used to direct sunlight onto the subject.

lights. This takes advantage of the unique characteristic of sunlight to be both directional and ambient at the same time. The technique selected to light the base capture image is often referred to as *board-to-board reflecting* (*Figure 1*). This technique is used to get light someplace other than the point light source (in this case the sun), and/or to have the light source appear to be farther from the subject than it actually is. Here, this technique was the best way to evenly light the subject with the best type of light—reflected sunlight.

This lighting technique was selected not primarily for aesthetic reasons, but rather due to economic and time constraints. All that was required were two light stands with light-disc holders and two reflectors. Setup and breakdown times were insignificant, and there was the added bonus of the reflected sunlight.

Another major theme of this chapter is the idea of a cinematic approach to still photography, rather than the more traditional still approach to still photography. The first premise of a cinematic approach to still photography is this: A still photograph is called a still photograph because the picture does not move, not because the objects in the photograph are not in motion. The central objective of a cinematic approach to still photography is to capture motion with stillness. The second premise is this: Engage the subject in a dialogue and fire the shutter frequently, with the images captured then becoming the result. This is the third premise: It is in absolute spontaneity that you get absolute truth. And the fourth premise: Know how the human eye works, and understand the way it chooses to "see" things. There are several more, but let's stick with these four for now.

By understanding and exploiting the knowledge of how the eye sees, we can control how the eye moves around the image, which creates the sensation of movement and dimensionality. In a nutshell, the eye first goes to patterns that it recognizes, then to areas of light to dark, high contrast to low contrast, high sharpness to low sharpness, in-focus to blur (which differs from high sharpness to low sharpness), and high color saturation to low color saturation. It is from this palette that we will paint.

Finally, before we begin the how-to aspect of this chapter, it is important to remember that even though the final intent is an image in black and white rather than color, the image will never cease being a color image, nor leave the RGB color space. With that said, the how-to part of this chapter begins.

How to

The steps listed below are designed to produce the most efficient workflow, offer the greatest control, and produce the best effect. In Photoshop as in most things, quicker is better as long as quality doesn't suffer. Learning keyboard commands and working efficiently is always a good idea. This chapter reflects this approach.

For the best results in this project, apply the following assumptions to your setup:

- You are working on a Sony Artisan CRT monitor, an Eizo LCD, or—at a minimum—a monitor calibrated with a hardware device such as the GretagMacbeth EyeOne or EyeOne Display. (Using the Adobe Gamma or ColorSync monitor-calibration utilities is not sufficient.)
- The proofing light source is a full-spectrum bulb (such as SoLux).
- All printing will be done using ICC profiles.

- Your workflow includes soft proofing.
- Your working color space is either Adobe RGB (1998) or ColorMatch RGB. (ColorMatch RGB is generally considered the best for photographic imaging workflows.)
- If the source file is a digital capture (the image was shot with a digital camera), the file format is RAW (when possible), and the camera's color space is set to Adobe RGB (1998).
- The final output device is a 1440/2880-dpi six-color inkjet printer, or ideally, a seven-color 1440/2880-dpi printer.
- The image file resolution is 360 ppi.
- Whenever possible, the final image is displayed under full-spectrum bulbs. (The best viewing color temperature for display is 4100K).
- Your working environment is controlled. The monitor's background color is set to medium gray, and there are no wild patterns or colors within your immediate field of view when you're doing color-critical work on the image.
- Adobe Photoshop CS (or later) is the image-manipulation software being used, and the operating system is the most current version of Mac OS X for Macintosh or Windows XP for PC.

If you have not already done so or are not in the habit of doing so, go to a neutral gray background in Photoshop. You do this by simply pressing "f." (Pressing "f" cycles among Photoshop's three display options. You can also select the Full Screen with Menu Bar option by clicking the middle of three buttons near the bottom of Photoshop's Toolbox. If for some reason the background is not gray, select gray as the foreground color, and Shift-click with the Paint Bucket tool in the background area that surrounds the image.) Using gray gives you an uncluttered and color-neutral background. Gray is specifically used to minimize chromatic induction (visual color contamination). A midtone (gray) is used to minimize contrast effects. By choosing a gray background, you can make the most informed and accurate decisions about how to change the color, contrast, and shade of the image you're working with.

Is there any time when you would choose black as a background option? Yes—when you want to see how much contrast is in an image and how much detail exists in its deep shadow areas. It is a good idea, however, not to use the black background for making color decisions.

Before we begin, remember that it is your eye and your sense of the aesthetic that you have to please, no one else's. The techniques used in this lesson may be universal, but the choices being made accomplish what was previsualized and are specific to this image. When you work on your own images, though taking notes is important, remember to play first. Remember, too, that you can enable Photoshop CS's History Log in the preferences to keep a record of what steps you took when editing an image.

Figure 2
The Proof Setup dialog with Custom selected for setting up a soft proof.

Step 1: Analyzing the image—developing a dynamic image-specific workflow

Before working on any image, it is important to know how the image was captured, how it was lit, and what type of light was used. It is also important to work with as clean a source file as possible. This image was captured in color (Adobe RGB) using a Nikon D1x with an 80–200mm lens in the RAW (.nef) file format.

I opened and sharpened the image in Nikon Capture 4.1, and saved it as a 16-bit RGB TIFF file. I chose Nikon Capture over Adobe's Camera Raw, even though Camera Raw has a much cleaner and far more intuitive graphical user interface (GUI), because Nikon Capture does a significantly better job of interpolation and de-mosaicing the actual Bayer array data of Nikon RAW files than does Adobe's Camera Raw. Also, Capture's Un-Sharpen Mask algorithms do a better job of sharpening Nikon RAW files.

When working on any image, whether it's a simple one or one that will be as complex as this one is about to become, it is very easy to be overwhelmed with the sheer amount of what needs to be done. The best way to start is making a list of what needs to be done. If your workflow is tablet-based, creating a strategy layer is an excellent idea (see below). Regardless of whether you use a drawing tablet or not, begin with a plan for the image.

Step 2: Setting up soft-proofing

Before beginning work on any image, soft-proof the image (however, this step is pointless unless you are working on a calibrated monitor). Soft-proofing is the process of loading the ICC profile for a specific printer and paper combination into Photoshop and using that profile to see on the monitor what the image will look like when printed. Soft-proofing saves time, money, and effort. It also allows for more accurate decisions when working with the image file.

1. Go to View>Proof Setup and select Custom. This brings up the Proof Setup dialog with Custom selected by default (*Figure 2*).

2. Clicking the Profile pull-down menu (located right under the Setup menu) shows a list of all the profiles available on your system. You choose the appropriate profile based on the final intent for the image. In this lesson,

Figure 4
Soft-proofing a Perceptual rendering intent.

Figure 5
Soft-proofing a Relative Colorimetric rendering intent.

Figure 6
The master RAW capture.

this image is intended to be a continuous-tone black and white that will have the tonality and quality of a classic fine-art black-and-white print from the 1930s and 1940s. For this image, therefore, the best paper choice is a fine-art cotton rag paper, and the best printer choice is a seven-color inkjet printer. The printer that will be used for this image is the Epson 2200 at a resolution of 2880 dpi, using matte black ink and printing on Epson Velvet Fine Art paper.

3. Once the appropriate ICC profile has been chosen, you must determine which rendering intent to use (*Figure 3*). For photography, there are two appropriate options: Relative Colorimetric

Figure 3
The Intent menu, containing rendering-intent options.

and Perceptual (in some cases you might also consider the Saturation rendering intent, but Saturation is really best used for aesthetic reasons, not color accuracy). The best way to determine what rendering intent to use is to toggle through them and see which one looks best on your calibrated monitor, using the best color-decision device—your eye. For this image the best choice is Relative Colorimetric (*Figures 4 and 5*).

Step 3: Correcting color cast—finding the black point and white point of an image

The biggest issue in this image is correcting for the color cast inherent in all digital RAW files. All digital capture has a color cast. This has to do with how data is interpolated from the digital camera's imaging sensor, be it CCD, CMOS, or a hybrid of the two (*Figure 6*).

1. Select Photoshop's Color Sampler tool from the Toolbox. Click the New Fill/Adjustment Layer icon at the bottom of the Layers palette and add a Threshold adjustment layer. The image is converted to black and white, with no color and no gray (*Figure 7*).

Figure 7
A Threshold adjustment layer renders the image in only black and white pixels.

Figure 8
The first significant areas of black appear in the lower left corner of the image.

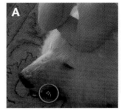

Figure 10
Color samplers marking the black point (A) and the white point (B) in the image.

2. In the Threshold dialog, move the slider all the way to the left, until the image is completely white. Now bring the slider back to the right until you see a significant area of black—not the first black pixel, but the first significant areas of black. We are doing this because we need to find both black pixels and white pixels that have some amount of color contamination. If we go for the first black pixel, we are guaranteed to find absolute pure black, but if we move in a little bit, we can find a black that also contains some level of color (*Figure 8*). This will also hold true if there is a white point to be found in the image, as is the case with this one.

3. With the Color Sampler tool still active, Shift-click in an area of black to add the first sample point, called a *color sampler* (*Figure 9*). Next, move the Threshold slider all the way to the right so that you see a pure black image. Now move the slider to the left until you see the first significant areas of white appear. Shift-click to create the second color sampler, which is the image's white point.

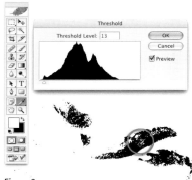

Figure 9
A color sampler is added to identify the darkest areas of the image.

4. Once the white point and black point are established and marked with color samplers, click the Threshold dialog's Cancel button. The white and black color samplers are visible in the image as crosshair targets #1 and #2 (*Figure 10*).

5. From the Layers palette's New Fill/Adjustment Layer pop-up menu choose Curves. Press Caps Lock to change the cursor from the standard icon display into a precise crosshair. This will make it easier to line up the cursor with the color samplers. Select the black eyedropper (Set Black Point) in the Curves dialog and click directly on color sampler #1 (*Figure 11*).

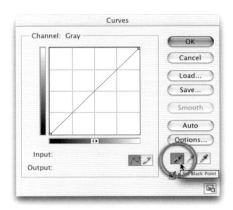

Figure 11
The Set Black Point eyedropper tool in Curves.

6. With Caps Lock still engaged, select the Curves dialog's white eyedropper (Set White Point) and click color sampler #2. Click OK to close the Curves dialog. By applying a Curves adjustment using the black point and white point of the image, we eliminate the color cast inherent in all digital RAW captures (*Figure 12*). What we should notice at this point is that the yellow-magenta cast is gone and there is a slight blue tint to the image.

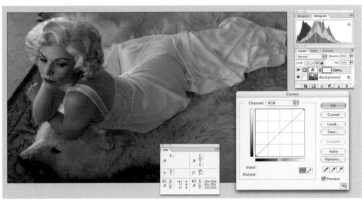

Figure 12
The image after the initial color cast has been removed by setting the black and white points with a Curves adjustment layer.

7. Next we're going to duplicate the image's Background layer by dragging it to the New Layer icon at the bottom of the Layers palette. Change the name of this layer to SKY LIGHT. We will now apply a third-party filter from nik multimedia called Skylight filter.

8. Go to Photoshop's Filter menu and select Skylight Filter from the nik traditional filters submenu. For this image, use the default setting of 25%. This filter works like a UV haze filter and an 85a warming filter (*Figure 13*). Once we have removed the color cast from the RAW file and the color cast from the reflected sunlight, we can begin to work on the first phase of lighting the image.

Figure 13
After applying the nik Color Efex Skylight filter to a copy of the Background layer.

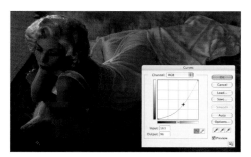

Figure 14
Creating a curve to darken all but the bright highlights in the image.

Figure 16
This is the approximate brush size that will be used to paint on the Curves 2 layer mask.

Step 4: Using Curves adjustment layers to create areas of light to dark

1. Add another Curves adjustment layer, Curves 2, again using the menu at the bottom of the Layers palette. Move the pointer to the center of the diagonal line in the Curves dialog, and click to create an anchor point. Drag the anchor point diagonally down toward the lower right hand corner, making sure not to flatten either end of the curve (otherwise known as *clipping* the curve). Now click OK to accept the change and close the Curves dialog. This Curves adjustment substantially darkens the image, with the exception of the extreme highlights (*Figure 14*).

2. With the Curves 2 adjustment layer active in the Layers palette, change the layer blending mode from Normal to Luminosity (*Figure 15*). This ensures that the adjustment layer affects only the lightness and darkness of the image, not the image's color. (Darkening an image generally increases the color's saturation. Using the Luminosity blending mode applies the adjustment to the gray value, the luminescence, of each pixel, preserving the color.)

Figure 15
The Luminosity blending mode applies an adjustment to only the brightness values in the image, leaving color values unaffected.

3. Now we can begin our first level of building light to dark. With the Curves 2 adjustment layer active, we'll paint in the layer's mask to control the application of the adjustment. Where the adjustment layer's mask is white, the adjustment is applied. Where the mask is black, the adjustment is not applied. Areas of gray in the mask reduce the effect of the adjustment. Select the Brush tool ("b"), and in the Brushes palette choose a feathered brush large enough to span the distance between the pupils of the eye (*Figure 16*). Press "d" to set the foreground color to white and the background color to black, and then press "x" to exchange the colors and place black in the foreground color swatch.

Figure 17
The image after painting in the layer mask for the Curves 2 layer.

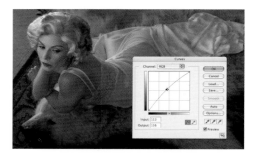

Figure 18
The Curves 3 adjustment.

Figure 20
The blurring effect is revealed only in certain areas of the image by painting on a layer mask.

4. Set the Brush's Opacity to 100%. (You can change a tool's opacity by simply typing a number. For example: 0 = an Opacity of 100%, 5 = 50%, and 2 = 20%.) We're now going to paint over the face at 100% Opacity. Change the Opacity to 50% ("5"), and paint in the area of the hair that surrounds the face, as well as the area of exposed skin on the back, arms, and hand. Now, increasing the brush size and selecting an Opacity of 20%, brush in the area along the back, across the gown, and down to the feet (*Figure 17*).

5. Now we're going to create a third Curves adjustment layer, Curves 3. In the Curves dialog, click the center point and move the curve toward the upper left corner, making sure that the arc of the curve is maintained and does not flatten along the top or left side of the graph (*Figure 18*). Click OK. We have now accomplished our first level of creating areas of light to dark. It is from this point that we can start to make some aesthetic changes to this image.

Step 5: Creating selective depth of field

1. Duplicate the layer named SKY LIGHT by dragging it to the New Layer button at the bottom of the Layers palette. Rename the new layer BLUR. Choose Filter>Blur>Gaussian Blur and move the Radius slider to the right until you have a significant amount of blur but can still discern the image through the Gaussian effect. For this image a radius of 8.8 pixels is optimum. Click OK (*Figure 19*).

Figure 19
Applying the Gaussian Blur filter to the BLUR layer.

2. Press "d" to ensure that the foreground color is set to black and the background color is set to white in preparation for creating a layer mask. To create a layer mask, click the Add Layer Mask button, second from the left at the bottom of the Layers palette, to add a layer mask to the BLUR layer. (Note that the foreground and background colors automatically swap when you start editing a layer mask.) Now, making sure that the layer

Figure 21
The cumulative effect of the bottom layers is merged into a new layer at the top of the Layers palette.

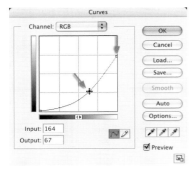

Figure 22
Bringing the highlight and midtone point down in a Curves adjustment layer.

mask is active, we can fill it with black by pressing Command-Delete (PC: Control-Backspace). Keep in mind that when you're working with a layer mask, you are working in grayscale and using only shades of gray to alter the mask and manipulate the image.

3. Click the BLUR layer mask thumbnail to make sure it is active. Select the Brush tool ("b") and set it to an Opacity of 70% ("7"). Paint over the upper part of the image with white, thus revealing the blurred effect, which appears to look like shallow depth of field. Change the Opacity to 50% ("5"). Brush the area from behind the model's knees all the way to the bear's arm. With an Opacity of 20% ("2"), paint the area just beneath the head of the bear, back into the area that we just brushed at 50%. What we now have is an image that looks like that shown in *Figure 20*.

4. Create a new layer with the shortcut Command-Option-Shift-N (PC: Control-Alt-Shift-N). In the Layers palette, name this new layer MERGED LAYER. Move this layer up to the top of the layer stack. We can now merge a copy of all of what we've done into one layer, while preserving the original layers. Press Command-Option-Shift-E (PC: Control-Alt-Shift-E) to merge a copy of all visible layers into the active layer, which in this case is the new empty layer (*Figure 21*). What we now have is our base image layer, which we can start to work on aesthetically.

   In the image that this example is based on, I did considerable retouching work on the woman's face, which entailed the addition of several more layers. For this tutorial, however, I will keep the focus on creating the classic glamour lighting effect and skip ahead to that part of the process.

Step 6: Further building areas of light to dark
In this step we're going to be using curves a little bit differently. Specifically, we're going to be using curves to diminish the apparent contrast of aspects of the image. One of the issues with which we must deal is that the background is still too bright in relation to the foreground. As light passes from a high point of light to dark, it develops a quality of flatness.

1. At the bottom of the Layers palette, again select Curves from the list of adjustments. In the Curves dialog, click the white point, located in the

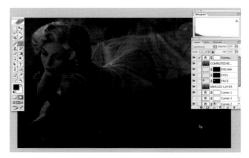

Figure 23
The effect of the previous Curves adjustment layer.

Figure 24
The darkening from the Curves adjustment layer is painted in behind the model.

Figure 25
The model's back, her lower legs, and the foreground are darkened.

upper right corner, and drag it downward. Next, add an anchor point in the middle of the curve and drag it on a diagonal toward the lower right corner (*Figure 22*). Click OK to accept the change and close the Curves dialog.

2. With the Curves adjustment layer active, Curves 4, in the Layers palette, change the layer's blending mode from Normal to Luminosity. As you can see, the adjustment layer substantially reduces the brightness of the entire image (*Figure 23*). Press "d" and then "x" to ensure that black is the background color. With the adjustment layer's layer mask active in the Layers palette, press Command-Delete (PC: Control-Backspace) to fill the mask with black, hiding the Curves adjustment.

3. Select the Brush tool, and set its Opacity to 70%. Press Tab to hide Photoshop's palettes. In the image, paint the area behind the subject, which shows the Curves adjustment at a reduced opacity (*Figure 24*). Change the Brush tool's Opacity to 50%, and apply the Brush to the area from behind the model's knees and lower legs to the lower right corner of the image. With an Opacity of 30%, paint the area from behind the bear head's ear to the edge of the area you just painted. Finally, change the Brush's Opacity to 20% and paint the area just behind the model's back (*Figure 25*).

Step 7: Selective lighting using Photoshop's Lighting Effects filter
We have now reached a point where we can no longer work in 16 bit, so the next step is to convert the image from 16 bit to 8 bit.

1. From the main menu bar choose Image>Mode>8-Bits/Channel to change the image's color depth.

2. Create a new layer and name it LIGHTING BASE LAYER. Make sure that it is positioned at the top of the layer stack. As we did earlier in the chapter, press Command-Option-Shift-E (PC: Control-Alt-Shift-E) to merge a copy of all visible layers into the active layer, which in this case is the new empty layer.

3. Duplicate the new layer by dragging it to the New Layer button at the

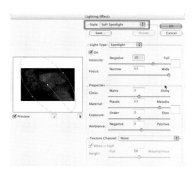

Figure 26
The Lighting Effects dialog with the lighting style set to Soft Spotlight.

Figure 27
Shaping the first spotlight to fall across the model's face.

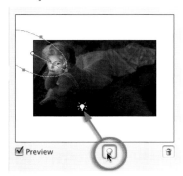

Figure 29
Adding another light source.

bottom of the Layers palette, and then choose Filter>Render>Lighting Effects to activate this extremely powerful but somewhat forgotten filter. From the Style pop-up menu at the top of the Lighting Effects dialog select Soft Spotlight for the lighting style (*Figure 26*).

4. Shape the first light by clicking each of the anchor points on the ellipse and dragging. Move and shape the first light to fall just across the model's face (*Figure 27*). When the first light is positioned where we want it, go to the Properties section of the dialog and move the Gloss slider to 100% Shiny. Move the Material slider all the way to Metallic. Increase Ambiance until you start to see the rest of the image. For this image, the value is 70.

5. Next, move the Exposure slider to –57. In the Light Type area of the dialog adjust the Intensity and Focus sliders to 68 and 3, respectively (*Figure 28*).

6. Add another light by clicking the light bulb icon located just below the image preview area, and drag the light bulb onto the image preview (*Figure 29*). For Light Type select Omni. Now move the Omni light source so that the center point is resting right on the model's chin, and decrease the light size by dragging inward on the light anchor points (*Figure 30*).

7. Click the light bulb icon again, and drag another light to the area just behind the model's head and above her left thigh. Again, select Omni as the Light Type. Decrease the Intensity of this light to +32 (*Figure 31*).

Figure 28
Setting the Exposure, Intensity, and Focus.

Figure 30
Setting the new light source to Omni, adjusting its size, and positioning it over the model's chin.

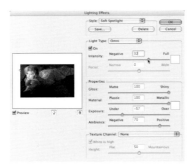

Figure 31
Adding another Omni light source just behind the model's head and above her left thigh.

Figure 32
The result of the Lighting Effects filter on the layer.

Figure 33
The result of selectively revealing areas of the layer where the Lighting Effects filter has been applied by painting on its layer mask.

8. One other area in this image that requires a light adjustment is the bear's eyes. Drag the light bulb icon from beneath the image preview to a spot just above the bear's eyes. Drag the anchors so that the light falls across the bear's face. Increase the Intensity of this light to Full and the Focus to Wide. Increase the Ambience to 88. Now click OK.. This Lighting Effects layer is not meant to be a finished product. Rather, there are some aspects of this layer that will contribute to the final image (*Figure 32*).

9. Add a layer mask to this layer and fill it with black. Use the Brush tool set to an Opacity of 30% with white as the foreground color. Paint over the areas across the eyes and part of the forehead. Reduce the Opacity to 20%, and decrease the brush size to a diameter that is slightly smaller than the lips and drag the brush over them. Using the same 20% Opacity, paint over the area behind the model's back and in front of her knees. Use an Opacity of 50% for the area around the bear's eyes (*Figure 33*).

10. Now we're ready to revisit an earlier step. In the Layers palette, duplicate the Curves adjustment layer created in step 6 (Curves 4) by dragging it to the New Layer button at the bottom the Layers palette. Move the new Curves adjustment layer (Curves 4 copy) to the top of the layer stack in the Layers palette and change the adjustment layer's blending mode from Luminosity to Soft Light.

11. Make the new Curves adjustment layer's layer mask active by clicking it in the Layers palette. With the foreground color set to white, set the Brush tool to an Opacity of 30% and the brush diameter to 200 pixels. Paint the area around the cheeks and neck, the back and arm, and the arm beneath the face (*Figure 34*).

Step 8: Adding the butterfly shadow
A common mistake when adding shadowing to images is not taking into account the color of the shadow.

1. Once again, create a new, empty layer at the top of the layer stack, and merge all of the visible layers into that layer. Using the Zoom tool, zoom in on the area of the nose and mouth. Now activate the Eyedropper tool,

Figure 34
The image after darkening the cheeks, neck, back, and arms by modifying the layer mask of Curves 4 copy.

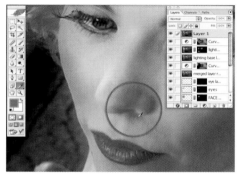

Figure 35
Sampling the shadow under the nose by clicking with the Eyedropper tool places that color into the foreground color swatch.

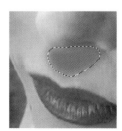

Figure 36
Selecting an area under the nose with the Polygonal Lasso tool.

Figure 37
After filling the feathered selection with the foreground shadow color.

and click once to sample the color of the shadow just below the nose. The foreground color now reflects the color of the shadow (*Figure 35*).

2. Create a new layer by clicking the New Layer icon at the bottom of the Layers palette. Select the Polygonal Lasso tool and make a selection like the one shown in *Figure 36*. Choose Select>Feather, and feather the selection by 5 pixels. The "marching ants" selection border will indicate the pixels that are at least 50% selected. Fill the selection with the foreground color using the keyboard shortcut Option-Delete (PC: Alt-Backspace). Use the shortcut Command-D (PC: Control-D) to deselect (*Figure 37*).

3. Use the Gaussian Blur filter (Filter>Blur>Gaussian Blur) to blur to the layer content a radius of 5.3 pixels.. In the Layers palette, lower the opacity of the shadow's layer until it matches the intensity of the original shadow, which we sampled to set the foreground color. An Opacity setting of 41% is appropriate (*Figure 38*).

Figure 38
Lowering the shadow layer's Opacity to 41% helps to create a more natural-looking shadow.

We've reached the conclusion of the main focus of this tutorial, which has been to show you how to create a classic lighting effect using Photoshop (*Figure 39a and 39b*). There is more, of course; with Photoshop there is always more.

Figure 39a
The "Stardust" image at the beginning of the journey down the RGB Road ...

Figure 39b
... and at the conclusion of this part of the journey.

Go to
www.peachpit.com/
dreamteam.html
to download files for
this chapter.

CHAPTER TWENTY-ONE

THE PHOTOSHOP CREATIVE COOKBOOK: FILTERS & BLENDING MODES

Ben Willmore

Ben Willmore is the author of the award-winning, best-selling book, *Photoshop CS Studio Techniques* (Adobe Press, 2004). More than ten years ago, Ben founded Digital Mastery, a company dedicated to helping people master Photoshop. Since then, he has personally helped over 20,000 design and photography professionals make the transition from blindly following step-by-step techniques to "Aha! I finally GET Photoshop!" Ben's breakthrough teaching style of "not just how—but why" has made him the in-house instructor of choice for such companies as America Online, Mattel, Mercedes-Benz USA, Adobe Systems, LexisNexis, and Fisher-Price. He is currently on tour with his hit seminar Photoshop for Photographers and is a member of the Dream Team at PhotoshopWorld, both produced by the National Association of Photoshop Professionals (NAPP). He is also a featured speaker at conferences in England and Australia, and writes for numerous publications, including a monthly column for *Photoshop User* magazine. His reputation as the "expert's expert" prompted NAPP's president, Scott Kelby, to say, "When we get stuck, we call Ben!"

Ben's home office is in a Swedish cope log home on the edge of a meadow perched at 8,100 feet in the Colorado Rockies, where he is often joined by a herd of elk and a lone coyote.

BOOKS
Adobe Photoshop CS Studio Techniques (Adobe Press, 2004).

BAD TELEVISION AND PHOTOSHOP—THE PERFECT COMBINATION

Photoshop is like the human brain. Most of us only tap into about 10 percent (in some cases much less) of its actual potential. If you are familiar with the "partial brain" theory, you've probably wondered what it takes to get at the unused portion of gray matter that resides, apparently useless, inside your skull. And if you're a regular user of Photoshop, you've probably wondered how to get at the part of Photoshop that seems to be reserved only for those pixel-head extremists who are permanently crouched over their computers, chained to their keyboards, goggle-eyed, into the wee hours.

In their vigilant quest to transform themselves from 10 percent Photoshop weaklings into full-throttle Photoshop superheroes, people often ask me how they can improve their skills. I tell them the plain, honest truth. Watch bad television, I say. Lots of it. Really crappy stuff, like on USA Network. In fact, the shoddier the program, the better you'll get at Photoshop. Needless to say, the same person who was previously very interested in what I had to say is now politely trying to find a way to get away from me as fast as possible.

But listen up, Photoshoppers. I'm not messin' with ya. You wouldn't believe what you can do with the potent combination of bad television and Photoshop. Practicing properly, you can metamorphose into a Photoshop butterfly, or stud, or maestro, or whatever you envision yourself as.

I'd like to share my personal Photoshop story—how I came to discover just how good bad television can be. For all the details, turn to page 289.

continued on next page

VIDEOS

The Master Series: Understanding Curves, Understanding Resolution, Understanding Channels, Advanced Layers, Blend Mode Magic, Color Correction (KW Computer Training; running time, 90 minutes). For Photoshop 7.0 and 6.0. Format: VHS/PAL. Available from www.digitalmastery.com or www.photoshopvideos.com.

SEMINARS & CONFERENCES

Photoshop for Photographers

PhotoshopWorld

CORPORATE TRAINING EVENTS

If you have a group of Photoshop users who are in need of training, Ben Willmore will come right to your door with a training event designed to meet your specific needs. See www.digitalmastery.com for more information.

MAGAZINE ARTICLES

Ben writes for the following magazines: *Photoshop User, Macworld, Mac Design, Design Graphics, Step-by-Step Electronic Design, Photo-Electronic Imaging (PEI), Professional Photographer,* and many more.

FREE STUFF

For regular doses of Ben's tips and tricks, sign up for his free Extra-Strength Photoshop tips at www.digitalmastery.com/tips.

PHOTOSHOP FILTERS FOR ALL AGES

To many people, Photoshop's filters are just a hodgepodge of special effects that can produce some exciting results but at times seem a bit useless or are just plain frustrating. They use the hit-and-miss approach, spending enormous amounts of time torturing their images while they blindly go through an endless procession of filters, oftentimes with lackluster results. And then there are the blending modes, which seem promising, but many people confess to cycling through the entire list (sometimes several times) before they can decide which one works best. Their hope is, of course, that all the effort will pay off and they'll hit the jackpot and get a stunning result.

Wouldn't it be nice, though, if you could get the results without all the guesswork? Well, you've come to the right chapter. My purpose here is to help you gain an understanding of filters and blending modes that will take a lot of wasted time and mystery out of the process and give you the ability to hit the jackpot every time. And also to let you in on what the pros already know—that filters and blending modes used together is the unbeatable marriage of features that will take your creativity to new levels you couldn't previously imagine.

But you can't use just any combination, because not all the blending modes and filters get along. You must first get to know them well enough to know which ones will work in harmony. In this chapter you'll find out how to think about blending modes and filters, and, most important, you'll learn which filters are synergistic with which modes. We'll start with an introduction to blending modes and then throw filters into the mix, which is when things start to heat up. But don't skip the part on blending modes, because your understanding of them is the key to making the magic work.

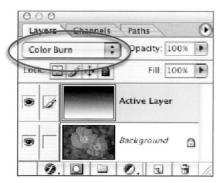

The Blending mode menu is found at the top of the Layers palette.

How to Think about Blending Modes

Photoshop's blending modes seem to mystify many users. Their job is to make the information on the active layer interact with the underlying image in a variety of ways. You don't have to know how each individual mode works; instead, it's usually more useful to have a general idea of how they are organized and to know what's unique about each grouping of modes. With that knowledge, you can start to apply these modes with some precision. So let's start by looking at what's unique about each blending mode grouping, and then we'll expand our knowledge to see how to use them with filters.

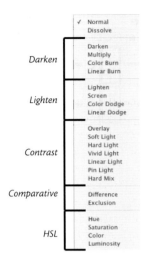

The Blending Modes are divided up into five groupings.

Darken Modes

This group consists of Darken, Multiply, Color Burn, and Linear Burn. With all of these modes, white disappears and anything darker than white has the potential of darkening the underlying image. The only differences among these modes are in the methods they use to darken the underlying image. Multiply mode acts just like ink by printing one image on top of the underlying image, as if you made two passes on an inkjet printer. Linear Burn works in much the same way but does it with more gusto, making it much easier to end up with pure black. Color Burn mode not only darkens but also increases the saturation of colors in the underlying image. Darken mode compares the active layer with the underlying image and allows only those areas that are darker than the underlying image to show up.

Lighten Modes

This group consists of Lighten, Screen, Color Dodge, and Linear Dodge. These modes are the exact opposite of the choices in the Darken group. With these modes, black disappears and anything brighter than black has the potential of lightening the underlying image. Screen mode acts just like light, as if you are projecting one image onto the same screen that another image is being projected onto. Linear Dodge works in much the same way but does it with more force, which makes it much easier to end up with solid white. Color Dodge mode not only lightens but also increases the saturation of colors in the underlying image. Lighten mode compares the active layer to the underlying image only allowing those areas that are lighter than the underlying image to show up.

Contrast Modes

This group consists of Overlay, Soft Light, Hard Light, Vivid Light, Linear Light, and Pin Light. All of these modes are combinations of the modes that are available in the Lighten and Darken groupings. With all these modes, 50% gray disappears, and areas brighter than 50% have the potential to brighten the underlying image (using one of the lighten modes), while areas that are darker than 50% have the potential of darkening the underlying image (using one of the darken modes). Hard Light is a combination of Multiply and Screen. Overlay is the opposite of Hard Light in that it uses the information on the underlying layers to change the contrast of the active layer. Soft Light is a mellower version of Hard Light. Linear Light is a combination of Linear Dodge and Linear Burn. Vivid Light is a combination of Color Dodge and Color Burn. Pin Light is a combination of Lighten and Darken.

Photoshop CS Introduces the Oddball: Hard Mix Mode
Adobe introduced Hard Mix mode in Photoshop CS. But in trying to shoehorn this new mode into the existing groupings, it created an oddball mixture of modes. Let's look at how it works, and then you'll see why it doesn't quite fit with the other contrast modes. This mode posterizes the underlying layers based on the Fill setting (found at the top of the Layers palette and often referred to as the Fill Opacity) of the layer that is using the Hard Mix blending mode. A high Fill Opacity will deliver extreme posterization, while lower Fill Opacity settings will deliver a smoother-looking image. If the brightness of the layer is near 50% gray, then the brightness of the underlying image will not change. Anything brighter than 50% gray will brighten the underlying image, while anything darker will darken it. A layer filled with 50% gray (RGB = 128, 128, 128) will neither brighten nor darken the underlying image, although varying the Fill Opacity will still control its posterization. Using Hard Mix mode with a 50% Fill Opacity often achieves results identical to what you get using the Vivid Light blending mode at 100% Fill Opacity. For that reason, I try Hard Mix and experiment with the Fill Opacity setting anytime I'm experimenting with the Vivid Light blending mode.

Comparative Modes
This group consists of Difference and Exclusion, which compare the active layer with the underlying image and attempt to show you where things are different (areas that are identical in both the active layer and underlying image become black). The main difference between the two modes is that Exclusion mode tends to maintain areas of 50% gray in the active layer as 50% gray. In both of these modes, solid black disappears.

HSL Modes
This group consists of Hue, Saturation, Color, and Luminosity. These modes break up the colors in the active layer into three parts—hue (which means basic color), saturation (which means how colorful), and luminosity (which means how bright)—and then they apply one or more of those qualities to

Original image before applying the filter

Result of applying the High Pass Filter

Result of fading the filter using Overlay mode

Result of fading the filter using Hard Light mode

Result of fading the filter using Vivid Light mode

the underlying image. Hue mode applies the basic color of the active layer to the underlying image without changing how colorful or bright the underlying image is. Saturation mode makes the underlying image just as colorful as the active layer. Color mode applies the color of the active layer to the brightness of the underlying image. Luminosity mode applies the brightness of the active layer to the colors in the underlying image.

Now that you have a general idea of why the blending modes are grouped the way they are, let's take a look at how they can become surprisingly useful when used in combination with particular filters.

Filters

If you experiment with the different filters available in Photoshop, you might start to notice that certain filters produce predictable results. Two examples are Filter>Other>High Pass and Filter>Stylize>Emboss. Both of those filters will always deliver a bunch of 50% gray, in many cases almost obliterating the original image. Lots of people like the idea of the embossed look but don't like all the gray that comes with it. This makes for a good occasion to use the contrast blending modes, and it will provide our first example of how to combine filters and blending modes. All of the contrast blending modes make 50% gray disappear while adding contrast to the image. In the example on the left, I started by choosing Filter>Other>High Pass; then I used a setting of 10 and then clicked the OK button. Immediately after applying that filter, I chose Edit>Fade High Pass, which allowed me to control how the High Pass filter would apply to the image. It's important to note that the Edit>Fade option is only available immediately after you apply the filter. If you perform more tasks in Photoshop and try to go back to the Edit>Fade command, it will be grayed out.

The Fade command acts as if the result of your last action (filter, adjustment, or whatever) is isolated onto a separate layer (even though it isn't) and allows you to choose a blending mode and opacity setting to use when applying that action. Since I had a lot of 50% gray after applying the filter, I experimented with the contrast modes because I knew that would cause the 50% gray to go away.

The Emboss and High Pass filters aren't the only culprits to cause problems. There are other filters that give you large amounts of black,

© PHOTOSPIN

Original image

Result of applying the Find Edges filter

Result of applying the Glowing Edges filter

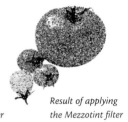

Result of applying the Mezzotint filter

Result of applying the Trace Contour filter

Result of applying the Dark Strokes filter

Result of fading the Find Edges filter with the Linear Light blending mode

white, and/or 50% gray without too many other shades getting in the way. In that case, lighten blending modes will make the black disappear, leaving the white areas to affect the image (just lower the opacity to lessen the effect), while the darken blending modes will do the opposite, making white disappear. The main filters that produce black and white are Stylize>Find Edges, Stylize>Glowing Edges and Pixelate>Mezzotint. Stylize>Trace Contour produces a bunch of white, which is great with the darken blending modes, and Brush Strokes>Dark Strokes produces a bunch of black. Or you can use the Conté Crayon filter (with low Foreground and Background Level settings), which will always give you a lot of 50% gray—great with the contrast modes.

Now let's look at what we can do by combining multiple filters to add texture to our images.

Creating Textures

The great thing about filters is that you're not limited to using just one. You can use multiple filters to create and apply texture to your images. Since we'll be using multiple filters, we won't be able to use the Edit>Fade feature, which reduces our control somewhat. But we can get a lot of that control back by working creatively with layers.

To start, create a new empty layer above the image to which you'd like to apply texture. Many of the filters we're about to use work only on layers that are not empty, so before continuing, choose Edit>Fill and set the Use pop-up menu to White. Now, with that new layer active, choose any one of the filters listed on the following page (a few of them use the foreground and background colors, so type "d" to make sure you don't get an unusual result). Those filters are unique in that they create detail even from a solid color.

Next, distort the image using any of Photoshop's filters. Once you have an interesting-looking result, apply the Stylize>Emboss filter, which adds dimension to the image and delivers large areas of 50% gray.

Finally, to apply the texture you've created to the underlying image, change the blending mode of the layer that contains the texture to one of the contrast blending modes (such as Overlay or Soft Light). Since the texture is isolated on its own layer, you can control where it applies to the image by painting with the Eraser tool.

Original image.

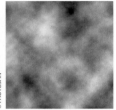

Result of applying the Clouds filter.

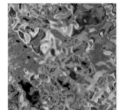

Result of applying the Chrome filter.

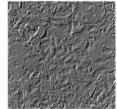

Result of applying the Emboss filter.

Result of setting the layer to Hard Light mode.

Result of lowering Opacity of the layer to 70%.

Result of using the Eraser tool on some of the texture.

The result of applying the filters that create something out of nothing. From top left to bottom right: Sponge, Add Noise, Mezzotint, Pointillize, Clouds, Halftone Pattern, Note Paper, Reticulation, Extrude, Tiles, Craquelure, Grain, Mosaic Tiles, Patchwork, Stained Glass, Texturizer.

- Artistic>Sponge
- Noise>Add Noise
- Pixelate>Mezzotint
- Pixelate>Pointillize
- Render>Clouds
- Sketch>Halftone Pattern

- Sketch>Note Paper
- Sketch>Reticulation
- Stylize>Extrude
- Stylize>Tiles
- Texture>Craquelure
- Texture>Grain

- Texture>Mosaic Tiles
- Texture>Patchwork
- Texture>Stained Glass
- Texture>Texturizer

There are many filters that will work fine as long as you apply them directly to the layer that contains your original image but these same filters will cause problems when working on a multilayered image. Every filter in Photoshop will only apply to the active layer, and most of Photoshop's filters will be unavailable when working on an empty layer. Let's take a look at how we can

Original image.

© PHOTOSPIN

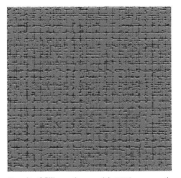

Result of filling a layer with 50% gray and then applying the Craquelure filter.

Result of changing the blending mode to Hard Light.

overcome those limitations by using a special set of filters that react well when applied on layers that are full of 50% gray. We'll start by filling a layer with 50% gray by choosing Edit>Fill and changing the Use pop-up menu to 50% Gray. Next, choose one of the filters listed below (with the foreground and background colors set to their defaults of black/white), and then change the blending mode of the active layer to one of the contrast modes.

- Artistic>Film Grain
- Artistic>Rough Pastels
- Artistic>Smudge Stick
- Artistic>Sponge
- Render>Lens Flare

- Render>Lighting Effects
- Sketch>Conté Crayon
- Sketch>Water Paper
- Stylize>Extrude
- Stylize>Tiles

- Texture>Craquelure
- Texture>Grain
- Texture>Mosaic Tiles
- Texture>Texturizer

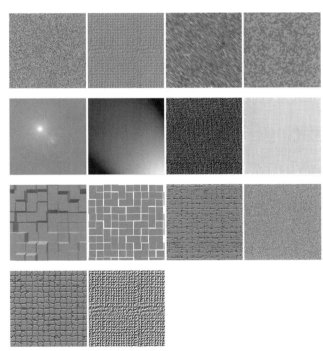

The result of applying the filters that work well with layers filled with 50% gray. From top left to bottom right: Film Grain, Rough Pastels, Smudge Stick, Sponge, Lens Flare, Lighting Effects, Conté Crayon, Water Paper, Extrude, Tiles, Craquelure, Grain, Mosaic Tiles, Texturizer.

Original image

Result of applying the Neon Glow filter.

Result of changing the blending mode to Vivid Light.

Result of placing a copy of the original image at the top of the layers stack and setting its mode to color.

Now let's explore a group of filters that are unique in that they use your foreground and/or background colors as the basis for the end result. With these filters, you can set your foreground/background colors to black, white, or 50% gray, depending on which blending mode you plan on using. Many of these filters also need to be applied directly to the layer that contains your original image. Most of the time, I'll duplicate the layer that contains the original image by pressing Command-J (PC: Control-J), apply one of these filters to the duplicate layer, and then experiment with the blending modes. If you work on a separate layer, you can press "v" to make the Move tool active and then hold down the Shift and Option keys (PC: Shift and Alt keys) then press the plus (+) or minus (-) keys to cycle through the choices available in the blending mode pop-up menu at the top left of the Layers palette. When using multiple layers, you can also duplicate the original layer, place the duplicate on top of the layers stack, and set its blending mode to Color to prevent any of the effects you create from changing the color or saturation of the original image. Just make sure that any effects you create appear below the layer that is set to Color mode.

Filters that use foreground (F) and/or background (B) colors

- Artistic>Colored Pencil = B
- Artistic>Neon Glow = F & B
- Distort>Diffuse Glow = B
- Pixelate>Pointillize = B
- Render>Clouds = F & B
- Render>Fibers
- Sketch>Bas Relief = F & B
- Sketch>Chalk & Charcoal = F & B
- Sketch>Charcoal = F & B
- Sketch>Conté Crayon = F & B
- Sketch>Graphic Pen = F & B
- Sketch>Halftone Pattern = F & B
- Sketch>Note Paper = F & B
- Sketch>Photocopy = F & B
- Sketch>Plaster = F & B
- Sketch>Reticulation = F & B
- Sketch>Stamp = F & B
- Stylize>Tiles = B
- Texture>Stained Glass = F

Okay, let's move on to the filters that are helpful when using the concepts I described above, even though they are not directly related to the blending modes we've been using.

Original image.

Result of applying the Minimum filter with a setting of 1.

Result of applying the Minimum filter with a setting of 2.

Result of applying the Minimum filter with a setting of 3.

Result of applying the Maximum filter with a setting of 1.

Result of applying the Maximum filter with a setting of 2.

Result of applying the Maximum filter with a setting of 1.

Minimum

This filter is great for controlling the thickness of lines. It attempts to minimize how much space white takes up. That means that anytime you have black lines on a white background (as I had earlier when I used the Find Edges filter), you can thicken up those lines with the minimum filter. I know it sounds like a paradox, using the Minimum filter to "maximize" lines, but if you think about minimizing white, which makes black take up more space, you'll easily remember which filter to use.

Maximum

Maximum is the opposite of Minimum, in that it maximizes how much space white takes up, causing it to encroach into any black lines that are in your image. This is great for those times when you'd like to make black lines thinner (remember, think about white with these two filters!).

Median

I use this filter as an alternative to blurring an image. It maintains crisp edges while throwing away tiny details. Anytime a filter gives you way too much detail, you might want to apply Median and then try the filter again so it will be looking at less detail.

Original image. *Result of applying the Find Edges filter.* *Result of applying the Median filter with a setting of 3 before applying the Find Edges filter.* *Result of changing the blending mode of the filtered layer to Color Burn.*

The Filter Gallery

Finally, if you find the Filter menu tiresome because there are just too many filters, and you'd like an easier way of sorting through them, try Filter>Filter Gallery. This will present you with a giant dialog containing little previews of each filter effect. You can quickly glance through them and visually select the one with the most desirable effect. Just beware that this feature is new to

The Filter Gallery dialog.

Original image.

Result of applying the six-step technique described here.

Photoshop CS and in some ways is not completely ready for prime time. The biggest drawback is that it doesn't show all the filters available in Photoshop, and for those folks with less powerful processors, it can slow things down to the speed of molasses.

An Example

Now that you have an idea of how I use the different filter and blending mode combinations, let's take a look at how I've used those ideas to create a complex effect.

The following steps produce a high-contrast image that has a slight painterly look. Each step in this technique involves duplicating the original image (which was on the Background layer), moving the duplicate to the top of the layers stack, applying a filter, and then changing the blending mode of the layer. Since there are six steps, you should end up with a total of six copies of the original, each with its blending set differently than the others. The only difference between the steps is which filter and blending mode were used. I'll just list the filter and mode used for each step to keep things simple.

Step 1

I applied the Watercolor filter, which produced a bunch of black, so I used Screen mode (knowing that black disappears in the lighten modes).

Step 2

I applied the Find Edges filter, which gave me a bunch of white, so I used Multiply mode to make the bright areas go away.

Step 3

I applied the High Pass filter, knowing that it was going to produce a lot of 50% gray, so I ended up using Hard Light mode.

Step 4

I applied the Colored Pencil filter using 50% gray, and as you can probably guess, I used a contrast blending mode (in this case Soft Light).

Step 5

I applied the Gaussian Blur filter, using Hard Light mode to add contrast.

Original image.

Result of applying the six-step technique described here.

Step 6

At that point I really liked what I had, but I thought the colors had shifted and had become too vivid. So I duplicated the original layer once more, put it on top of the layers stack, and set its blending mode to Color, which brought the colors back to their original look while keeping the brightness and contrast changes I had made with the filters. The creative process isn't a black-and-white road map. While I was going through this example, I may not have known exactly what I was going to end up with, but having a general idea of how the blending modes are organized, I had no problem figuring out the best modes to choose from during each step. With your newfound knowledge of filters and blending modes, and your understanding of which ones work together harmoniously, I hope that your relationship with these two features will be a lasting one, and one that results in the pitter-patter of tiny masterpieces running around your computer station.

Bad Television and Photoshop— the Perfect Combination

I try to make it a habit to watch as much bad television as I possibly can stand. It takes less than five minutes before I'm bored out of my skull. Funny thing is, the same happens when I try to concentrate on a single feature in Photoshop and just fiddle in an attempt to come up with new techniques (oh my god, that's my job!). But if I combine the two things that can put me to sleep faster than reading about Chinese calculus, an interesting thing starts to happen. Just as I begin to feel the first pangs of boob-tube monotony, I plop my laptop on my lap and start experimenting with Photoshop. I usually pick just one or two features and experiment until my brain starts looking for greener pastures, which usually takes about ten minutes. When that happens, I just change my glance and start paying attention to the TV again, and in about five minutes I'm mentally fresh to start playing in Photoshop again. I repeat this back-and-forth pattern until something forces to me stop (the phone, the bathroom, my stomach growling). When I'm experimenting in Photoshop, I try every single option available in the feature I've decided to explore. In doing this, I've come up with some rather interesting images.

Let's look at how this "waste of time" turned into something useful.

One time I decided that I was going to experiment with the Edit>Transform feature and nothing else. At first glance, it doesn't look like you could entertain

I started with a simple five-sided polygon.

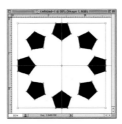

Then I rotated a few duplicates until I came up with this.

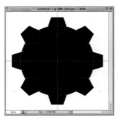

I added a circle to fill the middle.

Finally, I poked a hole in the middle with another circle and ended up with a gear, which I saved as a Custom Shape to use later.

I made another fancy gear using the ideas from a previous session.

After applying the layer styles I had created, things started to heat up.

yourself for four or five hours with just that feature. Not so if you have some truly horrid television to keep you company! On this particular night I discovered features I had used before, but whose possibilities I had never really explored. The main thing I came away with that night was a new understanding of how rotations work (they pivot around the crosshair that shows up in the middle of a layer) and how I could combine that simple idea with the Transform Again command (while holding down Option to duplicate the layer). At the end of that night, I was excited because I had learned how to make images like the ones that appear to the left.

That night was just the beginning. About once a week, I'd get back to the quality programming on USA Network and my ideas would slowly progress. For my next session, I chose to explore Photoshop's shape tools and nothing else. Well, after playing for a little while, I couldn't help but incorporate some of the ideas I had come up with in my previous session, and I started creating more intricate shapes than I first thought was possible. So you see, this method was causing its own evolution of sorts. My Photoshop brain was growing! Who knows what kind of creature I would end up as! I hoped I would still have two eyes, a nose, hands—that sort of thing.

After two relatively successful sessions of Photoshop and appallingly bad TV, I was hooked. My next session was dedicated to Photoshop's Layer Style feature, which I explored for almost six hours! At the end of that session, I couldn't help but combine the ideas I'd learned from my previous sessions, and I created the image below (sadly, I was also able to recite, line for line, almost every episode of *Walker, Texas Ranger*).

Now you might be afraid that I'm going to drag you through a whole year's worth of these sessions. Not true. We only need to explore one more until you can see where this started to lead. In my next session I began by playing with the shape tools again and creating some nice organic shapes. I then started to

I learned to rotate a duplicate multiple times to create this image.

Rotating and scaling multiple images was interesting.

A shape that I made by combining all I had learned about the shape tools.

I start to rotate duplicates of the shape just like I learned in my first session.

Rotating many copies made the image evolve into something that caught my attention.

My first rotation was a bit too busy-looking.

My second try was a little more successful.

Intertwining the simple shapes added complexity to them, which I really liked.

rotate duplicates of those shapes to create interesting compositions.

Then I started to add layer styles to give a little pop to the image. As I played more and watched even more bad television, I started to experiment with changing the colors of each object and trying different ways of rotating the shapes.

After getting to this point, I decided to start exploring a feature I'd never used before—vector masks. That's what I was going to devote this session to. I was committed to learning as much as possible about vector masks and was not afraid to spend hours doing so. Vector masks allowed me to make it look as if the shapes I had created were intertwined, when in reality I was just hiding part of a layer where I wanted it to look as if it was underneath another layer.

After watching literally six low-budget bombs on USA Network, I had created what (at least then) felt like a few masterpieces. When I showed the result of that session to a few friends, they all wanted to know how I had created the images. But since I had spent so much time learning about Photoshop's features and had gotten so in-depth with them, it was next to impossible to explain exactly how I had done it. I knew how to create this type of image with no problem, but that was because I really understood all the technology behind it. The next month, I heard about a juried art show that was going to happen soon. I decided to print a few of my images and enter them. A jury of artists picked two of my images to be shown! See what can happen if you just "waste your time" with bad television and Photoshop?

So it's your turn now. Get your computer and television at the ready. Channel surf until you get something you can stand for only about five minutes, turn on Photoshop, and get ready to start your own transformation.

This image was one of the two images accepted into the juried art show.

This is the second image that was selected.

PUBLISHER'S NOTE

We at Peachpit and New Riders are proud and honored to have the unique opportunity and immense pleasure of working with the Photoshop gurus featured in this book. Publishing a collection of work by the "dream team" of Photoshop artists and photographers has been a dream of ours for many years, and with this book, our dream has become a reality.

And what a team it is. Through our longstanding publishing partnerships with many of these talented people, we've come to see firsthand that there is more creative collaboration, more good will, and more camaraderie among Photoshop users than you'll find in almost any other creative community, with many close relationships dating back to the early days of Photoshop. Nowhere is this more evident than at PhotoshopWorld, a conference put on twice a year by the National Association of Photoshop Professionals and spearheaded by NAPP's fearless leader and extraordinary talent, Scott Kelby. Year after year, Scott and his creative, high-energy partners and staff assemble the best of the best to bring you uniquely inspiring, entertaining, and expert Photoshop instruction.

As publisher of Peachpit and New Riders, I want to personally express my thanks to everyone who contributed to making this dream come true: First and foremost, to Scott Kelby, who brought together the 21 contributing artists; to the artists themselves, of course, for their inspiring and enlightening work; to Seàn Duggan, for his scrupulous technical and development review of all the material; to Felix Nelson, who designed this beautiful book; to designer/compositors Ted LoCascio and David Van Ness, who executed (and tweaked) the design; to New Riders Executive Editor Steve Weiss, who from the beginning has shared in the enthusiasm and the vision; to Associate Managing Editor Becky Morgan and Production Editor Connie Jeung-Mills, who shepherded this dream into the land of tangible reality; to Designer Aren Howell, who helped at so many stages along the way; and finally, to the Photoshop community at large, to whom this book is dedicated.

Nancy Aldrich-Ruenzel
Publisher/Vice President
Peachpit Group, A Division of Pearson Education

CREDITS

SEÁN DUGGAN

Seán Duggan is a photographer, author and educator who combines a traditional, fine art photographic background with over a decade of extensive real-world experience in the field of digital imaging. He is co-author of *Real World Digital Photography, 2nd Edition* (Peachpit Press, 2003) and *Photoshop CS Artistry, Mastering the Digital Image* (New Riders, 2004), and an Adobe Certified Photoshop Expert. His Photoshop tutorial column can be seen regularly in *Mac Design Magazine* and he also writes articles on Photoshop and digital imaging for *Photoshop User*, *PCPhoto*, *Outdoor Photographer*, and *Digital Photo Pro* magazines.

In his twenty-year imaging career, he has been a studio and location photographer, worked as a custom black-and-white darkroom printer, and supervised the digital imaging department of a professional photo lab. Equally at home with both low-tech and hi-tech approaches, his visual tool kit includes everything from primitive pinhole cameras and wet darkroom alternative processes to 35mm and medium-format SLRs, digital SLRs, and advanced Photoshop techniques. His photographs have been exhibited at the Monterey Peninsula Museum of Art, the Center for Photographic Art in Carmel, California and at galleries and exhibitions throughout California.

He is an instructor in the photography departments of the Academy of Art University in San Francisco, and the University of California, Santa Cruz Extension in Silicon Valley, where he teaches regular classes on Digital Photography and Photoshop for Photographers. Seán provides Photoshop and imaging consulting services for photographers and companies, and also teaches annual workshops at the Palm Beach Photographic Workshops in Delray Beach, Florida, the Lepp Institute of Digital Imaging in Los Osos, California, and Golden Gate School of Professional Photography in Oakland, California.

For those students looking for a more focused learning experience, he also teaches custom digital photography and Photoshop workshops for individuals and small groups at his studio in the foothills of California's Sierra Nevada Mountains. For more information on Seán's photography, books and workshop schedule, please see his Web sites at www.seanduggan.com and www.digitalphotobook.net.

TED LoCASCIO

Ted LoCascio is currently the creative director for the Professional Digital Imaging Association (PDIA) and their publication *Great Output* magazine. Previous to PDIA, Ted held the position of senior designer at KW Media Group—publishers of *Photoshop User*, *Mac Design*, and *Nikon Capture User* magazines. Ted is also a successful freelance designer and illustrator, and was an instructor at the 2003 PhotoshopWorld conference held in Miami. Please visit www.lukasnmc.com for more information or e-mail t.lukas@knology.net.

COPYRIGHT OF AUTHORS

The book was produced by the authors and the design team using all Macintosh computers, including a Power Mac G5 Dual 2-GHz, a Power Mac G5 1.8-GHz, a Power Mac G4 1.25-GHz, a Power

Mac G4 733-MHz, and a Power Mac G4 500-MHz. We use Sony Artisan, LaCie Electron Blue 22, and Apple Studio Display monitors.

Page layout was done using Adobe InDesign 2.0. Section heads are set in 12 point Berthold Akzidenz Grotesk Light Extended. Body copy is set using CronosMM250 Light at 10 points on 12 leading.

National Association of Photoshop Professionals (NAPP)

The industry trade association for Adobe® Photoshop® users and the world's leading resource for Photoshop training, education, and news.

http://www.photoshopuser.com

PhotoshopWorld Conference & Expo

The convention for Adobe Photoshop users has now become the largest Photoshop-only event in the world. This is where you can see your favorite Dream Team authors in action.

http://www.photoshopworld.com

Adobe Photoshop Seminar Tour

Learn the latest Photoshop tips, tricks and cutting edge techniques on the Adobe Photoshop Seminar Tour, the nation's most popular Photoshop seminars. For upcoming tour dates and class schedules, visit the tour website.

http://www.photoshopseminars.com

KW Computer Training Videos

A series of Photoshop training videos and DVDs for beginners or for those seeking more advanced techniques are available from KW Computer Training. Visit the Web site or call 813-433-5000 for orders or more information.

http://www.photoshopvideos.com

PlanetPhotoshop.com

"The Ultimate Photoshop Site" features Photoshop news, tutorials, reviews, and articles posted daily. The site also contains the Web's most up-to-date resource on other Photoshop-related websites and information.

http://www.planetphotoshop.com

Photoshop Hall of Fame

Created to honor and recognize those individuals whose contributions to the art and business of Adobe Photoshop have had a major impact

on the application or the Photoshop community.

http://www.photoshophalloffame.com

Kelby's Notes

Now you can get the answers to the top 100 most-asked Photoshop questions with Kelby's Notes, the plug-in from Scott Kelby. Simply go to the How Do I? menu while in Photoshop, find your question, and the answer appears in an easy-to-read dialog. Finally, help is just one click away.

http://www.kelbysnotes.com

Mac Design Magazine

"The Graphics Magazine for Macintosh Users" is a tutorial-based print magazine with how-to columns on Photoshop, Illustrator, InDesign, Dreamweaver, Flash, Final Cut Pro, and more. It's also packed with tips, tricks, and shortcuts for your favorite creative applications.

http://www.macdesignonline.com

INDEX

INDEX

D

D1 digital tape format 122, 123
Dark Strokes filter 283
Darken blending mode 280–281, 283
darkening images 269, 280, 281
darkening techniques 189–191
daylight color balance 233
De-Interlace filter 126–128
default settings, restoring 31
defragmenting hard-drive partitions 234
deinterlacing images 126–128
depth
    adding 101
    creating 210
Depth map 86–87
depth of field, simulating shallow 81
desaturating colors 218
deselecting selections 30
design variables 105
designs, refining 105
designs, developing 107
detail, restoring 167, 192
Difference blending mode 281
Diffuse Glow filter 166, 286
digital camera bit depth 189
digital captures 186
    designing with 94
    high resolution 95
digital noise. *See* noise
digital photography 184–185, 187–194
Digital Video Professionals Association
        (DVPA) 119–120
dimensions, adding 210–216
Direct Selection tool 72, 219
disc map 134
Displace filter 14
displacement maps 14
display gamma 201
dock, displaying 6
Document Properties, Acrobat 240
documents, creating new 161

Dodge tool 178, 221
downloading images, from digital camera 234
drawing techniques 208–226
drop shadows 46, 102–103, 140, 218
    layer style 223
duotone images 17
DV technology 119
DVD format 132
DVD menus, designing
    constraints 133–134
    source material 134
DVDs, writing to 234
DVPA 119–120

E

edges
    blending 247, 251
    continuity 180
    isolating 166
    roughening 178
    rounded 181
    retouching 251
    sharpening 287
    softening 67, 165, 178, 217
editing, tracking 264
8-bit images 189
    from 16-bit 272
85a warming filter 268
Elliptical Marquee tool 69
embedding profiles, recommendations 197
Emboss filter 282
embroidery template 159
encaustic technique 158–169
Enhance per Channel Contrast option 237
Epson printers 198–199, 203, 204, 205
Eraser tool 180, 283, 284
    retouching edges 178, 251
erasing areas 226
Exclusion blending mode 281
experimenting 27–28, 51, 79–80, 105, 181, 277
exposure, locking 52
Extrude filter 284, 285

Eyedropper tool sample size 33
eyes
    rebuilding 254
    how they see 263

F

Fade command 28, 282, 283
feathering selections 67, 216, 275
    previewing with Quick Mask 68
    using context menu 68
Fibers filter 112, 286
File Browser 55, 162, 235–236
    PDF presentation 239
filling layers 285
filling with foreground color 275
film, replicating 187–194
Film Grain filter 285
Filter Gallery 28, 166, 287–288
filters
    predictable results 282
    applying multiple 283
    combining with blending modes 279,
        282–287
    layer requirements 284–285
    unsupported modes 31
Find Edges filter 283, 287
fine-art prints 266
flagging images 235
flattening layers 138, 257
flaws, correcting 60–61
flipping layers 107, 108
focusing viewer's attention 90
fonts, previewing 34–35
foreground, receding 217
foreground color, filter results 286
Full Screen mode 193, 248, 249, 264

G

Gaussian Blur 191, 270, 275, 288
    compared to Lens Blur filter 81, 87
    feathering selections 68
    Quick Mask selection 98

INDEX

INDEX

Photography that has the power to make you STOP.